Contents

For Kellie,
and all her queer personas

Preface

What a queer thing Life is![1]

All the world is queer save thee and me, and even thou
art a little queer.[2]

We're here because we're queer
Because we're queer because we're here.[3]

THE WORD QUEER HAS historically been used in a number of different ways: to signify something strange, as in the quote from P. G. Wodehouse; to refer to negative characteristics (such as madness or worthlessness) that one associates with others and not with the self, as in the quote from Robert Owen; and, as in the refrain from Brendan Behan which 'queerly' anticipates the ACT UP slogan 'we're here, we're queer, so get fucking used to it!', to denote one's difference, one's 'strangeness', positively. Similarly, queer has been used, sometimes abusively, and other times endearingly, as a colloquial term for homosexuality. So what exactly does this term mean when appended by the word 'theory'?

While Queer Theory may now be recognised by many as an academic discipline, it nevertheless continues to struggle against the straitjacketing effects of institutionalisation, to resist closure and remain in the process of ambiguous (un)becoming. Queer Theory does not want to 'straighten up and fly right' to have the kinks ironed out of it: it is a discipline that refuses to be disciplined, a discipline with a difference, with a twist if you like. In saying this, however, I do not mean to endow Queer Theory with some sort of 'Tinkerbell effect'; to claim that no matter how hard you try you'll never manage to catch it because essentially it is ethereal, quixotic, unknowable. Obviously Queer Theory does function in

v

specific – albeit complex and somewhat ambiguous – ways in particular contexts, and in relation to particular issues. And, as Alan McKee has pointed out, ignoring this because of a fear that any attempt to investigate the multifarious, multivalent, and contextually specific practice(s) of Queer Theory will result in assimilation, is politically dangerous and ethically suspect. Historically, says McKee, Queer Theory has been inscribed in a number of ways, and 'to write histories of Queer Theories is not the same thing as defining Queer Theory' (1999: 237). Consequently, this book does not attempt to define what Queer Theory is, but, rather, is concerned with providing an overview of what Queer Theories do, and a critical examination of how and why they have functioned in the specific ways that they have, and what kinds of effects have been produced as a result.

Rather than focusing narrowly on sexuality and/or sexual practices, the book aims to consider critiques of normalising ways of knowing and of being that may not always initially be evident as sex-specific – hence the inclusion of topics such as community, popular culture, race, and so on. This sort of approach is crucial, it seems to me, if we are to understand the broader significance of Queer Theory and the extensive range of ways in which notions of sexuality and gender impact – at times implicitly – on everyday life. Whilst the list of topics covered in the book is far from exhaustive, the theories and issues discussed do lend themselves to other applications. For instance, the analysis of the culturally and historically specific ways in which transsexualism and transgender have been understood and experienced may well prove useful for those interested in intersex issues. Likewise, the chapter entitled 'Queering Popular Culture' will provide students of literature with a range of theoretical and methodological approaches to (re)reading canonical texts, as would the genealogical account of the discursive construction of sexuality discussed most explicitly in the earlier chapters of the book. In effect, what this highlights is the interdisciplinary and/or rhizomatic character and potential of Queer Theory which, whilst having its roots in Gay and Lesbian Studies, need not be confined by disciplinary boundaries or what Deleuze and Guattari would refer to as arborescent structures.[4]

In short, the aim of the book is to queer – to make strange, to frustrate, to counteract, to delegitimise, to camp up – heteronormative knowledges and institutions, and the subjectivities and socialities that are (in)formed by them and that (in)form them.

NOTES

1. P. G. Wodehouse, *My Man Jeeves* (1919), quoted in Partington (1998: 740).
2. Robert Owen, to his partner W. Allen, on severing business relations (1928), quoted in Partington (1998: 503).
3. Brendan Behan, *Hostage* (1958), quoted in Partington (1998: 60).
4. For a more detailed discussion of the terms 'rhizome' and 'arborescent', see Deleuze and Guattari (1983).

1

The Social Construction of Same-Sex Desire: Sin, Crime, Sickness

I WANT TO BEGIN WITH the suggestion that sexuality is not natural, but rather, is discursively constructed. Moreover, sexuality, as we shall see, is constructed, experienced, and understood in culturally and historically specific ways. Thus we could say that there can be no true or correct account of heterosexuality, of homosexuality, of bisexuality, and so on. Indeed, these very categories for defining particular kinds of relationships and practices are culturally and historically specific and have not operated in all cultures at all times.

So, if there is no single correct account of sexuality, then contemporary views of particular relationships and practices are not necessarily any more enlightened or any less symptomatic of the times than those held by previous generations and this is important to keep in mind when we look at historical accounts of sexuality. It is very likely that fifty years from now people will cringe when they view current representations of lesbianism, or accounts of fetishism, in much the same way as we sometimes do when we encounter texts from the past. Given this, I want to avoid positing a developmental account of changing historical construc-tions of same-sex relations and instead offer what Foucault would call a genealogical analysis of sexuality as it has been lived and understood in Western culture over the last couple of centuries.

For Foucault, a genealogical analysis consists of a search for 'instances of discursive production . . . of the production of power and of the propagation of knowledge', which makes possible a 'history of the present' (Foucault 1980: 12). In other words, the task of the genealogist is to examine the random, provisional, and often discontinuous ways in which power has functioned or been

1

deployed and to analyse the forms of subjectivity that have been discursively constructed as a result. This sort of critical endeavour, then, enables us to understand the present – in all its complexity – in terms of the past(s) that inscribe it.

As I've said, sexuality is, according to poststructuralist theorists, discursively produced and classifications of sexuality (or even of what might be seen to constitute sex or sexuality) do not simply describe being, but rather constitute it in historically and culturally specific ways. Therefore, an analysis of the discourses surrounding and informing sexuality can provide clues as to why particular knowledges, practices, and subjectivities emerge when and where they do, and what purposes they might serve. Terms such as invert, queer, sodomite, sapphist, dyke, and so on, are cultural artefacts that are tied to ways of understanding and of being that are specific to a particular cultural milieu. Likewise, the term 'homosexuality' – and by extension, 'heterosexuality', which was developed later – is a relatively modern one. The former term was coined in 1869 by the Swiss doctor Karoly Maria Benkert, but, John Marshall has argued that it was not until about a century later that the term gained common popular usage.[1] Moreover, same-sex practices which we might conceptualise as or label 'homosexual' have been understood and experienced (or, one might say, constructed) quite differently in cultural contexts other than our own. David Halperin makes this point when he asks:

Does the 'pederast', the classical Greek adult, married male who periodically enjoys sexually penetrating a male adolescent, share *the same sexuality* with the Native American (Indian) adult male who from childhood has taken on many aspects of a woman and is regularly penetrated by the adult male to whom he has been married in a public and socially sanctioned ceremony? Does the latter share *the same sexuality* with the New Guinea tribesman who from the ages of eight to fifteen has been orally inseminated on a daily basis by older youths and who, after years of orally inseminating his juniors, will be married to an adult woman and have children of his own? Do any of these three persons share *the same sexuality* with the modern homosexual. (cited in Jagose 1996: 8)

What this quote suggests is that in many cultures same-sex relations have played an integral and socially acceptable function, but have nevertheless taken quite different forms.

During this period in Britain and most of Northern Europe, however, things were quite different. For example, in Britain sodomy was conceived of as a sin against nature until the late 1800s. The term sodomy, however, was not simply used to refer to anal sex – which is generally what is inferred today – but included practices such as oral sex and sex which involved the use of contraception. In short, it was used as an umbrella term to cover a range of practices which did not have procreation as their aim: that is, 'unnatural' forms of sexual relations. Obviously the term sodomy was derived from the biblical city of Sodom, an allegedly extremely wicked and corrupt place, the destruction of which is recorded in Genesis. Prior to the late 1880s in Britain the penalty for what was known as 'The Abominable Vice of Buggery' was death. It is important to note here, however, that during this time, laws were directed against acts and not against a certain category of persons – that is, homosexuals. As Foucault claims in *The History of Sexuality* Volume 1, it was not until the mid to late nineteenth century that particular acts came to be seen as the expression of an individual's psyche, or as evidence of inclinations of a certain type of subject.

Despite the fact that sodomy was not necessarily a gender-specific practice, historical documents nevertheless seem to indicate that it was most often men who were accused or convicted of sodomy. In records of the few rare cases of women being tried for the crime of sodomy, what becomes apparent is that the 'crime against nature' of which they were supposedly guilty, was 'acting like a man'. This is the case in the 1477 trial of Katherina Hetzeldorfer, a German woman who was drowned because she was said to have had a long-term sexual relationship with her female housemate, to have acted like a husband, to have made sexually aggressive advances towards other women, to have sometimes dressed in men's clothing, and to have made, worn, and used, a dildo (a 'prosthetic penis'). One of the interesting things about the trial notes is that Hetzeldorfer's crime has no name in the proceedings. Instead, it is implied that she was hanged for committing a 'crime against nature' (*crimen contra naturam*), for '*acting like a man*', and thus transgressing gender norms, rather than for being what we might now call a lesbian.*

In Britain this gendering of sodomy became more explicit when, in 1781, a law was passed stating that in order for a person to be convicted of sodomy 'penetration and the emission of seed' must be proved. The passing of such a law is illustrative of the growing conviction that since men were by nature sexually active and women were by nature sexually passive, then only men could commit sodomy: only they were capable of penetration (which is seen as active) and of emitting bodily fluids whose natural destination was reproduction.

In *The History of Sexuality* Volume 1, Foucault traces what I've referred to above as the shift from sodomy as a crime of which anyone is potentially capable, to an act that is the expression of an innate identity. He shows how, from the mid-nineteenth century onwards, medical analyses of various forms of non-procreative sex as categorisable perversions and deviations came to replace the religious association of undifferentiated non-procreative acts (sodomy) with sin. He says:

The nineteenth century homosexual became a personage, a past, a case history, and a childhood in addition to being a type of life, a life form, and a morphology, with an indiscreet anatomy and possibly a mysterious physiology. Nothing that went into his total composition was unaffected by his sexuality. It was everywhere present in him: at the root of all his actions because it was their insidious and indefinitely active principle; written immodestly on his face and body because it was a secret that always gave itself away. It was consubstantial with him, less as a habitual sin than as a singular nature . . . Homosexuality appeared as one of the forms of sexuality when it was transposed from the practice of sodomy onto a kind of interior androgyny, a hermaphroditism of the soul. The sodomite had been a temporary aberration; the homosexual was now a species. (1980: 43)

This shift in focus from sinful acts against nature that potentially anyone might commit as a result of 'man's' fallen state, to the notion of homosexuality as the basis of an individual's nature, raised the question of whether it was any longer just to criminalise and/or punish particular sexual activities. For example, in numerous books and articles published between 1864 and 1879,[2] Karl Heinrich Ulrichs, a homosexual German lawyer and social commentator, argued that same-sex love should not be regarded as criminal, sinful or insane. For Ulrichs, homosexuality, as we now call it, is congenital; it is the result of 'a kind of interior androgyny, a hermaphroditism of the soul' (Foucault 1980: 43). It is a simple fact of nature, Ulrichs argued, that some males are born with a strong feminine element or psyche – a condition he referred to as *anima muliebris virili corpore inclusa*. Similarly, he claimed, some females are born with a strong masculine drive. According to Ulrichs' theory, until a certain stage of inter-uterine development, the sexes are the same. At a particular point the foetus then becomes either male, female, or what Ulrichs called an Urning (a 'feminine' male who will be sexually drawn to men) or a Uringin (a 'masculine' woman who is sexually drawn to women). Ulrichs attempted to further support the claim that homosexuality is congenital by citing examples of 'feminine' inclinations in pre-pubescent Urnings. In one of his earliest published pieces he states:

The female habitus [the outwardly recognizable female essence] is quite particularly in us in our childhood, before we have been reared into an artificial masculinity, and before we have had the depressing experience that every expression of our female essence will be ascribed to us as a disgrace . . . before, that is, suffering under this external pressure, we began to carefully hide that female trait.

The Urning shows as a child a quite unmistakable partiality for girlish activities, for interaction with girls, for playing with girl's play-things. (cited in Kennedy 1997: 31)

Ulrichs also coined the term Dioning to describe what we now call a heterosexual man. Interestingly, he did not develop a term for heterosexual women since, along with most other thinkers of the time, Ulrichs presumed that feminine/heterosexual (and the two terms are interchangeable) women were not subjects of sexual desire, but merely passive objects. Ulrichs derived the terms Urning and Dioning from the names of the Greek gods Uranus and Dione and, in particular, from the speech made by Pausanias in Plato's *Symposium* in which two kinds of love are outlined: common love which is associated with Aphrodite, the daughter of Dione (the great mother goddess) and thus with the love of women; and heavenly love which is associated with the motherless (Uranian) Aphrodite, daughter of the omnipotent Zeus, and there-fore with the birth of a love in which the female has no part.

According to Ulrichs' thesis, Urnings/Uringins have the physical features of one sex and the soul or sexual instinct of the other and these forms of being are no less products of nature than the more common Dioning is. Therefore, Ulrichs argued, insofar as homo-sexuality is the result of nature, it cannot be unnatural. In fact it would only be possible to conclude that Uranian love (same-sex love) is unnatural, if one assumed that 'all men [sic] were born with the nature of the Dioning' (Ulrichs 1994: 36) – an assumption that Ulrichs argued vehemently against. Indeed, Ulrichs claimed that the Urning who satisfies his sexual drive with another male is behaving as naturally and thus as appropriately as the Dioning who satisfies his sexual drive with a woman. Ulrichs used this argument to counter the notion of same-sex love as a crime against nature, and to call for law reforms that would no longer allow the punishment of individuals on the basis of such a crime. It is unjust, he argued, to presume that there is only one form that nature takes and to judge one person in accordance with the natural laws of another. He writes:

You cannot study fish by comparing them to birds or vice versa, because they belong to different species... This prosecution [of Uranian love] is as senseless as... punishing hens for laying eggs instead of chicks, or cows bearing calves instead of laying eggs. The current day persecution of [Uranian] love is just as foolish as the persecution of heresy and witchcraft. It, too, was unsuccessful. 'You can drive nature out with a pitchfork, but it will always return!' Horace says. (Ibid.: 38)

Whilst Ulrichs' work did not immediately result in radical law reform, it was influential not only in the field of legal studies, but also in medical studies, as I will go on to illustrate. But before I do, I want to point out that whilst Ulrichs' writing may, on one level, have challenged normative opinions about same-sex relations, it nevertheless tended to reaffirm gender norms. For example, Ulrichs was primarily concerned with same-sex relations between men, even though he acknowledged the existence of women who were sexually drawn to other women. Consequently, an account of what we might now call lesbianism remains fairly underdeveloped in Ulrichs' work and is cast unquestioningly in masculine terms. Moreover, as I said earlier, for Ulrichs, men who love men are understood as having a female soul in a man's body, and women who love women as having a masculine psyche, or sex drive in a woman's body. This thesis leaves no room for 'masculine' homosexuals or for 'feminine' lesbians, nor, moreover, does it accord heterosexual women (that is, feminine women who are sexually attracted to men)[3] any active sexual agency. In fact, Ulrichs' thesis is firmly founded on dichotomies such as male/female, active/passive, subject/object, mind/body, and so on, which construct the world in terms of one valued term and its opposite. The problem with this sort of dichotomous logic will become more apparent in the following chapters. Another problem with Ulrichs' model is, as Marshall notes, 'it effectively eliminated the need for a homosexual concept' (1981: 135). This is because, insofar as the

Urning is understood as a female soul in a male body, then this person is closer to what we might call a heterosexual female (in a male body) than a homosexual male.

Despite what we might now identify as its shortcomings, Ulrichs' account of same-sex relations influenced the work of the best-known sexologists of the nineteenth century, including Richard von Krafft-Ebing, Havelock Ellis, Carl Westphal, Magnus Hirschfeld, and Sigmund Freud. And, as we shall see in due course, Ulrichs' notion of 'man-manly love'[4] as congenital ironically made way for the development of the notion of 'homosexuality' as an illness, pathology, or 'natural' aberration – that is, something that is no longer punishable by law, but that nevertheless calls for medical scrutiny, and ultimately for a cure.

Perhaps the best known of the Victorian sexologists to be influenced by Ulrichs was the German-Austrian psychiatrist Richard von Krafft-Ebing, who, in 1886 published the first version of the highly influential *Psychopathia Sexualis*[5] – a text whose aim was to name and classify every possible form of non-procreative sex and the subjects who participated in such practices. What informed Krafft-Ebing's early research on sexual pathology was an interest in forensic psychiatry. His was a medical rather than an emancipatory project and, in this sense, was significantly different from the work undertaken by Ulrichs. Nevertheless, since, as Harry Oosterhuis has noted, *Psychopathia Sexualis* was originally written for doctors and lawyers 'discussing sexual crimes in court' and to this end aimed to show 'that in many cases perversion was not a sin, or a crime, but a disease' (Oosterhuis 1997: 70), Krafft-Ebing's work did play an important role in legal reform. Whilst Krafft-Ebing's prime motivation was not justice for homosexuals he did, between 1882 and 1900, publish a series of articles on the legal aspects of same-sex love and, in the early 1890s, signed Magnus Hirschfeld's petition advocating the abolition of §175 (one of the German and Austrian laws criminalising 'unnatural vice').[6]

Like Ulrichs, Krafft-Ebing believed that homosexuality was congenital, but, unlike Ulrichs, he associated this innate condition with heredity and degeneration: sexual inversion, he said is 'a result of neuro-psychical degeneration' (cited in Gibson 1998: 85). Krafft-Ebing believed that homosexuals were less developed, in an evolutionary sense, than heterosexuals; that, in short, they exemplified a more primitive state of being. He supported this claim by proposing that humans had once been hermaphroditic and that since this was still the case with lower life forms, then individuals who displayed sexually ambiguous (or hermaphroditic) traits were therefore primitive, atavistic, or degenerate.[7] For Krafft-Ebing then, along with many of his contemporaries, homosexuals who blurred the normative boundaries of gender – 'either as masculine women or effeminate men – were regarded as "unfinished" specimens of stunted evolutionary growth, a status they shared with "savages" and certain types of criminals' (Terry 1995: 135).

Not all physicians or scientists who believed that homosexuality was innate were quite as scathing or as deterministic as Krafft-Ebing. For example, Havelock Ellis, a British sexologist and author of *Sexual Inversion*,[8] and *Studies in the Psychology of Sex*, played an important role in rethinking the notion of degeneration that was central to Krafft-Ebing's writings. Whilst Ellis clearly dismissed the suggestion that inversion – the term he used to refer to same-sex love – was purely acquired, he nevertheless seemed to be of the opinion that both nature and nurture had a hand in the construction of (homo)sexuality. Unlike Ulrichs who implied that same-sex love was normal, if uncommon, and Krafft-Ebing who claimed that it should be read as a symptom and sign of constitutional degeneracy, Ellis posited the notion of a congenital predisposition which he regarded as an anomaly or an abnormality, but not as a disease. In this sense, inversion, Ellis claimed, is analogous to colour-blindness or colour-hearing insofar as all three conditions are abnormal but are not necessarily 'morbid' or harmful.[9]

For Ellis then, sexuality was not understood as absolutely biologically determined even though, he claimed, a predisposition towards one form of sexual practice or another is apparent in all human beings. Such a predisposition does not, however, determine (although it will no doubt influence) the way one lives one's life. As Ellis puts it: 'It is probable that many persons go through the world with a congenital predisposition to inversion which always remain latent and unroused' (1908: 190). Given that a predisposition towards inversion does not necessarily lead to same-sex sexual relations, the question of what makes a homosexual a (practising) homosexual remains slightly unclear in Ellis' work, at least if one is looking for scientific or biological certainties.

What I meant when I said earlier that in Ellis' work on inversion both nature and nurture seem to play a part, is that whilst Ellis posits the notion of a predisposition to inversion, he also shows that cultural factors influence the ways in which this predisposition will be lived and experienced. A number of times throughout *Sexual Inversion* Ellis refers to a sort of sexual indefiniteness that is apparent at the time of puberty, which, like colour-hearing tends 'to become less marked, or to die out, after puberty' (Ibid.: 183, 187). This narrowing of sexual expression could well be explained by Ulrichs' claim that external pressures 'encourage' individuals to conform to social expectations and/or to hide forms of behaviour that are likely to be considered inappropriate. Whilst Ellis does not explore this issue, he does raise the question of what it is that might be said to excite or invoke (rather than discourage) a latent predisposition to inversion, and in doing so, shows, at least implicitly, that sexuality is, to some extent, affected by cultural factors. Ellis offers three examples of causes that excite inversion, but, citing the Berlin sexologist Albert Moll,[10] points out that such factors are unlikely to have such an effect if a person is not already endowed with a predisposition to inversion. The causes discussed are the school system, seduction, and disappointment in 'normal' love.

As Ellis tells it, the segregation of boys and girls during adolescence and the forming of bonds between young people of the same sex, makes school 'the great breeding-place of ... homosexuality' (Ibid.: 193).[11] Moreover, Ellis claimed that the education (and consequent 'masculinisation') of middle-class women which was part of the increasing push for women's rights in the early twentieth century, was responsible for the emergence of 'mannish' women[12] (inverts) who tended to exploit the natural passivity of womanly women (heterosexuals). Ellis says:

Women are, very justly, coming to look upon knowledge and experience generally as their right as much as their brother's right ... [H]aving been taught independence of men and disdain for the old theory which placed women in the moated grange of the home to sigh for a man who never comes, a tendency develops for women to carry this independence still further and to find love where they work. I do not say that these unquestionable influences of modern movements can directly cause sexual inversion ... but they develop the germs of it ... [T]he congenital anomaly occurs with special frequency in women of high intelligence who, voluntarily or involuntarily, influence others. (Ibid.: 147–8)

Again, this example illustrates my suggestion that inversion, as Ellis formulated it is, in part, effected by historically specific cultural factors, as does his discussion of both seduction and 'disappointment in normal love' as things that could be said to excite the predisposition to inversion.[13] In short, then, Ellis believed that since inversion was congenital, it could not be cured and should not be punishable: it was neither a sickness nor a crime. However, he was also of the opinion that since the innate predisposition to inversion was aroused by culturally and historically specific practices and forms of social life, it may be possible to lessen the potential for homosexuality by eliminating, or at least discouraging, things like sex-segregated schools.

Before we move on to look at some of the other positions elaborated by various sexologists I want to suggest that perhaps one of the most interesting things about Ellis' ideas is the extent to which they continue to circulate and to be given credence in contemporary Western cultures. How often have you heard it said, for example, that someone is a lesbian because her past relationships with men were unsuccessful, perhaps even disastrous? How common is the claim that homosexuals induct young people into homosexuality? And who could honestly say that they have not encountered the stereotypes of feminists as lesbians and of Women's Studies as a hot-bed of lesbianism?

Karl Westphal, a German psychiatrist, is another sexologist whose ideas are still in circulation today, although perhaps less prominently so than Ellis'. Westphal, like Ulrichs, Krafft-Ebing, and Ellis also believed that homosexuality was congenital and therefore should not be punished. However, Westphal took a position closer to Krafft-Ebing than to Ulrichs or Ellis, and suggested that whilst homosexuals should not be imprisoned, they would benefit from medical treatment since homosexuality was a deviation from 'normal' sexual development. In fact, many commentators have claimed that Westphal's work, first published in 1869, marks the beginnings of the medicalisation of homosexuality.

Westphal was also one of the first writers to describe extensively, and in medical terms, same-sex relations between women. In a case study published in 1869, Westphal suggested that the female invert was really a man trapped in a woman's body – an idea that was obviously derived from Ulrichs' work, and which, as we shall see in Chapter 5, could be read as a theory of transgender rather than homosexuality. For Westphal, a woman who desired other women was necessarily 'masculine', and so-called masculine women, were invariably inverts. Indeed, masculine appearance figured heavily in early definitions of the female invert as Lillian Faderman has pointed out.[14] For example, Krafft-Ebing described the female invert thus:

[She] may chiefly be found in the haunts of boys. She is rival in their play . . . The toilet is neglected and rough boyish manners are affected. At times smoking and drinking are cultivated even with a passion. Perfumes and sweetmeats are disdained. There is a strong desire to imitate the male fashion in dressing the hair and in general attire. (cited in Bland and Doan 1998: 47)

Similarly, Ellis lists (masculine) characteristics such as a disdain for feminine artifices, brusque energetic movements, direct speech, straightforwardness, a sense of honour, a masculine type of larynx and a preference for masculine simplicity in dress if not for male apparel, as typical of female inversion. In short, what we find exemplified here is Foucault's claim that nothing that went into the lesbian's

total composition was unaffected by [her] sexuality. It was everywhere present in [her]: at the root of all [her] actions because it was their insidious and definitely active principle; written immodestly on [her] face and body because it was a secret that always gave itself away. (1980: 43)

Obviously this view of lesbians as 'masculine' women still exists today and, one could argue, it has, to some extent, been reclaimed by (some) lesbians who take pleasure in performing what Judith Halberstam has referred to as female masculinity.[15] But whilst some of Westphal's claims still circulate in our culture, others are less apparent. For example, the idea that it is not only possible, but necessary to (at least attempt to) cure homosexuality is less common in contemporary Western culture than it was in Westphal's time, or, as I shall go on to discuss, in the 1950s and 1960s, although it still exists in what one might think of as fundamentalist discourses,[16] and, as the existence of films such as *But I'm A Cheer-leader* shows (see Chapter 3), the concept is far from alien to us.

Magnus Hirschfeld, whose work I will discuss in more detail in Chapter 5, was a sexologist whose approach and motivation were significantly different from Westphal's. Hirschfeld, a medical doctor, Jewish socialist, and advocate of homosexual rights, believed that the scientific study of homosexuality would destroy 'millenia-old religious superstitions and traditional morals' (Hirschfeld, cited in Steakley 1997: 135). In his early publications Hirschfeld, following Ulrichs, developed the notion of a third sex, who, rather than

11

being punished for their biologically determined drives, should be tolerated and treated justly. He later abandoned this idea and outlined instead a notion of what we might now call sexual pluralism which radically contravened the rigid nineteenth-century paradigm of sexual polarity.

In (at least) two ways Hirschfeld's contributions to the question and status of homosexuality were groundbreaking. First, insofar as he posited a notion of infinite sexual variability that he compared to the distinctiveness of fingerprints,[17] Hirschfeld totally undermined the distinction between 'normal' and 'abnormal' forms of sexuality and challenged the popular theory of constitutional degeneracy. Second, Hirschfeld used his scientific analyses to argue for the elimination of not only popular prejudices, but perhaps more importantly, legal ones.

In Berlin in 1897 Hirschfeld founded the world's first homosexual rights organisation, the Scientific-Humanitarian Committee, which had as its primary goal the repeal of the German sodomy statute, and, as its more general aim, the education of the populace on issues pertaining to same-sex relations. The organisation was dissolved, however, in 1933 by the Nazis. In 1919 Hirschfeld established the Institute for Sexology – again, the first of its kind in the world – and in 1928 became the founder and chair of the World League for Sexual Reform. Hirschfeld – whose tombstone was inscribed with the words *'Per scientiam ad justitiam'* (Through science to justice) – argued throughout his lifetime that attempts to cure homosexuality were pointless and misguided. What he did advocate though was a form of 'adjustment therapy' in and through which homosexuals would come to accept, embrace, and perhaps even celebrate their sexuality. In a sense, then, Hirschfeld's work could be said to be central to the development of what in the mid-late twentieth century came to be known as gay pride.

Some would argue that Edward Carpenter a British contemporary of Hirschfeld's who was also a socialist pioneer, the author of the influential *The Intermediate Sex* (1908), and the first president of the British Society for the Study of Sex Psychology founded in 1914, went one step further than Hirschfeld, suggesting, at least in a roundabout way, that inverts were superior to heterosexuals. In the above-mentioned text Carpenter states:

The instinctive artistic nature of the male of this [the homogenic] class, his sensitive spirit, his wavelike emotional temperament, combined with hardihood of intellect and body; and the frank free nature of the female, her masculine independence and strength wedded to thoroughly feminine grace of form and manner; may be said to give them both, through their double nature, command of life in all its phases, and a certain freemasonry of the secrets of the two sexes which may well favor their function as reconcilers and interpreters. (in Bland and Doan 1998: 51)

For Carpenter inverts (with the exception of what he refers to as the extreme types) were conceived of as more well-rounded, and thus as having greater insight into the variegations of human being than their more common (heterosexual) counterparts. Unlike many of the sexologists who were writing at the time, Carpenter did not seem particularly disturbed by the existence of women who exhibited so-called masculine characteristics including (active) sexual agency and/or pleasure. Indeed, in *Love's Coming of Age* (1896) – a text whose focus is the problem of opposite sex relations – Carpenter separates sex from procreation, arguing for the necessity of sexual pleasure for both parties. As Weeks (1981) has pointed out, such a position has important implications for women (of all sexual persuasions) and for male homosexuals[18] who, at this time in Britain were still punished by law for committing what were referred to as criminal acts of 'gross' indecency.

Carpenter's tendency to reverse the normative hierarchy between heterosexuality and homosexuality may have been unusual, but the association of lesbianism with masculinity in the work of the majority of the sexologists writing in the nineteenth to twentieth centuries tended, inadvertently, to have a similar effect. As Margaret Gibson (1998) has explained, it was a generally held belief at the time of such writings that the masculine intellect was superior to the feminine intellect. However, if this was the case, and if it were true that lesbians were masculine, then the lesbian intellect must necessarily be superior to that of the heterosexual woman, despite the fact that (female) homosexuals were simultaneously cast as degenerate and thus inferior to heterosexuals. Obviously the notion of the lesbian as a sort of an intellectual superwoman would present all sort of problems not only for normative cultural hierarchies but also for the controversies surrounding women's access to education that were raging at the time. Consequently, various theoretical attempts were made to overcome the tension inherent in the notion of the mannish woman, the most common of which involved depicting the lesbian brain as similar to, or sharing characteristics with, 'a non-white or lower-class masculine brain' (Ibid. 1998: 86). In short, many medical writers and social commentators drew on existing cultural hierarchies based on race and class differences in order to maintain the privileged position of white, middle-/upper-class, heterosexual masculinity and to veil over any contradictions in established theories of inversion that might pose a challenge to the status quo.

Perhaps the best known theorist of sexuality is Sigmund Freud, the founder of psychoanalysis. In one of his earliest papers on sexuality entitled 'The Sexual Aberrations' Freud notes the influence on his thinking of the work of sexologists such as Krafft-Ebing, Havelock Ellis, Hirschfeld, and others. However, whilst Freud's work undoubtedly engages with the ideas elaborated by these writers, it also diverges from them in significant ways. For example, for Freud the notion of degeneracy was considered of little value to a study of the aetiology of same-sex desire. Inversion, he claimed, 'is found in people who have no other serious deviations from the normal' (Freud 1996: 78). Indeed, it is often apparent in those who are 'distinguished by specially high intellectual development and ethical culture' (Ibid.: 78). Given this, Freud, unlike Krafft-Ebing, concluded that it is 'impossible to regard inversion as a sign of degeneracy' (Ibid.: 78).

Freud was also sceptical of the claim that inversion is simply innate and therefore fixed and unchanging.[19] For him, sexuality was understood less as an essence than as a drive. This is not to suggest, however, that Freud agreed with those who saw inversion as purely acquired and created solely by outside influences. Rather, according to Freudian theory, the (sex) drive[20] is shaped in and through the (social) development of human being. As Freud states, there are a whole range of possible sexual aims, object choices, and states of psycho-sexual being which are the products of each individual's psycho-sexual development and of the context in which such development occurs. Consequently, as Jeffrey Weeks notes,[21] Freud's work was ground-breaking in that it pointed to the fact that heterosexuality (as a culturally and historically specific institution) may well be a cultural necessity, but it is not something that is naturally preordained. As Freud put it:

From the point of view of psychoanalysis the exclusive sexual interest felt by men for women is also a problem that needs elucidation and is not a self-evident fact based upon an attraction that is ultimately of a chemical nature. (cited in Weeks 1981: 153)

Moreover, Freud was also aware of the impact of culturally specific ways of understanding sexuality on the lived experience of erotic life. In a passage that is interestingly reminiscent of Foucault's analysis of *aphrodisia* in ancient Greek culture,[22] Freud shows that the notion of object choice as central to the definition of sexuality is particular to twentieth-century Western culture rather than being natural and therefore universal.[23] Given that Freud was writing at a time when heterosexuality (founded, as it was, on the notion of object choice) was so naturalised as to be almost unquestionable, then insights such as these were radical, to say the least. Even today many people unquestioningly accept the idea that sexuality is defined and is definable in terms of the sex/gender of object choice. However, as we shall see in Chapter 3, once normative assumptions about sex/gender are undermined and/or the traditional focus on object choice is shown to be cultural rather than natural and inevitable, identity categories such as heterosexual and homosexual become almost impossible to maintain.

Chris Waters has argued that, whilst in Britain in the inter-war period (1920s and 1930s) sexological understandings of homosexuality were more influential than the work of Freud, by the 1950s psychoanalytic accounts of the aetiology of homosexuality had come to dominate – to varying degrees – the English-speaking world. What this meant was that the notion of homosexuality as innate was slowly superseded by an image of homosexuality as a form of arrested development that could be cured by therapeutic means. Waters suggests that this shift was, in part, the result of the discrediting of the work of sexologists such as Ellis by Freudians such as Ernest Jones, and, in part, the effect of the use of psychoanalytic paradigms by an increasing number of criminologists working on delinquency in the inter-war period. But Freudian psychoanalysis, as it was developed and practised by both Jones and his followers and by many of the British criminologists, was much more inclined to the view that homosexuality was more or less the sole result of environmental factors, and thus was inevitably susceptible to therapeutic intervention, than was Freud. Waters supports this claim by citing Jones' criticism of Freud's tolerant attitude toward one of his lesbian clients and by outlining the differences in approaches taken by Freud, and, for example, Thomas Ross, the British psychotherapist and author of a number of influential works, including *An Introduction to Analytical Psychotherapy*, published in 1932.

For Ross and others like him, the homosexual had merely been 'diverted from the heterosexual path' (Ross, cited in Waters 1998: 170), and thus, in and through therapy, could be put back on the straight and narrow. The importance of this shift in the understanding of the homosexual is, as Waters notes, that it consists of 'the construction of a new type of being . . . the refashion[ing] [of] the congenital invert as a treatable homosexual' (Ibid.: 170). And it is this figure that comes to loom large in the imaginations of post-war criminologists, legislators, and medical professionals, particularly in the USA. Not everyone agreed that homosexuality could, or should, be cured, or that magistrates should have the power to sentence people to psychiatric treatment. For example, Edmund Glover, the British criminologist and founder of the Institute for Scientific Treatment of Delinquency (1932), argued that therapeutic intervention was, for the most part, unsuccessful, and that most of the psychological problems suffered by homosexuals were the result of their marginalisation and persecution. In fact, in 1957, in his testimony to the Wolfenden Committee on Homosexual Offences and Prostitution,[24] Glover wrote, 'there is no answer to homosexuality save tolerance on the part of the intolerant anti-homosexual groups in the community' (cited in Waters 1998: 175).

Despite Waters' claim that the belief in the possibility of curing homosexuality in and through therapeutic intervention was much more wholeheartedly embraced in the United States than it was in Britain in the 1950s, Erin Carlston's study of medical discourses (particularly of the Freudian persuasion) on homosexuality in North America during this period suggests that they were far from uniform. There were, for example, those who continued to associate homosexuality with (inappropriate) gender, rather than with object-choice, but who simultaneously drew on psychoanalytic accounts of (arrested) sexual development in order to identify lesbianism as a refusal to renounce an active, self-defined subject position and/or sexuality. Dr John Meagher took such a position, thus conflating feminism and lesbianism in a move that even today is not uncommon. Meagher writes:

The driving force in many agitators and militant women who are always after their rights, is often an unsatisfied sex impulse, with a homosexual aim. Married women with a completely satisfied libido rarely take an active interest in militant movements. They have other interests, family and social, to use up their energy . . . The best biological and social assets to society are the complete she-women, and the complete he-men. (cited in Carlston 1997: 181)

The inevitable conclusion to be drawn from Meagher's words of warning is that 'appropriate' gender roles are crucial to the well-being of both the individual and society and that women who seem inclined towards lesbianism may avoid that tragic fate if society ensures that their energy is directed towards, and used up in, the service of heterosexuality. But, as Carlston shows, this was not necessarily a position shared by all those working in the field at the time. In the same issue of the journal in which Meagher's article appeared, Aaron Rosanoff, a Los Angeles-based psychiatrist, penned a piece condemning the coercion of so-called homosexuals into heterosexual marriage on the grounds that this would lead to the heredity perpetuation of homosexuality – 'the very thing that conventional society would wish to avoid' (Rosanoff, cited in Carlston 1997: 183). Indeed, the answer, as Rosanoff saw it, was not even to ignore homosexual behaviour, but rather, to 'encourage it, on eugenic grounds' (Carlston 1997: 183). I would suggest, however, that Rosanoff's position was not one that was shared by many in the post-war period. Indeed, from the 1940s onwards, therapeutic attempts to 'cure' delinquency of various kinds, including, of course, homosexuality, increased significantly. These therapies ranged from the so-called 'talking cure', to aversion therapy, to insulin-induced shock, to the use of chemicals such as Metrazol to provoke grand mal seizures, to the mutilation of the bodies of homosexuals in and through procedures such as castration.[25]

Despite the publication in the late 1940s and early 1950s of Alfred Kinsey's statistical survey – commissioned by the National Institute of Mental Health – of current sexual practices in the USA, which suggested that a large number of so-called heterosexuals had had, at some point in their life, same-sex liaisons of one sort or another, and that the majority of Americans fell somewhere between the strictly heterosexual and strictly homosexual positions at each end of the six-point scale that he elaborated, the notion of homosexuality as something opposed to heterosexuality nevertheless persisted. In a book entitled *Female Homosexuality: A Psychodynamic Study of Lesbianism*, published in 1954 – allegedly 'the only study that is based on investigations of lesbianism and lesbian practices in practically every part of the world'[26] – Frank Caprio argued that there is little point in ostracising, punishing, or

17

pitying inverts. Rather, the aim must be to understand that lesbianism, like other forms of inversion, is the symptom of a more
fundamental 'personality problem, associated with feelings of
sexual immaturity and insecurity' (1954: 299) that must be treated,
or, better still, prevented from occurring. Thus, says Caprio, it is a
parent's responsibility to prevent the development of homosexual
patterns by providing a 'wholesome family atmosphere', a sense of
security – particularly from their mothers – so that young women
will not seek 'substitute mothers' later in life, and ensuring that
their daughters do not form 'unnaturally close ties' with other
girls. In cases where homosexuality has not been avoided, Caprio,
drawing on the writings of psychoanalysts such as Ernest Jones and
Emil Gutheil, claims that it can, however, be cured because

many so-called homosexuals are really normal; they have simply got
off on the wrong track for one reason or another. They can be restored
to a normal sex outlook by sympathetic and expert treatment . . . at
the hands of a psychiatrist or psychoanalyst who believes in cure.
(Ibid.: 294)

Caprio concludes that whilst the majority of the lesbians he
encountered were cured in and through therapy, and thus went on
to become happily married, there were, and no doubt always will
be, a small minority who do not wish to be changed, and thus
prefer to refuse responsibility for their 'affliction' by claiming that
it is a congenital one. In this way, the homosexual is in fact refusing
to take up the 'normal' responsibilities associated with marriage
and family life. However, this refusal must, stresses Caprio, be overcome if young men and women are to avoid being caught in what
Robert Leslie described in his 1966 text *Casebook: Homophile*, as 'a
morass of twisted, warped desires . . . torments of unhappiness'.
As Leslie, the quintessential gender conformist,[27] puts it in the
Introduction to the book, the homosexual's life 'is not a life to
emulate, regardless of the claims made by the homophile apologists'
(1966: 16).

This notion of the homosexual as doomed to a life of torment,
suffering, loneliness, and so on, was not confined to so-called
medical tracts during this period. From around the 1930s on an
increasing number of novels and films appeared in which the
homosexual was constructed as a sad and twisted creature whose
perverse desires would inevitably lead to their tragic downfall, and
often their death. Perhaps the most famous of these is Radclyffe
Hall's *The Well of Loneliness*, originally published in 1928, and

found to be 'obscene' in both Britain and America and thus withdrawn. Hall's text has, over the years, evoked mixed feelings in gay and lesbian readers because of its depiction of Stephen, a disconsolate butch lesbian whose feelings remain unrequited. Nevertheless, it has been claimed that the text could, and should, be read as a critical commentary on the social and historical context in which Hall found herself, and as the forerunner of a genre of pulp fiction which, unfortunately, for the most part, sensationalised the tragic elements and forgot about the critical commentary. This sort of shift is probably most evident in novels such as Dean Douglas' *Man Divided* (1954), Fritz Peters' *Finistère* (1952), and Lilyan Brock's *Queer Patterns* (originally published in 1935, and reprinted in 1952 on the heels of the successful reprinting of *The Well of Loneliness* in 1951).[28] Films that constructed homosexuality similarly include *Fireworks*,[29] *Maedchen in Uniform*,[30] *The Killing of Sister George*,[31] *The Locket*,[32] *Young Man With A Horn*,[33] *Suddenly Last Summer*,[34] *Victim*,[35] *Advise and Consent*,[36] *The Detective*,[37] and most particularly, *The Children's Hour*.[38]

These representations of homosexuality and the medical and legal practices that they engendered gave rise to various civil rights groups such as the Mattachine Society, and the Daughters of Billitis (in the USA). It is groups such as these and the theoretical and political positions that they took which will be the focus of the following chapter.

NOTES

1. Marshall (1981)
2. Some of these were originally published under the pseudonym Numa Numantis.
3. The assumption is that all heterosexual women are 'feminine' since a 'masculine' heterosexual woman is a contradiction in terms in Ulrichs' account.
4. This is the title of a collection of Ulrichs' articles written between 1863–1865 and originally published under the above-mentioned pseudonym. The twelfth and last volume of *Man-Manly Love* was published in 1879 under Ulrichs' real name.
5. *Psychopathia Sexualis* was revised and expanded a number of times and seventeen editions were published in German between 1886 and 1924.
6. For further discussion of this issue see Oosterhuis (1997).
7. Krafft-Ebing was not alone when it came to the notion of an original

bisexuality or hermaphroditism which, in the nineteenth century was thought to exist only in less evolved human beings. In *Sexual Inversion* Havelock Ellis footnotes other medical writers who held this position, including Kiernan, Lydston, and de Letamendi.

8. This text was declared to be unscientific and was thus banned for obscene libel at the Old Bailey in 1898. Ellis then published *Studies in the Psychology of Sex*, a twelve-volume collection of which *Sexual Inversion* was one volume, in the USA in 1908.

9. See Ellis (1908) pp. 186–8.

10. Moll says 'He can only be seduced who is capable of being seduced' (cited in Ellis 1908: 191).

11. In a discussion of female inversion Ellis also suggests that prisons, workplaces in which employees live together, and theatres are also places that for structural reasons seem to encourage same-sex relations. See Ellis (1908) pp. 126–32.

12. For a description of the 'mannish' woman see Ellis (1908) pp. 133–47.

13. For further discussion of seduction and of disappointment in 'normal' love, see Ellis (1908) pp. 190–2.

14. See Faderman (1991), especially pp. 37–61.

15. See Halberstam (1997; 1998).

16. For example, ex-gay and/or Transformational Ministries, of which GayChange Webring lists thirty-six. These groups, which include Exodus International, Evergreen International Inc., and Homosexuals Anonymous, began to emerge in the early 1970s and currently have branches in the USA, the UK, Australia, Canada, Europe, and Asia. They all claim that conversion from homosexuality to heterosexuality is both possible and morally necessary. For more information see www.religioustolerance.org/homosexu.htm

17. In the second volume of *Sexual Pathology* (1918) Hirschfeld stated that there is 'absolutely no such thing as two individuals identical in their sexuality' (cited in Steakley 1997: 145).

18. Weeks (1981) p. 172

19. See, for example, Freud (1977b) pp. 140; 145–6.

20. I do not mean to suggest by this that there is an innate, identifiable, and discrete entity that one can call the sex drive. Rather, Freud speaks of 'an endosomatic, continuously flowing source of stimulation' (1977b: 82–3); that is, a process (rather than a thing) which lies on what he describes as the frontier between the mental and the physical.

21. Weeks (1981) pp. 153–4

22. Foucault (1987)

23. See Freud (1977b) p. 61 footnote. See also Marshall (1981).

24. For a more detailed discussion of this committee and its findings and effects see Weeks (1981) pp. 239–44.

25. For a more detailed account of the idea that homosexuality is curable, and the repercussions of this, see Birke (1982), and Reynolds (2002) who is specifically concerned with the Australian context.

26. This claim is made on the cover of the book in which it is stressed that this is a scientific study in which the author, a medical expert with years of experience in clinical research, has consulted with an array of international 'authorities on sexual abnormalities', and thus produced a text of 'inestimable value to all, professionals and lay readers alike, who are interested in acquiring a scientific understanding of this aspect of Sexual Behavior'.

27. The dedication in Leslie's book tellingly reads: 'To Nancy and the kids, who tiptoe as father works'.

28. For a more detailed discussion of pulp paperbacks of the 1950s and 1960s see Stryker (2001).

29. 1947, directed by Kenneth Anger.

30. Originally released in 1931 and directed by Leontine Sagan. The film was remade in 1958.

31. 1969, directed by Robert Aldrich.

32. 1946, directed by John Brahm.

33. 1950, directed by Michael Curtiz.

34. 1959, directed by Joseph L. Mankiewicz. Based on a play by Tennessee Williams.

35. 1961, directed by Basil Dearden.

36. 1962, directed by Otto Preminger, and based on a novel by Allen Drury.

37. 1968, directed by Gordon Douglas, and based on a novel by Roderick Thorp.

38. 1961, directed by William Wyler.

* I am indebted to Helmut Puff's article, 'Female Sodomy: The Trial of Katherina Hetzeldorfer (1477)', *Journal of Medieval and Early Modern Studies*, 30: 1, 2000, and would like to apologise to the author for failing to reference the text in an earlier version of this book.

2

Assimilation or Liberation, Sexuality or Gender?

IN THIS CHAPTER WE WILL examine a number of different ways in which same-sex relations were understood and experienced in the mid to late twentieth century, and touch briefly on the forms of political activism that emerged in the USA, the UK, and Australia as a result of these specific ways of knowing and of being. Rather than providing detailed accounts of particular groups and the protests and events they organised or participated in, I will proved a brief overview of some of the fundamental conceptual shifts that occurred and that affected different groups and individuals in heterogeneous ways. The reason for this is first, that detailed culturally specific histories have already been more than adequately elaborated,[1] and second, that it is impossible to do justice to the complexities and nuances of each group or movement and each specific cultural and political situation in a chapter of this length.

As I noted in the previous chapter, various humanitarian organisations concerned with the (de)criminalisation of homosexuality were active in Europe, the USA, and Britain in the first half of the twentieth century. The work of such organisations, combined with the increasingly public discussion of sexuality, paved the way for the emergence, in the 1950s, of what we might think of as the first homosexual civil rights groups. In the USA such groups formed what came to be known as the Homophile Movement. The groups most often associated with this movement are, of course, the Mattachine Society[2] which was established in Los Angeles in 1951, and the Daughters of Bilitis founded in 1955.[3]

The aims of the Mattachine Society were to bring homosexuals and heterosexuals together, to educate both homosexuals and heterosexuals, to lead a movement for legal reform, and to assist those who found themselves victimised on a daily basis in the context of entrenched homophobia, and McCarthyism. Similarly, CAMP (Campaign Against Moral Persecution) Inc, an Australian group founded in 1970, described their political agenda thus:

As far as the wider society is concerned, we should concentrate on providing information, removing prejudice, ignorance and fear, stressing the ordinariness of homosexuality and generally reassuring and disarming those with hostile attitudes. Concerning homosexuals, we think a policy of development of confidence and lessening of feelings of isolation and guilt, where they exist, is vital. (Poll, cited in Thompson 1985: 10)

In other words, we could say that groups such as these took, for the most part, what we would now refer to as an assimilationist approach to politics and to social change. The aim of assimilationist groups was (and still is) to be accepted into, and to become one with, mainstream culture. Consequently, one of the primary tenets of assimilationist discourses and discursive practices is the belief in a common humanity to which both homosexuals and heterosexuals belong. And this commonality – the fact that we are all human beings despite differences in secondary characteristics such as the gender of our sexual object choices – is the basis, it is claimed, on which we should all be accorded the same (human) rights, and on which we should treat each other with tolerance and respect. As Daniel Harris, citing Ward Summer, puts it:

Gay propaganda from the 1950s . . . is characterized by what might be called the Shylock argument, the assertion that a homosexual is not a . . . dissolute libertine well beyond the pale of respectable society, but 'a creature who bleeds when he is cut, and who must breathe oxygen in order to live'. (1997: 240–1)

In short, then, the assumption was/is that tolerance can be achieved by making differences invisible, or at least secondary, in and through an essentialising, normalising emphasis on sameness.

Often assimilationist groups drew on the writings of theorists such as Ulrichs, arguing that homosexuality is biologically determined and therefore should not be punishable by law. However, unlike Ulrichs, such groups allegedly tended to accept the medical model of homosexuality articulated by sexologists such as Westphal and Krafft-Ebing (see Chapter 1) and, as a consequence, sometimes represented themselves as victims of an unfortunate congenital accident who should be pitied rather than persecuted.

Thus, argues Harris, assimilationist groups relied heavily on what could best be described as 'the propaganda of powerlessness' (1997: 242).

In a sense, it may be perfectly understandable given the historically, culturally, and politically specific context in which they found themselves – one in which Cold War conservatism rubbed shoulders with the liberal humanist belief in democracy and humanitarianism – that these groups stressed sameness over difference, and assimilationist strategies over revolutionary ones. However, the notion of homosexuality as a biological 'accident' or anomaly which, whilst not being the fault of the individual, should nevertheless be policed and regulated, had tragic consequences for many. As Jeffrey Weeks has pointed out, and as I mentioned briefly in the previous chapter, the 'sickness model' of homosexuality necessarily involves the development and implementation of curative practices such as hypnotherapy, aversion therapy, insulin-induced shock therapy, the use of seizure-inducing chemicals, electric-shock treatment, religious indoctrination, and even castration, the removal of female reproductive organs, and lobotomies.[4] However, whilst some commentators have argued that in equating homosexuality with biology assimilationist organisations lent power – albeit inadvertently – to the normalising imperative of medical discourses and discursive practices, it is nevertheless true to say that groups such as the Mattachine Society and CAMP Inc spoke out and/or protested against the barbaric procedures associated with attempts to cure homosexuality.[5]

Assimilationist organisations also tend(ed)[6] to draw on the commonly held belief in a distinction between the public and the private spheres, arguing that sexuality is a private issue and is therefore outside of the domain of the law,[7] and that since sexual practices take place behind closed doors then they do not threaten the propriety of the public (political) domain, nor, by association, social relations more generally. One of the main problems with this sort of proposition is that it has the effect of depoliticising the private and the kinds of relations associated with it. So, for example, many feminists have argued that it is this kind of logic that has enabled rape in marriage to go unpunished, and domestic violence to be regarded as a personal issue that has nothing to do with the state and/or with hegemonic institutions and structures of power.

The claim that homosexuals are 'just like everybody else' and thus do not constitute a threat to normative society, and the proposition that homosexuality is congenital and a private matter, have led many social and political commentators to retrospectively describe assimilationist politics and those groups who promote(d) it, in negative, and often scathing terms. For example, Harris describes the Mattachine Society as 'cautious centrists who waved the flag and pledged "allegiance to church, state, and society"; a sentiment espoused in the Society's official slogan – "evolution not revolution"' (1997: 240). However, Martin Meeker has argued against this somewhat monolithic view of an organisation that changed over time, and consisted of a number of chapters which themselves were made up of diverse individuals. In fact, Meeker claims that the Mattachine Society adopted a practice of dissimulation, rather than simply promoting assimilation, donning a 'Janus-faced mask of respectability' which enabled them to 'speak simultaneously to homosexuals and homophobic heterosexuals and to communicate very different ideas to each population, during a time when the latter exerted considerable power over the former' (2001: 81). Interestingly, Meeker likens this practice to 'a good drag performance' (Ibid.: 117) that is recognisable for what it is to those 'in the know', but 'passes' undetected by those not familiar with the codes and conventions of gay (sub)cultures.

Obviously during this period there were gays, lesbians, and other sexual minorities who did not belong to homophile organisations or ascribe to assimilationist aspirations and agendas. For the most part, the groups that I've mentioned did consist of white, middle-class, 'well-educated' gays and lesbians and the views they put forward tended to reflect this as *Stonewall* (1995) illustrates. In fact, this film, directed by the late Nigel Finch, seems to suggest that such organisations were ideologically opposed to transsexuals, drag queens, and those gays and lesbians who frequented 'gay bars' and whose lifestyles were regarded as simply too radical or flagrantly confrontational. This dichotomy is embodied in the film in the figures of the Latino drag queen, LaMiranda, and the Columbia University graduate, teacher, and homophile organiser, Ethan, the two (potential and competing) lovers of the new kid on the block, Matty Dean who has fled the Midwest in search of sexual liberation in New York. Whilst it seems to me that the film uncritically reiterates this overly-simplistic (binary) myth of two tribes who go to war as much with each other as with heteronormative institutions, Chris Berry has nevertheless argued that the film reconfigures the legendary events that took place at the Stonewall Inn in June 1969, and in doing so, resists dichotomous logic, and queers history.

As you are no doubt aware, the Stonewall riots are often posited as the founding moment or the inauguration of the Gay (and Lesbian) Liberation Movement, and the associated death of the homophile movement. 'Stonewall' is, one could argue, a myth, as, according to Derrida, all origin stories are. But it is a myth that has taken on legendary dimensions. And, like traditional legends, the legend of Stonewall is all too often a story of saints and sinners that functions to canonise some and crucify others. However, as I said, Berry argues that Finch's *Stonewall* undermines this tendency in and through the proliferation of Stonewall legends that 'continue to reverberate and regain significance in the queer era' (1997: 137). The film opens, as Berry notes, with the pretty-in-pink lip-synching lips of LaMiranda who, once revealed in her entirety, tells the viewer:

See, there's as many Stonewall stories as there are gay queens in New York, and that's a shitload of stories, baby. Everywhere you go in Manhattan, or America, or the entire damn world, you're going to hear a new legend. Well, this is my legend honey, OK! My Stonewall legend.

This sort of logic, argues Berry, pervades the film and recasts history as perspectival, heterogeneous, always-already fiction-alised, and in short, 'fabulous'. History itself becomes a fabulous fable (or a myriad of often camp and contradictory fabulous fables) that no longer conforms to the (hetero)normative demand for a clear definition of, and distinction between, the real and the unreal, fact and fiction. Whilst Berry's analysis of the ways in which *Stonewall* (critically) engages with and destabilises or queers the codes and conventions associated with documentary, and by association with the re-presentation of historical events, may be convincing, his claim that the film resists oppositional logic could nevertheless be said to be debatable. This is because Finch's film – and to some extent Berry's article – tends to overlook the possibility that, as Meeker claims, homophile practice could be read as 'a good drag performance' (2001: 117) and instead equates drag (as epitomised by the figure of LaMiranda) with radicalism, diversity, and the demand for 'R-E-S-P-E-C-T', and sets it up in opposition to WASP standards of respectability, conservatism, and sameness (as epitomised in the figure of Ethan and the homophiles more generally). But there is of course the scene in which Bostonia, the 'chick with the dick', whilst uncharacteristically dancing with the leader of the Homophile Society whispers 'Between you and me, I do salute', to which the latter blushingly responds 'Between you and me, I'm honoured'. And perhaps this scene does, in a sense, bear witness to a relationship that was no doubt complex and contradictory, and, to the proposition made by Meeker that the Mattachine Society to some extent supported and aided the bar culture.[8]

Before we move on to an examination of Gay (and Lesbian) Liberation I want first to briefly discuss an aspect of bar culture that *Stonewall* fails to pay any sustained attention to, but which was not only well established at this time, but was politically important in the way it which it profoundly troubled gender norms. The phenomenon that I am referring to is butch/femme relations. In their analysis of the bar dyke community[9] in the USA in the 1940s and 1950s, Elizabeth Kennedy and Madelaine Davis claim that butches wore what were commonly regarded as masculine forms of clothing and their mannerisms – the way they walked, sat, spoke – were considered by themselves and others to be more 'masculine' than 'feminine'. However, for the most part, butches did not see themselves as women who passed as men, but as butches; that is, 'masculine' women who made explicit the existence of lesbianism, and who overtly resisted what they saw as heterosexist norms. In this way butches differed significantly from femmes who often did not visibly appear to be all that different from heterosexual women.

The visible resistance of butch women to heteronormative gender norms all too often resulted in persecution, and even violence. As one self-proclaimed black bulldagger dyke tells it, she was regularly harassed by the police for committing the crime of 'dressing like a man'. She writes:

I've had the police walk up to me and say, 'Get out of the car.' And they say 'What kind of shoes you got on? You got men's shoes on?' And I say 'No, I got on women's shoes.' I got on some basket-weave shoes. And he says 'Well, you're damn lucky.' Cause everything else I had on were men's – shirt, pants. At that time, when they picked you up, if you didn't have two or three garments that belong to a woman, you could go to jail . . . and the same thing with a man . . . They called it male impersonation or female impersonation and they'd take you downtown . . . It would give them the opportunity to whack the shit out of you. (cited in Kennedy and Davis 1992: 69)

As Kennedy and Davis tell it, because of severe harassment from police and the public, the butch role came to be identified with the defending of one's self and one's 'girl'. The role of the femme on the other hand, was, as one butch puts it, 'to help you with your black eye and split lip. You kick ass and she'd make you dinner. You never failed, or you tried not to. You were there, you were queer, and you were masculine' (Ibid.: 70).

Connected with this performance of gendered roles was the commonly held assumption that the butch was the physically active partner, initiator, and leader in sex, whose primary role was to give pleasure to her femme partner. No doubt this image of strongly defined and absolutely distinct roles was truer in theory than it was in practice, but dichotomies such as active/passive, subject/object, masculine/feminine, and so on, did have a huge impact on butch–femme relations and their possibilities at the time, and to some extent still do. Because of this it has been argued by feminists such as Sheila Jeffreys (1993; 1998) that butch–femme relations simply replicate(d) heterosexual relations, whereas Kennedy and Davis (amongst others) argue that butch–femme relations share(d) resonances with heterosexual sexual relations, whilst simultaneously challenging heterosexuality and heteronormativity.

The similarities that have been noted between butch–femme relations and heterosexuality include the centrality of gender polarity, the responsibility of the 'masculine' partner to sexually please the 'feminine' partner, and the idea(l) of the 'masculine' body as untouchable,[10] or at least the overlooking of the sensuality of that body in its entirety. The important differences include the fact that the butch–femme erotic system did not consistently follow the gender divisions of dominant culture. For example, in much writing of the time the butch's pleasure was represented as the result of giving pleasure to her woman,[11] whilst in heterosexual sex manuals, and popular cultural texts of the period the importance of a man giving pleasure to his woman may have been stressed but this was rarely represented as the ultimate source of his pleasure or as his primary sexual goal. Moreover, in butch–femme writings, the femme (unlike the heterosexual 'feminine' woman) was often described as highly sensual and/or sexual, and as someone who actively seeks out and experiences pleasure. What this seems to suggest is that the active/passive, subject/object dichotomies do not seem to neatly fit the butch–femme relation in the ways in which one might have supposed they would.

Given this, perhaps it is possible to conclude that whilst butch–femme sexual subcultures did not seem to accept normative beliefs, values, lifestyles to the extent that homophile groups such as the Daughters of Bilitis supposedly did, butches and femmes were nevertheless agents and effects of culturally and historically specific discourses. Butch–femme identities and relations did not exist outside of dominant regimes of power/knowledge and thus were not necessarily any more enlightened than their homophiles counterparts. Indeed, to suggest otherwise – as *Stonewall* could be said to in and through its use of liberationist rhetoric and its sentimentalisation of minority status – is to set up a dichotomous hierarchy that is divisive, reductive and overlooks the complexities of both identity and politics.

We will return to butch–femme relations and their changing political status a little later, but for the moment I want to move to the 1960s and 1970s and the emergence, in the West, of a range of radical political movements – the Anti-war Movement, the Black Power Movement, Women's Liberation, and student protest groups – of which Gay (and Lesbian) Liberation was one.[12] What these groups – which one might loosely describe as the New Left – had in common was a shift away from assimilationist strategies and the call for legal reforms. This is apparent in Carl Wittman's account of the defining principles of Gay Liberation as outlined in his *Refugees from Amerika: A Gay Manifesto* (1970). He writes:

Liberation for gay people is to define for ourselves how and with whom we live, instead of measuring our relationships by straight values . . . To be a free territory, we must govern ourselves, set up our own institutions, defend ourselves, and use our own energies to improve our lives. (cited in Adam 1995: 81)

For liberationists, then, the imperative was to experience homosexuality as something positive in and through the creation of alternative values, beliefs, lifestyles, institutions, communities, and so on. As Dennis Altman put it, 'gay liberation . . . is concerned with the assertion and creation of a new sense of identity, one based on pride in being gay' (1972: 109). Indeed, one could argue that the four key concerns shared by the majority of (liberationist) activists and organisations[13] were Pride, Choice, Coming Out, and Liberation.

The notion of Gay Pride is perhaps best captured in the theme song of *La Cage aux Folles*, 'I Am What I Am', which has since become something of a gay and lesbian anthem. In response to the image of homosexuality as a biological anomaly and something which one must at once justify and be ashamed of, liberationists claimed that one's identity 'needs no excuses', that, in fact, it is something to celebrate. As the anonymous author(s) of *Young, Gay, and Proud* put it, 'there is nothing wrong with being homosexual', 'we must say into the mirror every morning "I'm gay and I love myself"' (cited in Harris 1997: 254). Whilst the development of a positive image of homosexuality was unquestionably important both on a personal and a political level, there have nevertheless been various criticisms made of the assumptions on which such rhetoric is founded, and the discursive effects of such. For example, Harris argues that 'good-to-be-gay propaganda', with its focus on the importance of expressing oneself, gave rise to a somewhat unique fusion of 'two completely unrelated forces, politics and therapy' (Ibid.: 253), and is thus implicated in the contemporary addiction to therapy and the self-help industry.

Liberationists also attempted to replace the understanding of homosexuality as congenital with the notion of choice. The reasoning behind this shift is that the biological or 'no-choice' model of homosexuality allows gays and lesbians 'to be accepted only by representing ourselves as victims . . . of desires over which we have no control' (Sartelle 1994: 6). Associated with this is, of course, the implication that if one could choose to be otherwise, to be straight, then one would. Such a position, argues Sartelle, constitutes both the abdication of responsibility for one's own feelings and actions, and a capitulation to hegemonic heteronormative discourses and discursive practices which ultimately function to destroy (and/or to cure) difference. Again, one can see the importance of this shift, but at the same time the claim that one's sexual orientation is freely chosen has a number of drawbacks. As Harris notes, in many instances, the focus on choice fuelled anti-gay propaganda, giving homophobes and 'religious moralists the ideological loopholes they needed to attack a segment of the population once protected by the mawkish, if effective, rhetoric of powerlessness' (1997: 242–3). If sexual orientation was a choice, they argued, then it was possible for homosexuals to make the 'right' choice and to practise heterosexuality. However, one could argue that the distinction that Harris makes here between the protection supposedly offered by the 'rhetoric of powerlessness' and the inevitable backlash against the positing of homosexuality as one possible chosen sexual 'lifestyle' amongst many others, is somewhat tenuous. This is because, as Sartelle points out, the determinist argument fails to acknowledge the distinction between desire and action which is central to the claim (made by the conservative Right, and at times by more progressive groups such as feminists) that the fact that one experiences particular desires does not automatically give one the right to act on them.[14]

Associated with 'pride' and with the rhetoric of choice was the belief in the transformative power of 'coming out', of publicly declaring one's personal and political identity. As the anonymous authors of a piece in the Australian gay liberation newsletter, *Gay Pride Week News* (1973), write:

We believe that it is so important to remind everyone that you are a homosexual – COMING OUT – for yourself so you won't be subjected to anti-homosexual acts against yourself, and so other homosexuals who haven't come-out or are not confident of their homosexuality can realize other people are homosexuals and that they enjoy it. (cited in Jagose 1996: 38)

Once again, 'coming out' has its benefits and its disadvantages, but either way, the call to come out presupposes that such an action is in itself transformative and that the identity that one publicly declares is unambiguous – assumptions that poststructuralist theorists find inherently troubling.[15]

The concept that was fundamental to all liberationist groups and agendas was, of course, liberation which Altman defines as 'freedom from the surplus repression that prevents us from recognizing our essential androgynous and erotic natures' (1972: 83). In short, liberationists believed that in order to achieve sexual, and political freedom it was necessary to revolutionise society in and through the eradication of traditional notions of gender and sexuality and the kinds of institutions that informed them and were informed by them. Thus in its embracing of a transcendental 'utopian vision of liberated bodies and unrepressed psychic drives' (Reynolds 2002: 70) Gay Liberation promised freedom not just for those whose primary desire was for members of the so-called same sex, but for everyone.

As we now know only too well, Gay Liberation failed to attain this monolithic universalising state, which is not, of course, to suggest that liberationist groups did not bring about politically significant changes. This 'failure', many would now argue, is the result of a misconception of power, and we will examine this claim in more detail in the following chapter. However, at the time, it was often experienced and/or explained as a result of the movement's usurpation by white, middle-class, gay men, and of their sexist and misogynist agendas. As John Stolten put it in a scathing critique of gay male S/M:

Most gay male activists have chosen a completely reactionary strategy: seeking enfranchisement in the culture as 'really virile men', without substantially changing or challenging even their own misogyny and male-supremacist convictions. There are many ways in which gay liberation has become a full-fledged component of the backlash against feminism . . . Gay men do not simply like other men; they are like other men, as their antifeminism makes clear. (cited in Jeffreys 1990: 161)[16]

To what extent this may or may not have been the case is debatable, but it is nevertheless true to say that many women involved in Gay Liberation organisations became increasingly disillusioned and some turned instead to the women's liberation groups that had begun to emerge in the late 1960s and early 1970s. However, many women also found that feminist groups were not always as welcoming as they might have imagined they would be.

Early second-wave feminist groups in the USA, and the UK, tended, for the most part, to be reformist in character and during the early days of the more conservative women's liberation organisations lesbian members and issues were thought to be a hindrance to the movement in the same way that drag queens had been regarded by homophiles as an obstacle to acceptance by the heterosexual majority. One of the most written about examples of this sort of attitude is Betty Friedan's[17] coining of the term 'lavender menace' to describe those who allegedly undermined the credibility of feminism. This division between heterosexual and lesbian feminists, and the similar tensions between feminist and non-feminist lesbians is the focus of '1972', the second of three 'generational' stories of lesbianism in the film *If These Walls Could Talk 2*. The piece opens with documentary-type scenes from women's liberation marches and cuts to a house shared by four young lesbian women, the founders of a college feminist group from which, in time, they find themselves ousted because of their sexuality. The women, who are understandably angered and hurt by the treatment received at the hands of their 'sisters' nevertheless reiterate the divisive logic of 'us and them' when they are confronted with butch–femme bar dykes, one of whom Linda falls in love with.

The perceived rejection of lesbians from women's liberation organisations triggered the formation of groups of lesbian feminists, one of which – Radicalesbians, formerly 'Lavender Menace' – wrote, in 1970, the now (in)famous position paper 'Woman-Identified Woman'. The aim of the group, as their manifesto states, was to create

a new sense of self. That identity we have to develop with reference to ourselves, and not in relation to men. This consciousness is the revolutionary force from which all else will follow . . . For this we must be available and supportive to one another . . . Our energies must flow toward our sisters and not backwards toward our oppressors . . . It is the primacy of women relating to women, of women creating a new consciousness of and with each other, which is at the heart of women's liberation, and the basis for the cultural revolution. Together we must find, reinforce, and validate our authentic selves.[18]

In calling on women to devote their energies first and foremost to other women, such groups – sometimes implicitly and sometimes not – promoted an idealised view of female relations in which lesbians had far more in common with heterosexual women than they did with gay men.[19] Gender, then, not sexuality, was seen as the basis of political coalition by activists such as these. However, as has been well documented, it often seemed that to be a heterosexual woman-identified woman was a contradiction in terms. This tension was probably most apparent in now notorious paper on 'political lesbianism' penned in 1979 by the Leeds Revolutionary Feminists. They wrote, 'We do think that all feminists can and should be political lesbians. Our definition of political lesbian is a woman-identified woman who does not fuck men. It does not mean compulsory sexual activity with women' (OnlyWomen Collective 1984: 5).

It seemed, then, during this period, that far from being detrimental to feminism, lesbianism was by definition tantamount to the embodiment of feminism in its most ideal form.[20] However, as is made apparent in '1972', what actually constituted (or should be understood as) lesbianism was a rather bloody bone of contention. For example, radical activists such as the Leeds Revolutionary Feminists argued that any woman could (potentially) be a political lesbian since lesbianism is less a sexual identity than a political position: as Jill Johnston put it, 'lesbians are feminists not homosexuals' (cited in Adam 1995: 101). Janice Raymond, in a position that mirrors that taken by the feminist lesbians in '1972', took this distinction one step further, criticising those who defined their lesbianism in terms of sexual desire and aligning them with heterosexual conservatives.[21] As a consequence of this sort of moralising rhetoric, many working-class lesbians, lesbians of colour, butches and femmes, 'sex positive' lesbians, and/or those whose lesbianism had been shaped in and though bar culture felt alienated from movements to which they also, or might have otherwise, belonged.[22]

As many feminists have since pointed out, political lesbianism paved the way for the concomitant desexualising of lesbianism and the policing of lesbian sex. For example, the Leeds Revolutionary Feminists' critique of heterosexual penetration as a key factor in the oppression of women was adopted by many political lesbians and used to condemn penetrative sex between lesbians on the grounds that penetration is, by definition, phallocentric. For radical feminists such as Raymond, Daly, and others then, 'acceptable' sex was sex that did not in any way mimic heterosexual sex, that is, sex that did not involve the objectification of one's lover, the use of phallic objects, or role-play of any kind. However, at the same time that such groups and political agendas were common, there was also another important strand to 1970s' feminism which, as Kimberley O'Sullivan points out 'was sex positive, anti-guilt and where a lot of lively discussion about sex, desire and fantasy took place' (1997: 116). This strand of feminism led, of course, to the publication of pro-sex magazines such as *On Our Backs* (in the USA), and *Wicked Women* (Australia), to the production of (amongst other things) lesbian porn, sex toys for women, and lesbian S/M. The tensions between these different ideological strands of feminism (which nevertheless sometimes overlapped) is often referred to as 'the Sex Wars'.[23]

To cut a long and exceedingly complex and contradictory story short, feminism and Gay Liberation became increasingly factionalised in Australia, the UK, and the USA throughout the 1980s, with all sorts of groups expressing their sense of alienation from what were, for the most part, white, middle-class movements. This is not, however, to suggest that Gay Liberation or lesbian feminism, or pro-sex feminism were/are discrete, monolithic, coherent entities, nor is it to suggest that such movements (loosely speaking) did not include in their ranks working-class lesbians, women of colour, Jews, and so on. Indeed, as theorists such as Linda Garber (2001), Chela Sandoval (1991), and the Combahee River Collective

(1983) have pointed out, black, Chicana, Jewish, Third World, and working-class, women played crucial roles in such movements from their inception but their participation is often obscured in and through the (re)production of homogenising accounts of complex political, geographical, and ideological histories. Rather, what I am gesturing towards is the increasing emphasis on difference that seemed to pervade sexual, gender, race and/or class politics in the 1980s, and the concomitant turning away from grand-scale utopian visions.

NOTES

1. See, for example, Jeffrey Weeks (1977; 1981) on the UK; Kieran Rose (1994) on the Republic of Ireland; Robert Reynolds (2002), Craig Johnston (1999), Denise Thompson (1985; 1991) and Graham Willett (2000) on Australia; and Adam (1995), Harris (1997), and D'Emilio (1983) on the USA.
2. For a detailed account of the Mattachine Society, see D'Emilio (1983) and Eric Slade's documentary *Hope Along the Wind* (2001).
3. For a detailed account of the Daughters of Bilitis and the group's relation to literary discourses, see Schultz (2001).
4. For further discussion, see Weeks (1977).
5. See, for example, Meeker (2001); Reynolds (2002).
6. The reason behind this attempt to evoke both the past and the present is that I want to indicate that what I am offering here is not a developmental historical movement from assimilationism to something else. Obviously, whilst the groups that I am discussing could be said in one sense to be assimilationist, this does not mean that they may not have simultaneously embraced radical and contradictory ideas and practices. Similarly, whilst queer politics may present itself as anti-assimilationist this is something of a misnomer as McKee (1999) argues, and as I illustrate in the following chapter.
7. As Chetcuti (1994) has noted, advocates of the decriminalisation of homosexuality almost always stress the privacy of homosexual acts. As a result, argues Chetcuti, 'private homosexual acts' have, in many parts of the Western world, been decriminalised, but this has not necessarily halted the persecution of homosexuals in public.
8. This is one of five propositions that Meeker (2001) makes in his attempt to rethink the commonly held image of the Mattachine Society and its relation to Gay Liberation. The other four propositions are: that the politics of the Mattachine Foundation mixed the radical with the conservative; that the Society's practice was daring and effective; that the society successfully built coalitions with sex

reformers; and that the Society's leaders were active and effective throughout the 1960s.

9. For filmic accounts of pre-Stonewall bar dyke communities in Canada and California respectively see *Forbidden Love: The Unashamed Stories of Lesbian Lives* (1992) directed by Aerlyn Weissman and Lynne Fernie, and *Last Call at Maud's* (1993) directed by Paris Poirier. For a critical analysis of these and other such films, see Hankin (2000).

10. This image of the 'untouchable' is particularly associated with the figure of the stone butch. See, for example, Halberstam (1998); Feinberg (1993).

11. For an explicit example of this, see Lee Lynch's poem *Stone Butch* in Nestle (1992) p. 405.

12. For a more detailed account of the political context in which Gay Liberation organisations formed in the USA, the UK, and Australia respectively, see D'Emilio (1983); Weeks (1977); and Wotherspoon (1991).

13. In saying this I do not mean to conflate what was in reality a heterogeneous range of organisations and forms of activism. For an account of the important political and socio-economic differences that gave rise to different models of Gay Liberation in different countries, see Adam (1995).

14. Sartelle quotes Cal Thomas, an opponent of gay rights, who says of the determinist argument: 'I don't think it legitimizes homosexual practice and behavior any more than the discovery of heavy doses of testosterone in a male justifies his adultery or promiscuity' (1994: 3).

15. Creet (1995), Phelan (1993), and Sedgwick (1990) have all critically engaged with the coming out narrative.

16. For similar critiques of the alleged sexism and misogyny of gay (male) politics see Jeffreys (1990); Frye (1983).

17. Friedan, the author of the influential *The Feminist Mystique* (1963) was at the time (1970) the national president of NOW.

18. This excerpt was taken from a copy of the entire manifesto which can be found at http://carnap.umd.edu/queer/radicalesbian.htm

19. This sort of agenda also played a central role in the development of separatist politics and communities. For detailed culturally specific accounts of lesbian separatism, see Doyle (1996); Ion (1997).

20. See, for example, Abbott and Love (1972).

21. See O'Sullivan (1997).

22. See Moraga (1983); Nestle (1992).

23. For a more detailed account of the Sex Wars, see Duggan and Hunter (1996); Faderman (1991); Healey (1996); and O'Sullivan (1997).

3

Queer: A Question of Being or A Question of Doing?

IN THE PREVIOUS CHAPTERS we focused on the ways in which homosexuality and lesbianism have been discursively produced in the West over the past two hundred years or so, and examined the various theoretical and/or political responses, positions, and strategies that evolved as a result of dominant understandings of sexuality, subjectivity, social relations, and the connections between them. In this chapter we will undertake a similar task, examining the social, theoretical, and political conditions that enabled the emergence of what has come to be known as Queer Theory. In addition to this we will consider the many and varied ways in which the term queer has been understood, and discuss the theoretical and political effects of these diverse uses. Whilst it is important to acknowledge the existence of a range of queer activist groups such as ACT UP, Queer Nation, OutRage, PUSSY (Perverts Undermining State Scrutiny), Transsexual Menace, Lesbian Avengers and Transgender Nation that formed in the 1990s and shaped Queer Theory and its practice, it is not within the bounds of this chapter to discuss these groups and their various forms of activism in any detail.[1]

As I discussed in Chapter 2, from the late 1970s on, gay and lesbian movements, like feminist movements, were challenged by those who felt frustrated and marginalised by the assumption that sexual preference or gender should (unquestionably) take precedence over other aspects of identity. Women of colour, for example, expressed their distrust of the white feminist focus on gender, claiming that politically and socially they had as much, if not more, in common with (the struggles of) men of colour than with white women, who, they noted, continued – in some respects

37

at least – to reap the benefits of colonisation. Increasingly, the ethnic model of identity and politics discussed in the previous chapter was 'criticized for exhibiting white, middle-class, hetero-normative values and liberal political interests' (Seidman 1995: 124). Consequently, as we shall see in Chapter 4, writers such as Cherríe Moraga and Gloria Anzaldúa argued for the necessity of a focus on the intersectionality of racial, sexual, gender, and class identities. Such a focus necessarily involves the problematisation of the notion of a unitary lesbian and/or gay identity and community,[2] which, as we saw in the earlier discussion of the 'lesbian sex wars', was becoming increasingly implausible. Connected to the challenging of unified, essentialising, and universalising identities was a critique of binary oppositions such as homosexuality/heterosexuality, male/female, and so on.

Eve Kosofsky Sedgwick's critique of the tendency to understand sexual identity on the basis of the gender of one's sexual object choice is an example of the changing theoretical and political milieu that the politics of difference engendered. In her landmark text, *The Epistemology of the Closet* (1990) Sedgwick, claiming that such forms of designation reaffirm, rather than challenge, hetero-normative logic and institutions, writes:

It is a rather amazing fact that, of the very many dimensions along which the genital activity of one person can be differentiated from that of another (dimensions that include preference for certain acts, certain zones or sensations, certain physical types, a certain frequency, certain symbolic investments, certain relations of age or power, a certain species, a certain number of participants, and so on) precisely one, the gender of the object choice, emerged from the turn of the century, and has remained, as *the* dimension denoted by the now ubiquitous category of 'sexual orientation'. (1990: 8)

This sort of counter-hegemonic logic is also apparent in the writings and practices of many of those now associated with 'sex radicalism'. Pat Califia, for instance, argued in 1983 in an article published in *The Advocate*, that the terms, lesbian, gay man, and heterosexual, are limited and limiting as a category of sexual iden-tification.[3] Califia, a proponent of sadomasochism, claims that sadomasochistic practices transgress the allegedly inviolate line between gay men and lesbians, and that sex between the two is something other than heterosexual since the gender of one's object choice is no longer the defining factor. Sharon Kelly uses the same sort of argument to claim that she (who usually has sex with so-called heterosexual men) and her sometimes sex partner Richard (who usually has sex with so-called gay men) are, in fact, queer.[4] As Annamarie Jagose notes, citing Jan Clausen, some bisexual theorists have made similar claims. Clausen says: 'bisexuality is not a sexual identity at all, but a sort of anti-identity, a refusal (not, of course, conscious) to be limited to one object of desire, one way of loving' (cited in Jagose 1996: 69).

These are just a few examples of the many and varied challenges to gay and lesbian theory and/or politics, to feminism, and to identity-based politics in general that proliferated in the 1980s and that engendered what some have called a politics of difference. The 1980s also saw the popularisation of the work of Michel Foucault and an increase, particularly in academia, of poststructuralist accounts of subjectivity and social relations. The impact of such theoretical shifts has been significant, not least of all in regards to notions of sexual identity and politics. Given this, let's now look at some of the fundamental tenets of poststructuralism.

Poststructuralism is most often associated with a rejection, or at least a critique, of humanist logic and aspirations. It therefore involves a rethinking of concepts such as 'meaning', 'truth', 'subjectivity', 'freedom', 'power', and so on. Poststructuralist theorists such as Foucault argue that there are no objective and universal truths, but that particular forms of knowledge, and the ways of being that they engender, become 'naturalised', in culturally and historically specific ways. For example, Judith Butler, and Monique Wittig argue (in slightly different ways) that heterosexuality is a complex matrix of discourses, institutions, and so on, that has become normalised in our culture, thus making particular relationships, lifestyles, and identities, seem natural, ahistorical, and universal. In short, heterosexuality, as it is currently understood and experienced, is a (historically and culturally specific) truth-effect of systems of power/knowledge. Given this, its dominant position and current configuration are contestable and open to change.

Poststructuralism is critical of universalising explanations of the subject and the world. Jean-François Lyotard's *The Postmodern Condition: A Report on Knowledge* (1984) is a case in point. In this text Lyotard argues that what we perceive as truth is constructed as such in and through its conformity with universalising accounts – or grand narratives as he calls them – of subjectivity and sociality that govern particular cultures at particular times. One such narrative embraces the notion of human being (and of history) as evolving towards an enlightened or ideal state of being. As a result, (political) actions, artworks, scientific 'discoveries', particular lifestyles, and so on, are judged on the basis of whether or not they supposedly contribute to, or inhibit, such progress. As we saw in the previous chapters, political theory and/or activism often attempts to validate itself in these sorts of terms. The liberationist agenda, for example, is most often driven by the image of a singular and supposedly universally achievable goal or state – sexual freedom – which presumably is understood and experienced (at least fundamentally) in the same way by all human beings. Lyotard and other poststructuralist theorists are, however, critical of grand narratives and the logic that they attempt to (re)produce and/or legitimate on the grounds that they lead to totalising or universalising discourses and practices that leave no room for difference, for complexities, or for ambiguity. Consequently, poststructuralist theorists tend to concentrate on the local and the specific, and eschew universal and ahistorical accounts of oppression, definitions of homosexuality, blueprints for freedom, and so on.

Rather than reproducing the logic of what Luce Irigaray has called an Economy of the Same, poststructuralist theorists are concerned with developing analyses of the differences within and between people, and the ways in which these are constructed and lived. Foucault's genealogical account of the ways in which sexuality (in its many forms) has been discursively produced in historically and culturally specific ways is an example of this. In *The History of Sexuality* Volume 1, for instance, Foucault, refuting what he refers to as the 'repressive hypothesis' – the idea that sex, as an instinctual drive, has been repressed by oppressive institutions, and thus is in need of liberation – critically analyses the ways in which educational establishments, discourses, and discursive practices, construct adolescent sexuality in and through the division of time and space not only in the school, but also in the home, in work life and recreation, and in all aspects of daily life. Moreover, in texts such as *Discipline and Punish: The Birth of the Prison*, Foucault demonstrates how grand narratives, or what he might call normalising discourses, constitute difference solely in terms of degrees of difference from the norm that is the ideal. It is this sort of logic that engenders and legitimises the representation of homosexuality as an aberration from heterosexuality (the norm/ideal).

The focus on difference both between and within subjects

necessarily involves a critique of, and challenge to, the humanist notion of the subject as a unique, unified, rational, autonomous individual whose relations with others are secondary and whose desires and actions are transparent to him or herself. For post-structuralist theorists there is no true self that exists prior to its immersion in culture. Rather, the self is constructed in and through its relations with others, and with systems of power/ knowledge. But insofar as the humanist subject is constituted in and through the privileging of certain aspects of the self which come to represent the self as naturally superior, and the simulta-neous splitting off parts of the self deemed inappropriate and the projection of these onto others, such a being is, as Naomi Scheman argues both 'engorged' and 'diminished' (1997: 126), privileged and threatened. As will become apparent throughout this text, this tension engenders all sorts of forms of social problems.

There are a range of poststructuralist accounts of subjectivity ranging from the psychoanalytic account of the split subject, to the Foucauldian notion of the subject as an agent and effect of systems of power/knowledge,[5] to the idea of rhizomatic (un)becoming developed by Deleuze and Guattari,[6] but what each share is a rejection of the belief that the subject is autonomous, unified, self-knowing, and static. As a result, poststructuralists are critical of the liberationist ideal of the liberation of the true self and of sexuality as a singular unified force that has been repressed.[7] Moreover, as we shall come to see, poststructuralist theorists and queer theorists find identity politics inherently problematic.

The humanist model of the subject is also founded on a dis-tinction between the mind and the body; it exemplifies what is sometimes referred to as Cartesian dualism. The assumption is that identity is located in consciousness, and that the body is simply a material receptacle that houses the mind or spirit. Ulrichs' theory of inversion as a female soul/mind in a male body is an example of mind/body dualism, and the liberationist assumption that ideology colonises the mind of the individual, and that the goal of politics is (through processes such as consciousness raising) to free the mind, and hence the self, from the repressive con-straints of dominant culture, is yet another. But poststructuralist theorists argue that changing your life is not simply a matter of changing your mind. This is because we embody the discourses that exist in our culture, our very being is constituted by them, they are a part of us, and thus we cannot simply throw them off. Indeed,

41

as we shall see in Chapter 5, both Maurice Merleau-Ponty and Judith Butler argue that the body is my being-in-the-world and as such is the instrument through which identity is performatively generated. It is in virtue of having/being a body that is discursively produced in and through its relation to culture, that I am an 'I'.

The notion of ideology as a tool with which the masses are 'brainwashed', is tied, in the grand narratives associated with left politics, to an understanding of power as something that the ruling elite alone can possess and wield to the detriment of the majority of the population, and, of course, to a model of subjectivity informed by Cartesian dualism. Power, on this model, is repressive; it is negative and dis-enabling. Foucault, however, has argued that power is productive rather than simply oppressive, and should be understood as a network of relations rather than something one group owns and wields in order to control another.[8] In short, Foucault, like poststructuralist theorists in general, is critical of dichotomous logic, of, for example, the (humanist) distinction between rulers and ruled, power and powerlessness, that seems to inform much of the homophile and gay and lesbian theory that we discussed in the previous chapters. An important example of this is the claim that:

Where there is power, there is resistance, and yet, or rather consequently, this resistance is never in a position of exteriority in relation to power... The existence [of power relationships] depends on a multiplicity of points of resistance: these play the role of adversary, target, support, or handle in power relations. These points of resistance are present everywhere in the power network. Hence there is no single locus of great Refusal... or pure law of the revolutionary. Instead there is a plurality or resistances... [which] by definition... can only exist in the strategic field of power relations. (Foucault 1980: 95–6)

In other words, for Foucault, unlike liberationists, resistance is inseparable from power rather than being opposed to it. And since resistance is not, and cannot be, external to systems of power/knowledge, then an oppositional politics that attempts to replace supposedly false ideologies with non-normative truths is inherently contradictory. There can be no universally applicable political goals or strategies, only a plurality of heterogeneous and localised practices, the effects of which will never be entirely predictable in advance.

It is this sort of focus on the constructed, contingent, unstable and heterogeneous character of subjectivity, social relations, power, and knowledge, that has paved the way for Queer Theory. So what exactly is Queer Theory? What do we mean when we use the term queer? Is queer an attitude, an identity, a particular approach to politics? Rather than attempting to define what queer is – which, as we will come to see, would be a decidedly un-queer thing to do – the remainder of this chapter is dedicated to the examination of a number of, often contradictory, examples of the ways in which this term has been used by contemporary theorists and activists.

In the same way that feminists and/or poststructuralist theorists have developed, and continue to develop, a broad range of critical responses to liberal humanism which are at times competing and contradictory, 'queer theorists are a diverse lot exhibiting important disagreements and divergences' (Seidman 1995: 125). Nevertheless, it is possible to identify similarities in the ways in which Queer Theory and politics are understood and practised.

So, let us begin with some fairly typical explanations of queer. For Chris Berry and Annamarie Jagose, 'Queer is an ongoing and necessarily unfixed site of engagement and contestation' (1996: 11). Or, as Jagose puts it in her book entitled *Queer Theory*, 'Queer itself can have neither a fundamental logic, nor a consistent set of characteristics' (1996: 96). In his book, *Saint Foucault*, David Halperin also refrains from pinning down the term queer, arguing instead that:

Queer is by definition *whatever* is at odds with the normal, the legitimate, the dominant. *There is nothing in particular to which it necessarily refers.* It is an identity without an essence. 'Queer' then, demarcates not a positivity but a positionality *vis-à-vis* the normative . . . [Queer] describes a horizon of possibility whose precise extent and heterogeneous scope cannot in principle be delimited in advance. (1995: 62)

This is a sentiment shared by a range of other writers. According to Cherry Smith, for example, queer 'defines a strategy, an attitude . . . [Q]ueer articulates a radical questioning of social and cultural norms, notions of gender, reproductive sexuality, and the family' (1996: 280). Similarly, Lisa Duggan argues that Queer Theory does not simply develop new labels for old boxes, but rather, carries with it 'the promise of new meanings, new ways of thinking and acting politically – a promise sometimes realized, sometimes not' (1992: 11). In each case, Queer (Theory) is constructed as a sort of vague and indefinable set of practices and (political) positions that has the potential to challenge normative knowledges and identities.

Halperin goes on to explain that since queer is a positionality rather than an identity in the humanist sense, it is not restricted to gays and lesbians, but can be taken up by anyone who feels marginalised as a result of their sexual practices. Queer could include, suggests Halperin, 'some married couples without children . . . or even (who knows?) some married couples *with* children – with, perhaps, *very naughty* children' (1995: 62). Likewise, the anonymous authors of a pamphlet entitled 'Queer Power Now' that was produced and circulated in London in 1991, state, 'Queer means to fuck with gender. There are straight queers, bi-queers, tranny queers, lez queers, fag queers, SM queers, fisting queers' (cited in Smith 1996: 277). In short, then, whilst queer is not an essential identity, it is nevertheless, according to both of these accounts, a provisional political one. Given this, it seems that the term queer, as Halperin and the authors of 'Queer Power Now' use it, functions in similar ways to the term 'political lesbian' which we discussed in the previous chapter.

For Gabriel Rotello, the former editor of *Outweek*, however, queer does denote an identity. Rotello says, 'When you're trying to describe the community, and you have to list gays, lesbians, bisexuals, drag queens, transsexuals (post-op and pre), it gets unwieldy. Queer says it all' (cited in Duggan 1992: 21). So, despite the claim made by Duggan, it appears that queer does function, at least at times, as a new, and less wordy, label for an old box. One of the problems with this particular use of queer as an umbrella term is that it does little if anything to deconstruct the humanist understanding of the subject. Worse still, it veils over the differences between, for example, lesbianism and gayness, between 'women', between transsexualism and cross-dressing, and ignores differences of class, race, age and so on, once again positing sexuality as a unified and unifying factor. As Gloria Anzaldúa puts it:

Queer is used as a false unifying umbrella which all 'queers' of all races, ethnicities and classes are shoved under. At times we need this umbrella to solidify our ranks against outsiders. But even when we seek shelter under it we must not forget that it homogenizes, erases our differences. (1991: 250)

In effect, then, the term queer can at times be used in such a way as to imply the existence of some sort of queer solidarity that has triumphed over the kinds of political divisions discussed in the previous chapter. The use of queer as an umbrella term can, as Halperin has noted,[9] have the effect of (mis)representing us as one big happy (queer) family.

Right at the other end of the queer continuum we find groups such as Queercore, a loose coalition of radical anarchist and/or punk queers for whom the term queer defines not a specific sexuality, 'but the freedom to personalize anything you see or hear then shoot it back into the stupid world more distorted and amazing than it was before' (Cooper 1996: 295). In fact, unlike Rotello, for whom the terms gay and lesbian, and queer appear synonymous, Johnny Noxzema and Rex Boy, editors of the queerzine *Bimbox*, state in no uncertain terms that for them gay and lesbian, and queer are as antithetical as you can get. In the editorial to a 1991 edition of *Bimbox*, they write:

You are entering a gay and lesbian-free zone . . . Effective immediately, BIMBOX is at war against lesbians and gays. A war in which modern queer boys and queer girls are united against the prehistoric thinking and demented self-serving politics of the above-mentioned scum. BIMBOX hereby renounces its past use of the term lesbian and/or gay in a positive manner. This is a civil war against the ultimate evil, and consequently we must identify us and them in no uncertain terms . . . So, dear lesbian womon [sic] or gay man to whom perhaps BIMBOX has been inappropriately posted . . . prepare to pay dearly for the way you and your kind have fucked things up. (cited in Cooper 1996: 292)

These 'radical' queers claim what they presume to be an outsider status; they do not want to be assimilated into heteronormative culture which is what they see as being advocated by lesbians and gays. In fact, as Cooper puts it, 'They don't pretend for a moment that they can alter the dominant culture – gay or straight. They don't want to . . . They're trying to create an alternative culture in and around it' (Ibid.: 296). What the quote from Noxzema and Boy makes clear is that the term queer can be used to reinforce, rather than deconstruct, the ways in which identity and difference are constructed in terms of binary oppositions, of us and them – oppositions which are never neutral, but are always hierarchical. The queer subject of this kind of discourse reaffirms his or her identity in opposition to the supposedly normative other – a gesture which is inherent in liberal humanism, and which poststructuralist theorists are eager to avoid. Consequently, particular uses of the term queer can even, as Halperin notes, 'support the restigmatization of lesbians and gays . . . who can now be regarded . . . as benighted, sad, folks, still locked – *unlike* the postmodern, non-sexually labeled, self-theorized queers – into an old-fashioned, essentialized, rigidly defined, conservative, specifically sexual . . . identity' (1995: 65).

The Chicago-based activist group Queers United Against Straight Acting Homosexuals (QUASH) take a similar position to the editors of *Bimbox*. They likewise believe that gay and lesbian politics and activism all too often plays into the hands of normative culture, reinforcing its values, beliefs, and status. In short, they are critical of what they see as the assimilationist agenda of gay and lesbian politics and activism. They state:

Assimilation is killing us. We are falling into a trap. Some of us adopt an apologetic stance, stating, 'that's just the way I am' (read: 'I'd be straight if I could'). Others pattern their behavior in such a way as to mimic heterosexual society so as to minimize the glaring differences between us and them. (QUASH, cited in Cohen 1997: 445)

QUASH go on to argue that no matter how much money queers make, or what kinds of corporate or professional positions queers might hold, they will never share the legal rights accorded to heterosexuals. Moreover, they argue that the concerns that are particular to queers will continue to be ignored and/or under-funded, and they will be bashed and persecuted by those whose being and whose actions epitomise the cultural logic of hetero-normativity. For QUASH, then, like the editors of *Bimbox*, assimilation is a deadly myth that must be shattered.

As Alan McKee has noted, the refusal to define queer apparent in the quotations from Halperin, Smith, Jagose, Berry, and Duggan, often goes hand in hand with this sort of virulent attack on assimilationism. In a critical analysis of such assumptions and associations, McKee problematises some of the key tenets found in much of the writing that calls itself Queer Theory. The first of these is the belief that naming something constitutes a form of closure, or of assimilation: that, for example, what is transgressive about queer is its ephemerality, and any attempt to 'explain what must forever escape meaning' (McKee 1999: 236) inevitably goes against the grain of the post-identity ethos of Queer Theory. This sort of position may seem attractive to those well versed in the limits and dangers of singular universalising accounts of politics and political activism, but, according to McKee, it too has its (all too often unacknowledged) dangers. McKee's argument is that the claim that Queer Theory is indefinable belies the fact that Queer Theory courses are taught in academia, and that some articles are chosen for inclusion in such courses, and for publication in Queer Theory journals and books, whereas other are not. In other words, some sort of sense of what queer is (or is not) is at work in the judgements being made in these institutional situations. 'Queer is not an entirely empty signifier', says McKee: 'in the face of a resolved and insistent unknowability, it remains clear that Queer *means*' (Ibid.: 237).

In denying this, as McKee notes, we fail to recognise or acknowledge how and why particular knowledges, practices, identities, and texts, are validated at the expense of others. In other words, the refusal to define queer, or at least the ways in which the term is functioning in specific contexts, promotes a sense of inclusivity which is misleading, and worse still, enables exclusory praxis to go unchecked. Steven Seidman shares McKee's concerns and asks what kinds of politics and/or ethics Queer Theory is implicitly promoting – a point which he claims queer theorists are suspiciously silent about. Indeed, Seidman argues that unless we seriously think through this question and refrain from simply reiterating enigmatic calls for fluidity, ambiguity, indefinability, and so on, Queer Theory will be little more than an anarchistic social ideal, or a form of libertarianism founded on a democratic pluralist ideal. In either case, Queer Theory will be no less problematic than the humanist system that it claims to be attempting to work against.

Second, McKee identifies a number of dichotomies that seem to play a central, although not always explicit, role in much Queer Theory. For example, despite the Foucauldian critique discussed earlier, assimilationism is often represented as conservative and as the opposite of resistance, which, by association, is posited as radical. Tied to this is a distinction between gay and lesbian theory and/or politics which is seen as epitomising the former, and Queer Theory and/or politics which is presumed to be somehow inherently transgressive. But as Lee Edelman, whom McKee cites, states, '"Queer" as the endlessly mutating token of non-assimilation (and hence as the utopian badge of a would-be "authentic" position of resistance) may reflect a certain bourgeois aspiration to be always *au courant*' (1999: 242). What Edelman means by this is that ironically, despite the fact that queer theorists insist that there is 'no single locus of great Refusal . . . or pure law of the revolutionary' (Foucault 1980: 96), this insistence, coupled with the associated image of queer as 'the endlessly mutating token of non-assimilation', functions to position queer (as it is understood here) and, by association, those who practise it, as quintessentially resistant, and, of course, as superior to, or more enlightened than, the so-called non-queer. So again, it is apparent, as McKee argues, that the term queer does inform the ways in which a range of practices and identities are interpreted, judged, evaluated, and positioned: queer does signify in specific, if unacknowledged, ways.

The problem, then, is that the unacknowledged meanings attached to this term and its usage do tend to privilege the values, desires, and aspirations of particular people and groups, and to overlook, or silence those of others. Consequently, some theorists and activists have accused Queer Theory and/or politics of repeating the same sort of exclusionary logic that is often associated with the Homophile Movement, with liberationist politics, and with second wave feminism.[10] Harriet Wistrich, for example, states 'I don't use the term [queer]. I associate it with gay men', and Isling Mack-Nataf says, 'I'm more inclined to use the words "black lesbian", because when I hear the word queer I think of white, gay men'[11] (both cited in Smith 1996: 280). Julia Parnaby goes so far as to claim that queer, a 'movement based almost solely on a male agenda' (1996: 5),

is far from the revolutionary movement it would like itself to be, it is little more than a liberal/libertarian alliance – neither of which is noted for its commitment to feminist politics ... [Q]ueer offers us [lesbian feminists] nothing. It is yet one more face of the backlash, trying to pass itself off as something new. (Ibid.: 10)

In summary, then, Queer Theory and/or activism has been accused of being, among other things, male-centred, anti-feminist, and race-blind.

Whether or not one agrees with these criticisms, it does seem valid enough to suggest that at times Queer Theory and politics are informed by, and inform, an overly simplistic distinction between what or who is deemed to be queer, and what or who is not. So, for example, we find dichotomies such as 'us' and 'them', queer and heterosexual, queer and gay/lesbian at work in many accounts of queer practice and/or identity. As a result, all heterosexuals, it is often implied, are situated in a dominant normative position, and all gays and lesbians simply aspire to be granted access to this position, whereas all queers are marginalised and consciously and intentionally resist assimilation of any kind. Of course, this sort of logic is reiterated in the work of anti-queer theorists such as Parnaby who simply reverse the hierarchy – but then Parnaby never does claim to be writing from a poststructuralist position.

Cathy J. Cohen is one of a number of contemporary critics who is critical of dichotomous logic and of the (re)production of 'narrow and homogenised political identities . . . that inhibit the radical potential of queer politics' (1997: 441). Instead of focusing primarily on sexuality, Cohen calls for a 'broadened understanding of queerness . . . based on an intersectional analysis that recognizes how numerous systems of oppression interact to regulate . . . the lives of most people' (Ibid.: 441). Such an approach would undermine dichotomies such as heterosexual/queer in that it would demonstrate that heterosexuals have multiple subject positions and thus not all heterosexuals are situated socially, politically, economically, in the same way. Cohen mentions, for example, heterosexual women who are on welfare, single mothers, and/or women of colour. She asks how, as queer theorists, we might begin to understand the position(s) of such women who, whilst being heterosexual, do not fit the ideal image of heterosexual femininity and are thus often perceived as something other than 'normal'. She also asks how queer theorists and/or activists relate, politically, to those whose sexuality may be deemed queer, but who, at the same time, see themselves as members of other communities, that is, communities formed around race, class, disability, and so on. In raising these kinds of questions Cohen challenges the notion of a homogenized identity on which (queer) political practice can be founded, and calls instead for a politics based on intersectional analyses of identity and its relation to prevailing systems of power/knowledge.

What the various uses of the term queer that we've looked at thus far seem to indicate is that the question of what, or who, is queer is as contentious as the definitions of lesbianism discussed in the previous chapter. If, as Halperin has suggested, queer is a positionality (rather than an innate identity) that potentially can be taken up by anyone who feels themselves to have been marginalised as a result of their sexual preferences, then one might argue that the majority of the world's population is (at least potentially) queer. But, as Elizabeth Grosz has warned, queer could consequently up end being used to validate what she regards as ethically questionable sexual practices and identities at the same time that it denigrates so-called conservative forms of same-sex relations. She says:

'Queer' is capable of accommodating, and will no doubt provide a political rationale and coverage in the near future for many of the most blatant and extreme forms of heterosexual and patriarchal power games. They too are, in a certain sense, queer, persecuted, ostracized. Heterosexual sadists, pederasts, fetishists, pornographers, pimps, voyeurs, suffer from social sanctions: in a certain sense they too can be regarded as oppressed. But to claim an oppression of the order of lesbian and gay, women's or racial oppression is to ignore the very real complicity and phallic rewards of what might be called 'deviant sexualities' within patriarchal and heterocentric power relations. (1994b: 113)

One way of avoiding the problems associated with the notion of queer as an identity – albeit a non-essential, provisional, and frag-mented one – is, as Janet R. Jakobsen suggests, to 'complete the Foucauldian move from human being to human doing' (1998: 516). What Jakobsen means by this is that it may be more productive to think of queer as a verb (a set of actions), rather than as a noun (an identity, or even a nameable positionality formed in and through the practice of particular actions). This seems to be the position taken by Michael Warner who says that queer is not just a resistance to the norm, but more importantly, consists of protesting against 'the idea[l] of normal behavior' (1993: 290). Queer, in this sense, comes to be understood as a deconstructive practice that is not undertaken by an already constituted subject, and does not, in turn, furnish the subject with a nameable identity.

So what exactly is deconstruction? The term deconstruction is often associated with the French philosopher Jacques Derrida. Deconstruction could be said to constitute a critical response to the humanist belief in absolute essences and oppositions. The idea that heterosexuality is a naturally occurring and fundamental aspect of one's identity, and, moreover, that it is the polar opposite of homosexuality, is one example of humanist ontology. Decon-struction works away at the very foundation of what Derrida refers to as Western metaphysics (a historically and culturally specific system of meaning-making), by undermining the notion of polarised essences. It is important to note, however, that decon-struction is not synonymous with destruction: it does not involve the obliteration and replacement of what is erroneous with that which is held to be true. In other words, a deconstructive approach to the hierarchised binary opposition heterosexuality/homosexuality would not consist of reversing the terms or of attempting to somehow annihilate the concepts and/or the relation between them altogether. Rather, a deconstructive analysis would highlight the inherent instability of the terms, as well as enabling an analysis of the culturally and historically specific ways in which the terms and the relation between them have developed, and the effects they have produced. So, for example, a deconstructive reading of heterosexuality as something that has been represented as natural and/or original, discrete, and essential, would show that heterosexuality is dependent on its so-called opposite (homosexuality) for its identity. In other words, heterosexuality (and/or the 'natural') includes what it excludes (homosexuality and/or the 'unnatural'); homosexuality is internal to heterosexuality (and vice versa) and not external to it as a humanist account of identity and meaning would claim. The 'two', then, are never discrete, and thus the opposition no longer holds. As Diana Fuss puts it:

Sexual identitites are rarely secure. Heterosexuality can never fully ignore the close psychical proximity of its terrifying (homo) sexual other, any more than homosexuality can entirely escape the equally insistent social pressures of (hetero) sexual conformity. Each is haunted by the other. (1991: 4)

It is this haunting/haunted relation, says Seidman, 'which ultimately accounts for the extreme defensiveness, the hardening of each into a bounded, self-protective hardcore and, at the same time, the opposite tendency towards confusion and collapse' (1995: 131). Deconstructing the presumed opposition between homosexuality and heterosexuality, the 'unnatural' and the 'natural' is important, then, because it enables us to acknowledge the constructedness of meaning and identity and thus to begin to imagine alternative ways of thinking and of living. At the same time, it enables us also to ask why it is that in particular cultural contexts being is divided up in this (arbitrary) way, and who it is that benefits from the cultural logic that (re)produces these kinds of divisions. As Seidman puts it:

Queer theory is less a matter of explaining the repression or expression of a homosexual minority, than an analysis of the Hetero/Homosexual figure as a power/knowledge regime that shapes the ordering of desires, behaviors, social institutions, and social relations – in a word, the constitution of the self and society. (Ibid.: 128)

It is this view of Queer Theory as a deconstructive strategy that Sue-Ellen Case has in mind when she says that Queer Theory, at least as she conceives it, works 'at the site of ontology, to shift the ground of being itself, thus challenging the Platonic parameters of Being – the borders of life and death' (1991: 3). The distinction between life and death, Case argues, not only structures Western metaphysics, but also plays an integral part in the politics of sexuality – most particularly in the denigration of homosexuality on the grounds that it (unlike heterosexuality) is a sterile or non-reproductive, and unnatural relationship. Consequently, homosexuality is constructed as anathematic to 'the family' as the cornerstone of heteronormativity, and, by association, to blood (lines) as that which enable(s) the passing on of private property and racial purity, at least when it sticks to the appropriate path carved out for it by phallocentric systems of power/knowledge. Case writes:

Queer sexual practice . . . impels one out of the generational production of what has been called 'life' and history, and ultimately out of the category of the living. The equation of hetero=sex=life and homo=sex=unlife generated a queer discourse that reveled in proscribed desiring by imagining sexual objects and sexual practices within the realm of the other-than-natural, and the consequent other-than-living. In this discourse new forms of being, or beings, are imagined through desire. And desire is that which wounds – a desire that breaks through the sheath of being as it has been imagined within a heterosexist society. Striking at its very core, queer desire punctuates the life/death and generative/destructive bipolarities that enclose the heterosexist notion of being. (Ibid.: 4)

For Case then, Queer Theory and practice are vampyric in that they consist of a perverse form of blood letting, of the abject[12] transgression of boundaries between the proper and the improper. To some, Case's argument may, no doubt, seem strange, odd, peculiar, eccentric even, but given that this is one of the many definitions of the term queer offered in the *Shorter Oxford English Dictionary*, then perhaps we could say that Case's article practises what it preaches. Queer is also defined in this text as 'not in the normal condition, out of sorts, drunk', and, of course, as a slang term for 'homosexual'.[13] If we turn to queer as a verb (to queer) we find 'to quiz or ridicule, to spoil, put out of order'.

For the remainder of the chapter I want to examine *But I'm A Cheerleader* in order to think through some of the possible ways in which we might, spoil, quiz, disorder, denaturalise, or, in a word, queer, heteronormativity. The cheerleader referred to in the film's title is seventeen-year-old Megan, the only child of a middle-aged and exceedingly straight Christian couple whose philosophy is that there is a 'single path', and that one must abide by all that is 'natural, healthy, and sacred'. Despite Megan's demure 1950sish appearance and seemingly naïve manner, her parents and friends nevertheless feel that there is something not quite right about her, and there are all sorts of signs that suggest that their suspicions may be well founded. Megan, for example, is a vegetarian who eats tofu, has posters of Melissa Etheridge on her bedroom wall and pictures of girls in bikinis in her locker, likes the art of Georgia O'Keefe (which, it is claimed, is full of vaginal motifs), and, does not get much pleasure from the slavering attentions of a boyfriend who seems to think that his tongue belongs anywhere but in his own mouth. Consequently, Megan's parents call on the expertise of 'True Directions', an organisation that works hard to get those who are bent – even in the slightest – back on the straight and narrow. Thus enters Mike (played, ironically, by RuPaul), an ex-gay who wears very short shorts and a 'straight is great' T-shirt.

When Megan and her parents arrive at True Directions – which is something like a cross between a rehabilitation centre and a school camp – they are introduced to Mary, the Director of the programme and mother of the overtly camp Adonis-like Rock. Mary declares that Megan's parents may well have caught the problem just in time since 'it's much more difficult once they [young gays and lesbians] have been through all that liberal arts brainwashing' at college. Thus begins the five-step programme of normalisation – itself a form of the most overt 'brainwashing' imaginable.

Step One, of course, is (self-) confession: Megan must admit to herself, and to a room full of boys dressed in blue, and girls dressed in pink, that she is indeed a homosexual. What the film makes clear is that the process of naming inevitably involves (re)constructing oneself in and through humanist identity categories – often imposed by others – and moreover, bracketing off or veiling over all the aspects of oneself that do not seem to fit neatly with such a designation. This scene also nicely illustrates Foucault's claim that the technologies of self-examination, confession and self-decipherment are aspects of a particular form of self-formation that he calls a hermeneutics of desire. In *The History of Sexuality* Volume I, he describes how, through the process of self-examination as 'an infinite extracting from the depths of one-self' (1980: 59), it is supposed that one comes to know the truth of oneself. The subject who knows him or herself is at the same time able, or, perhaps more importantly, obliged, to make pronounce-ments concerning him or herself, and this is what Foucault has in mind when he speaks of confession as being 'at the heart of the procedures of individualization' (Ibid.: 59). Moreover, according to Foucault, the obligation to confess has been embodied or nor-malised to such an extent that we no longer see it as an effect of a power that circumscribes us. In fact, the opposite is the case. Insofar as we experience subjectivity as autonomous and internal, we presume that self-expression has been repressed by oppressive social systems and that self-confession is, therefore, liberatory (Ibid.: 60). Confession then, Foucault argues, is a truth-effect of power, rather than a therapeutic practice of freedom, and thus it is a normalising mode of self-formation in which individual bodies are constituted as both objects and instruments of power.

Perhaps even more importantly, Foucault's analysis demonstrates that such technologies create a disjunction between self-knowledge and the interpretation of that knowledge by others, since the processes of self-examination, confession, and interpretation take place within a network of power relations that function to identify, classify, and evaluate individuals in accordance with normative criteria. The confession, as Foucault describes it, is a structurally asymmetrical ritual that presupposes the presence or virtual pres-ence of an authority figure – in this case Mary – who interprets and evaluates in order to 'judge, punish, forgive, console, and rec-oncile' (Ibid.: 61–2).

Step Two involves 'rediscovering your gender identity', and con-sists of the girls learning to use a vacuum cleaner and become pro-ficient at household chores, to apply make-up, to walk, talk, and sit in a 'ladylike' fashion, to change nappies, and ultimately, to desire, dream about, and constantly rehearse, getting married. Likewise, the boys are schooled (by RuPaul) in the art of wood chopping, car mechanics, target shooting, spitting, ball sports, and the regular readjustment of their genitals. Despite the fact that this part of the programme is referred to as the 'rediscovery' of one's gender identity – because, as Mary says, 'we're all *latent* heterosexuals' – what the film shows is that far from being 'natural', gender is learnt, often, with much difficulty and somewhat 'unsuccessfully'. Step Three is family therapy and here we find the queering of what one might refer to as the 'myth of origins', or the logic of cause and effect, and of psychotherapy as a practice founded on such logic. During the family therapy session each 'soldier' whose duty it is to 'fight against unnatural desires' is required to identify their 'root', that is, the thing that caused them to deviate from the one 'true direction'. For example, Graham's root,[14] is the fact that her 'mother got married in pants'; for Sinead it was being born in France; Clayton's mother let him 'play in her pumps'; whereas Joel's root is 'traumatic breasts'. These explanations of the various 'causes' of homosexuality engage with, and ridicule, the stereotypes of ethnicity, gender, mother/child relations, and so on that abound in our culture and that inform the ways in which sexuality is commonly understood and experienced. At the same time the viewer is made aware that the search for the 'cause' of homosexuality – which involves a form of (self-) scrutiny that is never directed at heterosexuality – draws on, and reaffirms the idea that heterosexuality and homosexuality are discrete and opposed entities and that the former is natural whereas the latter is an aberration. It could also be argued that the film's parodying of the humanist search for origins constitutes a deconstructive critique of the logic of cause and effect.[15]

Step Four, 'demystifying the opposite sex', and Step Five, 'simulated sexual lifestyle', also involve learning how to perform gender and heterosexuality in seemingly appropriate ways. In the final step of the programme Graham and Rock, dressed in flesh-tone bodysuits adorned with fig leaves come to symbolise both sexual difference and heterosexuality as Edenic and/or God-given. At the same time, the gender norms that are presumed to be intrinsic to heterosexuality are shown to be historically and culturally specific when Mary dictates, in soft porn clichés, the moves that the couple must make, declaring to the sensitive and thoughtful (and thus 'unmanly') Rock that 'foreplay is for sissies. Real men go in, unload, and pull out.' Indeed, in the lead-up to this scene, it becomes abundantly clear that what inspires the entire 'true directions' programme is Mary's virulent desire to both 'cure' and disavow her son's homosexuality. Whilst this may be read, at one level, as a comment on the lengths that some parents will go to in order to drag their perverse offsprings back onto the straight and narrow, on another level it highlights the self-defeating, but nevertheless dangerous and damaging character of dichotomous logic and the various forms of bigotry it engenders.

In foregrounding the mechanisms in and through which gender, sexuality, ethnicity, and the relations between them, are culturally constructed, *But I'm A Cheerleader* could be said to render strange, or queer, the 'truths' or norms that structure contemporary forms of knowledge and of being. In this sense, *But I'm A Cheerleader* – or at least the reading of the film that I have proposed – could be understood as an exemplification of Queer Theory as 'a theoretical perspective from which to challenge the normative' (Goldman 1996: 170).

NOTES

1. For a detailed discussion of these groups see Smyth (1992); Lucas (1998); Berlant and Freeman (1996).
2. Moraga and Anzaldúa (1981)
3. Califia (1983b)
4. Kelly (1996)
5. For example, Foucault writes, 'The individual is an effect of power, and at the same time, or precisely to the extent to which it is that effect, it is the element of its articulation. The individual which power has constituted is at the same time its vehicle' (1980: 98).
6. For an overview of various theories of the self, see Mansfield (2000).
7. See, for example, 'The Repressive Hypothesis', in Foucault (1980).
8. See Foucault (1980) pp. 92–102.
9. Halperin (1995) p. 64
10. For a range of contestatory responses to queer, see Jagose (1996) pp. 101–26.
11. See also Smith (1993).
12. For an account of the notion of abjection, see Kristeva (1982).
13. This definition is not in the main body of the above-mentioned dictionary, but is contained in the addenda, p. 2654.
14. Graham (played by Clea Duvall) is the rebel grrrl whom Megan falls in love with.
15. For examples of such critiques, see Nietzsche (1974), Aphorism #360, 'Two Kinds of Causes Which Are Confounded'; Nietzsche (1989: 45); and Derrida (1978).

4

Queer Race

RACE, LIKE GENDER, AND SEXUALITY, often tends to be regarded as something natural and innate. Indeed, the *Shorter Oxford English Dictionary* defines race as 'a group of persons, animals, or plants, connected by common descent or origin'. This text also cites the 1774 definition of race as 'one of the great divisions of mankind, having certain physical peculiarities in common'. Race, however, is not a concept that has always existed in the Western imaginary. In fact, theorists such as Soibhan Somerville, Linda Alcoff, and Tim McCaskell have argued that 'race', like 'sexuality' emerged as a classificatory concept in the era Foucault refers to as the Classical episteme. The aim of this chapter is to critically examine the emergence of the notion of race, the different and sometimes conflicting uses of the term, and the ways in which race intersects (or otherwise) with ideas about sexuality.

Historically, argues Somerville, the science of race emerged alongside of, or perhaps more particularly, in conjunction with, sexological accounts of sexuality in the eighteenth century. An explicitly pernicious example of the science of race – or of 'scientific racism' as McCaskell calls it – can be found in the classificatory system developed by the Swede Charles Linnaeus in his *General System of Nature*.[1] Originally Linnaeus proposed the existence of four basic colour types which he ordered in the following way: White Europeans, Red Americans, Yellow Asians and Black Africans. But, as Tim McCaskell notes, by the tenth edition of this text Linnaeus had attributed character traits to each race. For example, 'White' Europeans were gentle and inventive, 'Red' Americans obstinate, 'Yellow' Asians melancholy and covetous, and 'Black' Africans indolent and negligent (McCaskell, online, no page numbers in original).[2] What we see here is what McCaskell identifies as the three fundamental assertions central to biological determinist accounts of race science. First, the idea that there are distinct racial groups who are identifiable by their physiological characteristics. Second, that psychological traits such as intelligence, morality, and character are also racially specific. And, third, that these physical and psychological differences are the cause of cultural and linguistic differences among different racial groups.

McCaskell argues that alongside the popularisation of such beliefs during the Enlightenment there also existed an increasing concern with racial purity and fear of miscegination. Consequently, in many states in the USA, for example, interracial marriages were deemed illegal. The categorisation of people on the basis of race, and the imperative not to mix genres[3] were further developed, McCaskell claims, by evolutionary theorists such as Darwin, Haeckel, and Lamarck who argued that since all races were involved in a battle for survival of the fittest, some would inevitably dominate whilst others would die out, and by the Eugenics movement which concerned itself with the task of (re)producing racially 'good stock'. Obviously these discourses were drawn on to justify a whole range of atrocities such as slavery, physical abuse, and even genocide.

As Foucault has pointed out, the scientific attempt both to define race and ensure racial purity was inextricably bound up with the construction of gender and sexuality. In the nineteenth century, he claims, racism involved or engendered

a whole politics of settlement, family, marriage, education, social hier-archization, and property, accompanied by a long series of permanent interventions at the level of the body, conduct, health, and everyday life, [which] received their colour and their justification from the mythical concern with protecting the purity of the blood and ensuring the triumph of the race. (1980: 149)[4]

Consequently, (white, middle-/upper-class) women were constructed in and through these discourses and discursive practices as pure beings whose role in life was to reproduce within the ideal bounds of heterosexual marriage. Thus women who engaged in sexual relations outside of this sacrosanct institution, or women who chose not to marry and reproduce, were considered impure and a danger to the health and well-being of the human (read white) race, as were homosexuals whose (non-reproductive) sexual practices were constructed as 'akin to treason' since, as McCaskell explains, they allegedly 'wasted and exhausted the "germ plasm" that carried the strength and abilities of the [white] race'

(McCaskell, online). What we get a glimpse of here, then, is the coincidence between racism, sexism, and homophobia, which is integral to what I am referring to throughout this book as hetero-normativity. Given the inextricable relation between these forms of social organisation and regulation, one can conclude that any attempt to undermine heteronormativity must necessarily tackle issues of race and its historically and culturally specific relation to sexuality and gender.

One of the ironies of race science is that the harder biologists tried to define race, the more obvious it became that such a task was in fact impossible, thus undermining the notion of race (as genetic) altogether. As Henry Louis Gates Jr. puts it:

Race, as a meaningful criterion within the biological sciences, has long been recognized as a fiction. When we speak of the 'white race' or 'the black race', 'the Jewish race' or 'the Aryan race', we speak in biological misnomers and, more generally, in metaphors. (cited in Miles 1997: 134)

Nevertheless, the idea that race is a biological attribute continues to haunt the popular imagination and unfortunately is still used by some to argue for the innate superiority of one group over another. For example, in a book entitled *Race, Evolution, and Behavior* (2000), Philippe Rushton, a Canadian-based professor of Psychology, argues that there are three types of people: Orientals, Whites, and Blacks, and that these 'races' are distinguishable on the grounds of brain size, IQ, personality (under the heading of which Rushton compares levels of aggressiveness, impulsivity, and so on), matu-ration (which includes a consideration of motor development, skeletal development, age at first intercourse, age at first pregnancy, life span, and so on), social organisation (which Rushton under-stands in terms of marital stability, law abidingness, and mental health), and reproduction (which includes a comparison of penis size, the frequency of intercourse, permissive attitudes, rate of sexually transmitted diseases and of HIV/AIDS infection). In almost every case 'black' people come off worst, and 'orientals' best. So, for example, Rushton claims that black people have small brains and big penises, Asian people have small penises and big brains and white people, as Wendy Pearson puts it 'apparently sit nicely in the middle, not sacrificing penis size for brain size or brain size for penis size'.[5] What is important to note, however, is that these 'descriptions' of anatomical differences are far from neutral, and this is, in part, because of the association of physiology with psychology which I mentioned earlier. Indeed, in heteronormative Western discourses a big penis connotes extreme permissiveness, animality, criminality, and so on, even though no such association has ever been scientifically proven. Likewise, it is supposed that the bigger the brain, the bigger the intellect, and although once again this correlation has no basis in 'scientific fact', it most definitely continues to inform dominant ideas about race and gender differences, and the relations between them.

I now want to explore the white Western construction of the 'oriental' other apparent in Rushton's work, and in Western culture more generally, and outline the implications of such a construction in and through a discussion of David Cronenberg's M. Butterfly. According to Edward Said (1996), Orientalism is a Western system of thought and/or an academic discipline which projects ontological and epistemological distinctions between 'the Orient' and 'the Occident', and European concepts and values onto the body of the 'oriental' other (Edgar and Sedgwick 1999: 323–4). Thus, for example, Orientalism constructs the figure of the 'oriental' man as feminine, asexual, weak, and the 'oriental' woman as eager to be dominated and strikingly exotic. In other words, Orientalism regulates the race, gender, and sexuality of the oriental other in the service of its own white Eurocentric (sexual) fantasies by (re)producing stereotypical images of 'Asianness' that overlook or deny a huge range of complex cultural histories and differences. So, for example, when Rushton makes statements about 'orientals' he does not distinguish between people from Taiwan, China, India, Japan, Malaysia, Cambodia, South Korea, Hong Kong, and so on, nor does he seem to recognise the existence of Anglo-Asians, Black-Asians or other possible hybrid subjects, or of other differences based, for example, on class.

In an insightful reading of M. Butterfly, Teresa de Lauretis discusses the role of fantasy[6] in the construction of the other, the self, and the kinds of social relations that orientalist fantasies (such as Rushton's) tend to (re)produce. De Lauretis describes fantasy as an activity 'based on the capacity for imagining and imaging' (1999: 306), which tends to transgress the supposed boundary between the real and the phantasmatic. Drawing on Freudian psychoanalysis, she writes:

Psychic reality is everything that in our minds takes on the force of reality, has all the consistency of the real, and, on the basis of which, we live our lives, understand the world, and act in it. Fantasy is the psychic mechanism that structures subjectivity by reworking or translating social representations into subjective representations and self-representations. (1999: 307)

In other words, dominant cultural narratives, or 'public fantasies' as de Lauretis calls them, are internalised, psychically invested, and become part of one's sense of self, and one's way of knowing, experiencing, and interacting with the world and others. Orientalism is one such public fantasy.

Cinema, says de Lauretis, is one of the modes in and through which public fantasies are taken up and rearticulated, and *M. Butterfly* is evidence of this. Indeed, one could argue that Cronenberg's film not only enacts this process, but more important still, deconstructs specific individual and collective fantasies (and the ways in which these inform one another) and their effects. In particular, the film critically engages with the orientalist fantasy surrounding and informing not only Puccini's opera *Madama Butterfly* (1904),[7] but also, various other (significantly different) versions of this story of a relationship between a Japanese woman and a white Western man.[8] According to de Lauretis, Cronenberg's film, which is based on a play by Chinese-American playwright David Hwang, 'evokes the figure of Butterfly as a cliché, a stereotype set in a threadbare orientalist narrative, which, nevertheless, like many other public fantasies, still has the power of "something deeply felt and experienced"' (1999: 316). This stereotype of the submissive Asian woman, becomes, argues de Lauretis, a fetish: an individual and cultural fantasy imag(in)ed in order to ward off the fear of castration – a theme which I will discuss in much more detail in Chapter 10. In the very first encounter that takes place between René Gallimard, a French diplomat, and Song Liling who plays the part of Madame Butterfly in the opera of the same name, the latter gives voice to this public fantasy. In response to René's confession that he is deeply moved by the 'pure sacrifice' of the story of Butterfly which, to him, 'is very beautiful', Song says 'Why yes, to a westerner. It is one of your favourite fantasies isn't it, a submissive Oriental woman, and a cruel white man?' 'I don't think' so, replies René in an attempt to disavow this (racialised sexual) fantasy which, as Song's words make clear, is both an individual and a collective one. But Song is unwilling to let the matter rest, and further articulates the racially specific character of this fantasy by posing the following question:

What would you say if a blonde cheerleader fell in love with a short Japanese businessman: he marries her, then goes home for three years, during which time she prays to his picture and turns down marriage to a young Kennedy. Then, when she learns that he has remarried, she kills herself? Now I believe you would consider this girl to be a deranged idiot. Correct? But, because it is an Oriental who kills herself for a Western man, you find it beautiful.

M Butterfly mobilises this orientalist stereotype – or 'cultural truism' as Cronenberg describes it – in which race, gender, and sexuality are inextricably bound, in order to make explicit the ways in which a particular colonialist public fantasy can structure not only the imperialist subject's – in this case René Gallimard's – desire for what bell hooks describes as 'a bit of the Other' (1992b: 22), but also the mutual, but nonetheless devastating, desire that Song recognises, experiences and articulates: she says, 'the Oriental woman has always held a certain fascination for you Caucasian men . . . That fascination is imperialist, or so you tell me . . . but sometimes it is also mutual.' The reciprocity of such desires and fantasies are, of course, troubling, particularly given that the notion of reciprocity – of 'she wanted it too' – is in itself a fantasy all too often used to justify the mistreatment of others. However, Song is at once scornful of this fantasy, and complicit in it, and it is this tension that enables the viewer to regard her as something other than the (sex) slave of a cruel colonialist master, even though René is ironically and yet tellingly unable to see beyond the limited and limiting image of the perfect woman that exists nowhere except in his own psyche but which nevertheless comes to dominate his entire life.

In order to make sense of the relationship that develops between Song and René, and in particular the fact that Song – who unbeknownst to René is male-bodied – supposedly gives birth to a Chinese baby with blonde hair, it is necessary to understand that orientalism constructs oriental sex as exotic and shrouded in mystery. This public fantasy, and its effect on individual subjects, practices, and relationships are nicely illustrated in the following excerpt from *Chorus of Mushrooms*, a novel by the Japanese-Canadian author, Hiromi Goto.

We were . . . drinking lemon gin. I had opened his clumsily wrapped present and now his hands were inside my blouse and mine around his neck. He smelled like Dial soap.
'Do you like the T-shirt?' Hank asked.

'Yes, thank you. I'm sorry I didn't get you a present for our three week anniversary.'

'You could give me something now.'

'Oh Hank. I already told you, I don't want to go all the way yet.'

'We don't have to. Aren't there special things you can do without going all the way?' he asked, looking at me with half-closed eyes.

'What do you mean, special things?'

'You know,' he said, squirming in his trousers. 'Like Oriental sex.'

'What's Oriental sex?' This was a first.

'I don't know. *You* should know. You're Oriental, aren'tchya?' He was getting grouchy about my obtuseness, my unlearned innate sexuality.

'Not really,' I said. 'I think I'm Canadian.'

'Ahhh, you don't have to be embarrassed. I won't tell anybody if we do stuff.'

'What stuff?' I was going to lose it. And Hank was really nice, at heart, too.

'You know. The Oriental kinky stuff. Like on "Shogun".'

(Goto 1994: 122)

Likewise, it is the fantasy of 'oriental sex' that enables Song to avoid ever being naked in her sexual encounters with René, and presumably, to engage him in anal sex without him (supposedly) ever being aware that this is the case. In the court scene in which René is charged with espionage – and finally, twenty odd years after his time in Beijing, comes to realise that Song is male-bodied, and a spy for the Chinese government – Song responds to the prosecutor's inability to conceive of a sexual relationship in which one partner is completely oblivious to the sex of the other, thus: 'He never saw me completely naked. René never explored my body. He was responsive to my ancient oriental ways of love, all of which I invented myself for him.' What we see here is the (different) ways in which this fantasy engenders particular actions, relationships, and identities. For René the fantasy of oriental sex (and its articulation of a specific form of femininity) make possible a relationship with an ideal(ised) (necessarily non-white) woman, whereas for Song, it enables a (homo)sexual relationship with a straight man, and the justification of what in China during the cultural revolution would have been considered to be an unacceptable relationship, on the grounds that it allows 'her' to procure intelligence information for the communist government. In a sense, rather than promoting a theory of power in which one party (the oriental other) is completely oppressed by the dominant party (the colonialist), *M.*

Butterfly articulates a Foucauldian vision in which René and Song could both be seen as agents and effects, victims and saboteurs, of dominant cultural fantasies. So, for example, Song at once embodies the role of the fetishistic fantasy object, and simultaneously queers the Western imag(in)ary that constructs her insofar as she, the perfect woman, is male-bodied.

The orientalist fantasy of sexual domination which structures René's sense of self as well as his relationship with Song is, nevertheless, inextricably bound up with the colonialist fantasy of political domination. This is most apparent when René, in a discussion with the Consulate General about current Anglo-Asian relations, (mis)interprets (and conflates) the individual/sexual and the political character of those he defines as orientals and, as a result, seriously miscalculates future events with which the contemporary viewer is painfully familiar. He says:

In their hearts the Chinese don't even like Ho Chi Minh. Deep down they're attracted to us. They find our ways exciting. Of course, they'd never admit it, but the orientals will always submit to the greater force. So, if the Americans demonstrate the will to win, the Vietnamese, believe you me, will welcome them into a mutually beneficial union.

Whilst we, with the benefit of hindsight, may declare this reading to be a fantasy rather than a reality, what *M. Butterfly* relentlessly articulates is the dissolving of the one into the other. Psychic reality, as de Lauretis claims, consists, of 'fantasies' which take on the force of reality insofar as they form the basis on which we live our lives and understand ourselves and the world. Nowhere is this more clear than in René's desire for, and love of Butterfly/Song; a desire/love which is infused with fantasy and yet is never simply delusional. Indeed, there is something about René's desire/love that haunts and thus troubles (love) relations generally, and that is, the role that fantasy plays in the (en)gendering of the (always already racialised) beloved.

René, as I have suggested, embodies dominant (orientalist) public fantasies about gender, race, sexuality, and the relations between them, and projects these onto the body of Song. In the final scene of the film in which René performs *Madama Butterfly* to an audience of prison inmates this (phantasmatic) construction of the other – and, by association, its impact on the self – is verbally acknowledged and performatively affected. For example, René says:

There is a vision of the orient that I have of slender women in ...
kimonos who die for the love of unworthy foreign devils; who are
born and raised to be perfect women; who take whatever punishment
we give them and spring back strengthened by love unconditional. It
is a vision that has become my life.

And indeed, it has, as we see in René's transfiguration into a 'living
legend, the fantasy of Butterfly' (de Lauretis 1999: 323) the perfect
woman, who of course, dies at the hand of the man who has created her. But there is a twist, since it is 'René Gallimard, also
known as Madame Butterfly' who dies, and the suicide weapon,
rather than being a traditional Japanese *seppuku* dagger (a symbol
of honour), is a shard of mirror, a symbol, at least in the West, of
narcissistic self-love. de Lauretis sums up well the ways in which
this scene (and the film as a whole) queers orientalism when she
writes:

Western man looks into the mirror and sees the face of his other(s),
an orientalist pastiche of Chinese and Japanese costume and makeup.
This is the stereotype of the racial, cultural, and gendered other that
he himself has constructed for his civilization, his history, his desire;
and he is finally consumed like Frankenstein by his own creation ... In
René Gallimard's end – his name is the epitome of Western philosophy and high French culture: René for Descartes and Gallimard for
the French publishing company – the discontents of Western civilization have come full circle, and the aggression it had displaced onto its
colonized others now turns around upon itself, upon the colonizer.
The once mighty man is reduced to a pathetic figure in drag slumped
on the prison floor in a heap of coloured rags. (Ibid.: 324)

In short, then, white Western masculinity, like oriental femininity,
is shown to be the parody of an unachievable and self-defeating
idea(l) or fantasy that is both shared and lived out in specific ways
by individuals.

Not only have theories of race failed to explain so-called racial
differences in biological terms, race, as theorists such as McCaskell
and Ian Barnard have argued, and *M. Butterfly* illustrates, is an
unstable and shifting fantasy. For example, McCaskell claims that
at one time in Canada Irish people were considered to belong to a
different race and Ukranians were not thought of as white.
Similarly, Barnard tells us that Japanese people were designated as
'honorary whites' by the apartheid government (in South Africa)
despite the fact that to Europeans such as Gallimard 'orientals' are
by definition non-whites, and that some Latin American people

are considered white in their own countries but are described as 'Hispanic' in the United States (1999: 205). Nevertheless, notions of race have continued to play a part in anti-racist theory and politics, and in gay and lesbian theory and politics. Moreover, the ways in which race is constructed in and through these discourses is, as I pointed out in my discussion of *M. Butterfly*, inextricably bound up with the elaboration of particular idea(l)s about sexuality and gender. It is to this set of relations and the specific ways in which they are played out that we will now turn.

In his article 'Queer Race', Barnard argues that 'the construction of sexuality is usually treated separately from the construction of race, as if each figuration of subjectivity could develop independently of the other' (Ibid.: 200). In effect, what Barnard is highlighting is the tendency for Gay and Lesbian Studies theorists to focus primarily on sexuality, for theorists of race to focus primarily on race, for feminists to focus primarily on gender, and so on, and the associated tendency for readers to classify writers such as Gloria Anzaldúa, for example, who writes about race, sexuality, and gender, as race theorists. This latter tendency is evidenced by the fact that Anzaldúa rarely appears in canonical lists of queer theorists such as Sedgwick, Butler, de Lauretis, Bersani, Califia, Warner, Watney, and so on, despite the fact that she used the term queer in interesting and important ways in her 1987 text *Borderlands/La Frontera: The New Mestiza.*

One of the problems with disassociating race, gender, and sexuality and focusing primarily on one of the terms is that such an approach can lead to the production of accounts of race that are (at least implicitly) sexist and/or homophobic, theories of gender that are (at least implicitly) racist and/or homophobic, and analyses of sexuality that are (at least implicitly) racist and/or sexist. For example, Barnard, like Anzaldúa (1987; 1991), Cohen (1997), Ng (1997), Moraga (1983; 1996), Goldman (1996), Namaste (1996) and many other theorists,[9] argues that in focusing almost solely on sexuality, lesbian and gay theorists and activists, and queer theorists, have not only overlooked race, but have 'white-washed' the figure of the 'homosexual'. Barnard writes:

Any Western politics, no matter how coalitional its compass, that defines itself in terms of . . . sexual orientation only . . . will be a white centered and white dominated politics, since, in the West, only white people can afford to see their race as unmarked, as an irrelevant or subordinate category of analysis. (1999: 202)

At the same time these race-blind theorists and activists have allegedly fantasised a gay community that, in short, is homogeneous, and thus (at times) alienates all those who do not fit with the figure of 'the homosexual'; that is, non-whites, lesbians, disabled gays and lesbians, working-class gays and lesbians, transsexuals, intersexed people, and so on.

In *Welcome to the Jungle: New Positions in Black Cultural Studies* (1994), Kobena Mercer has argued that although white gays derived inspiration from the black liberation movement – even to the point of adopting the notion of Pride and translating 'Black Pride' into 'Gay Pride' – this debt has never been explicitly acknowledged.[10] Moreover, he argues that issues pertaining to race have, by and large, been marginalised within predominantly white gay and lesbian groups and/or theories. Consequently, Mercer claims that dominant forms of gay activism were (and still are) often inappropriate for non-white people. For example, he tells of how in 1982 in Britain the Gay Black Group published an article which questioned the ethnocentric assumptions behind the exhortation to 'come out'. The authors pointed out that the ties that black gays and lesbians often have with their families, and the support that they provide for one another in a racist environment are something that they may not be prepared to jeopardise in order to declare their sexuality. The group argued that for the most part, middle-class white gays and lesbians do not seem to have the same need for family support, and that their political consciousness is more likely to be 'dominated by the concern with sexuality in an individualistic sense' (Mercer 1994: 132–3). More recently Cathy Cohen, writing in response to the call to deconstruct identities rather than proclaiming them, argues that 'Queer theorizing which calls for the elimination of fixed categories of sexual identity seems to ignore the ways in which some traditional social identities and communal ties can, in fact, be important to one's survival' (1997: 450).

Concomitantly, it has been suggested by some writers and activists that various forms of nationalism, in focusing on race to the detriment of sexuality and gender, tend to be homophobic and/or racist. For example, Cherríe Moraga has argued that, on the one hand '"Queer Nation",[11] whose leather-jacketed, shaved-headed white radicals and accompanying anglocentricity were an "alien nation" to most lesbians and gay men of colour' (1996: 298), while, on the other, Chicano Nationalism 'never accepted openly gay men and lesbians among its ranks' (1996: 298). Similarly, theorists such as Kobena Mercer, Henry Louis Gates Jr., and Darieck Scott, amongst others, have claimed that they have experienced racism in the so-called gay and lesbian community, and homophobia in black nationalist[12] movements.[13]

Kobena Mercer offers an explanation for black homophobia when he claims that traditionally the racial power exercised by colonialism denied certain so-called masculine attributes to black male slaves and, as a result, (some) black men have adopted particular patriarchal values and characteristics such as physical strength, sexual prowess, and control, as a means of survival. Mercer writes, 'The incorporation of a code of "macho" behavior is thus intelligible as a means of recuperating some degree of power over the condition of powerlessness and dependency in relation to the white master subject' (1994: 137). However, the embodiment of 'macho' characteristics and values has meant that homosexuality (understood as effeminacy) has been seen by some black men as something that may threaten and weaken their position both socially and politically. Thus for some involved in the Black Power movement, to be gay was to be a race traitor, it was an act of betrayal. There are obviously similarities (and important differences) between this sort of position and the disdain for transsexuals and drag queens apparent among members of various homophile groups,[14] and the construction, and fear, of the 'lavender menace' by some early second-wave feminist organisations.[15]

This seeming tension between blackness and gayness brings me to what Barnard describes as the 'black gay versus gay black' debate. Before I outline this debate in any detail, it is important to note that it is a conflict which has taken place among gay African-Americans and not so much between black gays and straights. The debate pits gay identity against black identity in order to determine which is more formative, and consequently, like the additive model of identity which I will discuss later in the chapter, could be said to be indicative of an inability to recognise the complex intersections of race and sexuality, as well as of other things like gender, class, physical ability, age, religion, and so on.

In an article entitled 'Black Gay *v* Gay Black' Lloyd Jordan argues that 'black gays believe that gay blacks hate their own race ... and ... give their loyalty to the gay rather than to the black community' (1990: 25). Lloyd quotes an African-American gay man who says that 'while gay blacks may have sex with us ... deep down inside there is not real love, *real* love is reserved for whites' (cited in Jordan 1990: 30). In effect then, the term 'gay black' as it is used in these debates, refers (usually negatively) to someone who is considered to be more gay than black, or to put his sexuality before his race. The implication is that such a person is not really black at all, at least not politically, or in spirit.[16] Conversely, the term 'black gay' refers to a person who is first and foremost black, but who is also gay. As Darieck Scott points out in an article entitled 'Jungle Fever?: Black Gay Identity Politics, White Dick, and the Utopian Bedroom', the trouble with this debate is that it is founded on the belief that

the only available option [is] subordinating one characteristic to another, as if identity cannot be expressed except as an undisturbed center around which satellite qualifiers revolve. The integrity of the two concepts, 'black' and 'gay' is maintained without problematizing the exclusions of either – exclusions which are of particular import to the construction of black gay identities: namely, that in the vast majority of African-American self-representations, and in most images of African-Americans which circulate in American culture, 'blackness', especially male blackness, is almost definitionally masculine and constitutively heterosexual; and in the overwhelming majority of gay self-representations and images of gay men, the image of 'gayness' corresponds to that of white men. (1994: 301)

Scott takes his discussion of the limitations of this essentialising logic one step further by critically analysing the ways in which gay inter-racial relationships have been (negatively) constructed. In short, Scott argues that in the terms of the above-mentioned debate the 'gay black' is set up in opposition to the 'black gay', and this opposition is evaluated in terms of a hierarchy. Further, connected to this are other hierarchical oppositions such as Afrocentrist/interracialist, and blacker-than-thou/snow queen. Here, the snow-queen or interracialist (the black man who is sexually attracted to white men) is seen as the ultimate traitor, the worst form of gay black. This way of thinking is nicely illustrated in the following message from a 'black acquaintance' left on the answering machine of a self-proclaimed snow queen, after an encounter the previous evening in a racially mixed gay night-club. The caller says: 'Hello R . . . You should know better than to be with that tacky white man. You let down the black community. I am so disgusted at that silly queen that I saw you with. Can't you find a black partner, you bastard!' (cited in Taylor 1996: 1).

69

Scott claims that all too often in black nationalist discourses produced by gay men, the black partner in an interracial couple is assumed to detest blackness and therefore to hate himself and to loathe his 'brothers'. He is thought to be

beguiled, enchanted, by the white standard of beauty, by 'whiteness' itself, and consequently has an exclusive desire for a lover with Nordic features. Moreover, his political, social, and cultural allegiances are to 'white' gay politics, to white gay men, and to 'white' cultural forms. (Scott 1994: 299–300)

In other words, the desire for white men, as it is constructed in and through the gay black v. black gay debate, is fundamentally conceived of as a 'desire for the oppressor, and a capitulation to subjugation' (Scott 1994: 308).[17] As you may have noticed, there are similarities (as well as important differences) between this position and the claim made by political lesbians such as the Leeds Revolutionary Feminists that women who are attracted to, or who participate in sexual relations with, men, are reinforcing their own oppression (see Chapter 2).

Conversely, says Scott, love between black men is often constructed in gay nationalist discourses as emotionally and politically healthy, even revolutionary if one accepts Joseph Beam's claim that 'black men loving black men is the revolutionary act of the eighties' (cited in Scott 1994: 303) – a slogan which Marlon Riggs intensifies in his documentary *Tongues Untied* which ends with Beam's words, but this time the 'the' is underlined, and the historical reference is dropped. Thus the statement reads: 'Black men loving Black men is <u>the</u> revolutionary act', suggesting that there is something essentially and universally revolutionary about homosexual relations between black men.

One of the problems with this canonisation of homosexual relations between black men is that idealising the relation necessarily involves overlooking the possibility that other differences (and inequalities) might exist between people of the same race, gender, and sexuality, such as differences in class, wealth, occupation, education, age, body-image, physical ability, religion, health, and so on. Consequently, in an attempt to move beyond the essentialising humanist logic that informs the idealisation of sexual relations between men (or women) of the same race, Scott calls for a recognition of 'colored contradictions', that is, the differences between and within black gay men.

Similar problems informed by the separation of race and sexuality have also occurred among other 'non-white' groups. For example, in an article entitled 'Race Matters', Vivien Ng relates the story of the murder of a gay Vietnamese man (Truong Loc Minh) by a gang of white men in California in 1993. In the *Los Angeles Times* the incident was described as a gay bashing, and Truong's ethnicity was mentioned only once. In the Chinese-language *International Daily*, on the other hand, the incident was described as a case of Asian bashing and there was no mention of the victim's sexuality (Ng 1997: 222). In his critical analysis of the two accounts of the case, Eric C. Wat argues that neither report is wrong or untrue as such. Rather, he claims that each is mediated by racial and cultural assumptions about gay men and about Asian men. The trouble, as Wat sees it, is that gay Asian men 'are run over at the intersection of racism and homophobia' (cited in Ibid.: 222). What he means by this is that in the dominant Asian-American imaginary, there is an implicit association of gayness with whiteness and Asianness with heterosexuality. Wat problematises this association when he convincingly demonstrates that Truong's murder cannot ultimately be understood simply as either an example of homophobic violence, or as a case of racism. In short, Wat, like Scott, calls for a more complex analysis of the intersections between race and sexuality.

Similarly, Barnard argues that cultural categories such as race, sexual orientation, class, gender, and so on, do not exist independently of one another, rather, they operate, he claims, as interlocking systems. In saying this Barnard is not suggesting, however, that each of us has a number of discrete base identities – for example, an ethnic identity, a racial identity, a gender identity, a sexual identity, a class identity and so on – which simply exist side by side. If one did take this kind of position and reiterate what Elizabeth Spelman has referred to as 'the ampersand problem',[18] one might describe oneself, for example, as a disabled, indigenous, working-class, lesbian, mother. One could then argue that one was quadruply oppressed, and thus more oppressed than, for example, a white, working-class, disabled, lesbian, mother, who in turn is more oppressed than a white, working-class, disabled, heterosexual, mother, and so on and so forth. But, as Gloria Anzaldúa claims in her critique of the additive model of identity and oppression, 'Identity is not a bunch of little cubby holes stuffed respectively with intellect, sex, race, class, vocation, gender. Identity flows between, over, aspects of a person. Identity is a . . . process' (1991: 252–3).

71

There are indeed a number of problems with the additive model of identity and oppression. As the example of the various kinds of disabled mothers shows, this sort of logic involves the positing of hierarchies of oppression without recognising that the implications of being positioned in one of the above ways are significantly different from being positioned in another. In other words, the additive model of identity and of oppression cannot account for the complex, multiplicitous, and contradictory character of subjectivity(s), social relations, or oppression. It cannot explain why, for example, one's sexuality is always raced: why, being positioned as a black homosexual man is significantly different from being positioned as a black heterosexual man, and/or being positioned as a white homosexual man. It is not simply that the black gay man is 'doubly' oppressed whereas the black straight man and the white gay man are 'singly' oppressed on the basis of race and sexuality respectively. Rather, the lived experience of sexuality, for example, is, in each case, significantly different since race, class, sexuality, and so on, inflect and/or infuse one another. As Barnard puts it, sexuality is always already racialised, and race is always already sexualised. 'Thus, race and sexuality are not two separate axes of identity that cross and overlay in particular subject positions, but rather, ways to circumscribe systems of meaning and understanding that formatively and inherently define each other' (1999: 200).

What we find then in the work of Barnard, Scott, and Wat is a call for an analysis of what Kimberlé Crenshaw[19] has called intersectionality, that is, the complex interaction between a range of discourses, institutions, identities, and forms of exploitation, that structure subjectivities (and the relations between them) in elaborate, heterogeneous, and often contradictory ways. This is a task that, despite claims to the contrary, theorists such as Namaste, Barnard, Cohen and Anzaldúa claim Queer Theory has, by and large, failed to respond to with the required level of vigilance and commitment. Anzaldúa writes, it is white middle-class lesbians and gays 'who have produced queer theory and for the most part their theories make abstractions of us colored queers . . . Their theories limit the ways we think about being queer' (1991: 251).

Rather than immersing ourselves further in the question of Queer Theory's race blindness – and thus, in effect, its 'un-queerness' – I want to turn now to the idea of racial (im)purity. Obviously the image of a nexus of mutually constitutive and yet non-conflatable systems of gender, sexuality, race, class, and so on, outlined in the work of Barnard and others, leads one to the conclusion that racial purity is an impossible (but nevertheless highly influential) public fantasy. Kevin Thomas Miles, however, goes one step further and argues that the notion of purity is not something that simply structures racist discourses, but rather, is an intrinsic aspect of Western metaphysics and/or humanist logic. Miles claims that the dichotomy purity/impurity, is aligned in this system with rationality/irrationality and thus, he writes, 'There can be no coming to terms with the myth of racial purity if we do not come to terms with the myth of pure reason and its magical power to destroy monstrous ideas' (1997: 142). Whilst Miles does not seem particularly interested in Queer Theory *per se*, his thesis nevertheless illustrates the extent to which a critique of single-axis accounts of identity is integral to the queering of humanism more generally (and vice versa), and thus of heteronormativity. Queer Theory must therefore become, and remain, monstrous, as Sue-Ellen Case has rightly argued (see Chapter 3).

Of late, the notion of hybridity[20] – a term originally used to refer to the selective breeding of plants – has come to be seen by some as useful to the attempt to undermine the idea(l) of racial purity. In particular it seems to have enabled (some) 'mixed-race' people to describe themselves, for example, as neither Australian nor Asian, nor as a simple combination or amalgamation of the two, but rather as a sort or 'third term' which belongs to both and simultaneously neither.[21] But, as Homi Bhabha (1996) has noted the problem with using the term hybridity as an empirical description is that it then becomes (at least potentially) generalisable to the point where it loses any political import that it may have originally had – a problem, which, as we saw in the previous chapter, is also apparent in the use of the term queer as a descriptor that can be applied to anything or anyone considered to be 'non-normative'. Thus Bhabha argues for an understanding of hybridity as a strategy or a practice which in various ways establishes space(s) for being neither (European) Self nor (indigenous) Other.

In her discussion of what she refers to as 'New Asian Queer Funk', Audrey Yue seems to articulate a specific example of Bhabha's understanding of hybridity and/or Barnard's notion of queer race. According to Yue:

New Asian Queer Funk is a style that expresses a politics . . . [It] is loosely associated with a pastiche of heterogeneous Asian cultural

forms ... [I]t is an attitude, a style, and a politics driven by the forms
of New Asia, global queering, and indigenised diasporic funk ... [I]t
is an emergent event that produces a mobile and transient culture.
(2000: 43)

One aspect or example of New Asian Queer Funk, is 'sticky rice'.
As Yue sees it, 'sticky rice' refers to a sexual practice modelled
on 'diasporic postnational regionality' (Ibid.: 44). In other words,
'sticky rice' is a term used to describe a relationship between Asian-
Australian same-sex couples. However, since the term diaspora
refers to dispersion, and since the relationships that Yue is discussing, first, take place outside of Asian nation–states, and, second, occur between people whose race cannot be encapsulated
in single terms (that is, Asian or Australian), then 'sticky rice'
functions as a strategy of/which queer(s) race, rather than being
an empirical description of a desire for a person of one's 'own
kind' – that is, the kind of desire that is sometimes seen as revolutionary by, for example, those who share the position of Riggs
mentioned earlier.

As is apparent in the above quotation from Yue, the notion of
hybridity is often associated with the idea of diaspora. This term,
which means to disperse or scatter, has been used by many postcolonial theorists[22] to articulate the ways in which various (specific)
forms of postcolonial hybrid identity and social relations are lived
and experienced. But whilst this critical term has been seen as
enabling by some, others such as Gayatri Gopinath nevertheless call
for a queering of the (all too often unquestioned) assumptions and
associations that inform it and are informed by it. In an analysis of
Shyam Selvadurai's novel *Funny Boy* (1994), Deepha Mehta's film
Fire (1996), and the popular Hindi film *Hum Aapke Hain Koun*
(1993) which nicely illustrates the idea that sexuality is inextricably
bound up with other discursive constructs such as race, gender,
nation, home, and so on, Gopinath develops the notion of queer
South Asian diasporic subject(ivities) in order to counteract or
challenge 'dominant diasporic articulations of community and
identity [which] intersect with patriarchal nationalist logic'
(1997: 471), and/or with heteronormativity. Gopinath's thesis reaffirms the problems associated with focusing primarily on race
which I discussed earlier, and goes one step further by illustrating
that even postcolonial accounts of diasporic subjectivity can and
do fall prey to modernist logic with its singular fantasies of cultural
and political progress: fantasies, which at least implicitly, all too

often structurally exclude queer bodies. Thus, what is important about Gopinath's contribution to this particular field of critical enquiry is that her articulation of a queer diasporic imaginary undermines hegemonic heterornormative constructions of nation and diaspora, by performatively evoking the spectral figure of the 'impossible subject'; that is, the subject who is necessarily excluded from – but is nevertheless internal to – and whose appearance thus destabilises, these monologic discourses.

Despite the many and varied interventions into race(ism) that have been made during the past century – some of which I have outlined in this chapter – 'race still means things' (Barnard 1999: 206), or, as Linda Alcoff writes, 'racialized identities have as much political, sociological, and economic salience as they ever had' (2001: 269). The question, then, is why is this so: why is it that race(ism) seems so inexorable? Alcoff's response to this question is that 'race operates pre-consciously' (Ibid.: 271). Before we consider Alcoff's thesis which is influenced by the work of Maurice Merleau-Ponty (which I discuss in more detail in the following chapter), I want first of all to explore an anecdote which anticipates, it seems to me, Alcoff's explanation.

In his article 'The universalization of whiteness: racism and enlightenment', Warren Montag puzzles over an event that occurred in 1774 and which was subsequently recorded by Janet Schaw, a 'Scottish "lady of quality"' (1997: 281) in her diary.[23] Schaw, describing her arrival in Antigua, and the short journey on foot that followed from the ship to the hotel, writes that 'a number of pigs ran out at a door and after them a parcel of monkeys. This not a little surprised me, but I found that what I took for monkeys were negro children, naked as they were born' (cited in Ibid.: 281). According to Montag, Schaw who apparently embraced Enlightenment principles, was 'neither ignorant nor vicious' (Ibid.: 282) despite what we might think given her momentary (mis)interpretation of black children as monkeys. In fact, Montag claims that Schaw was a product and an exemplar of the Scottish Enlightenment (which one could describe as a system of specific public fantasies), and that her (mis)reading of racial difference attests to and/or is the result of this. If this is the case, then Schaw's (mis)interpretation is less a perceptual error, or a moment of perceptual confusion that is quickly rectified once she realises that the figures that crossed her path are really children, and more a mode of perception which (like all perceptions) is already imbued with historically and culturally specific values, fantasies, desires, aspirations, fears, and so on. Let me explain this by returning to Alcoff's phenomenological analysis of racial embodiment.

Drawing on Merleau-Ponty's work on bodily-being-in-the-world, Alcoff argues that knowledge is 'tacit and carried in the body' (2001: 272) rather than being something that is separate from the body and is processed by and stored in one's cognitive faculties. Perception, then, is the term used to describe this bodily-knowing: perception is structured by and 'represents sedimented contextual knowledges' (Ibid.: 272). What this means is that we perceive ourselves, others, the world, and the relation between them, in and through the grids of intelligibility that exist in our culture, and which we have embodied, which, in effect, we are. But this perception occurs, for the most part, at what you might call a subliminal, or pre-conscious (bodily) level. Thus, Alcoff claims that 'the process by which human bodies are differentiated and categorized by type is a process preceded by racism, rather than one that causes and thus "explains" racism as a natural result' (Ibid.: 272). In other words, Alcoff is less interested in the humanist notion of ideology as something that is imposed from the outside, than in the (Foucauldian) idea of a 'racial common sense' which forms a sort of cultural backdrop against which we all act, and in which we are all in varying ways and to varying degrees, implicated. Consequently, the aim of Alcoff's article is to make explicit the tacit 'perceptual practices involved in racialization [which] are . . . almost hidden from view' (Ibid.: 275), so that we can critically analyse the dominant collective fantasies that engender our individual actions, interactions, identities, ways of seeing, knowing, and being.

Drawing on Merleau-Ponty's account of the blind-man's stick as an instrument in and through which he habitually perceives rather than consciously interprets the world, Alcoff argues that interpretation is inseparable from perception. She says: 'Our experience of habitual perceptions is so attenuated as to skip the stage of conscious interpretation and intent. Indeed, interpretation is the wrong word here: we are simply perceiving' (Ibid.: 276). Let's consider this claim by returning to the story of Janet Schaw's encounter in the streets of St Johns, Antigua, and in particular her perception of black children as monkeys.

As I said earlier, Montag reads Schaw's report not as a singular and idiosyncratic example of racism, but rather, as an effect of a

conflict at the heart of dominant social narratives or public fantasies which (in)formed Schaw's (bodily-)being-in-the-world. This
conflict concerns the 'concept of universality as it actually functioned in the epoch of the Enlightenment' (1997: 285). Drawing
on the work of Etienne Balibar,[24] Montag explains that the univer-
salism inherent in humanism necessarily involves the positing of a
definition of the human, and, by association, an 'infinite process
of demarcation between the human, the more than human, and
the less than human' (Balibar, cited in Ibid.: 286). It is the border
between the human and the non-human at which, according to
Montag, Schaw stumbles; at which her perception oscillates (she
perceives the figures as both non-human and human).[25] But
Montag goes further than Balibar and argues that dominant
Enlightenment discourses collapsed the supposed distinction
between white and black into the categories of the human and the
non-human respectively. Thus 'whiteness' was constructed less as a
racial characteristic than as 'the very form of human universality
itself' (1997: 285). In other words, 'whiteness' as humanness
becomes central to what Alcoff describes as a historically and culturally specific 'structure of . . . perception [which] helps constitute
the necessary background from which [one knows oneself and
others]. It makes up a part of what appears to me as the natural
setting of all my thoughts' (2001: 275). Whiteness, then, is rarely
spoken as such, but nevertheless functions – in hegemonic and
some anti-hegemonic discourses – as the (embodied) 'principle of
perfection' (Montag 1997: 291), the tacit figure of the human
against which 'all (other) races have fallen short . . . Whiteness is
itself the human universal that no (other) race realizes' (Ibid.: 292).

If we accept this thesis which articulates a complex understanding of the relation between race(ism), public fantasies, and what
Alcoff describes as 'the micro-processes of subjective existence'
(2001: 273), then it becomes possible to argue, as Montag does,
that the perception that Schaw recorded in her diary over two
centuries ago was not hers alone. Rather:

> it was a [perception] that enveloped her, a [perception] that saw
> through her, the [perception] of an implacable whiteness confronted
> with beings that it could not reduce to its truth. It is the perception of
> a universal that stumbles on what it has left out, on the remainder that
> it cannot acknowledge except by projecting it beyond the limits whose
> existence it was designed to mask. (Montag 1997: 292)

And, as Montag notes, and as we've seen throughout this chapter, we are, of course, still – in varying ways, and to varying degrees – caught up and/or implicated in these perceptual practices and tacit knowledges which we cannot simply reject in and through conscious choice. Rather, what is necessary, as I said earlier, is to make explicit the existence of tacit knowledges which, for the most part, structure our perception, our identities, our actions, our relations with others, at a fundamental pre-conscious level, and which, all too often seem almost immune from critical analysis. One such structuring principle is, of course, whiteness.[26]

In one sense the troubling of (hegemonic) race(ist) perception and of the public fantasies that (in)form it and are (in)formed by it could be said to constitute queer practice. However, if we (re)turn to the criticisms of Queer Theory often made by 'non-white' cultural critics, it becomes apparent that this area of critical practice and those who participate in it would also benefit from an ongoing rigorous examination of the ways in which whiteness structures queer political perceptions and practices. As Phillip Brian Harper puts it in his address to the Queer Black Studies in the Millennium Conference:

What is currently recognized as Queer Studies is unacceptably Euro-American in orientation, its purview effectively determined by the practically invisible – because putatively non-existent – bounds of racial whiteness. It encompasses as well . . . the abiding failure of most supposedly queer critics to subject whiteness itself to sustained interrogation and thus to delineate its import in sexual terms, whether conceived in normative or non-normative modes. In other words, to speak personally, it bothers me less that white practitioners of queer critique tend not to address the significance of racial non-whiteness in the phenomenon of sex and sexuality they explore (though one often wishes they would – and indeed some do). It bothers me less though that they fail to do this, then that they tend not to address the effects of racial whiteness on the very manifestations of those phenomena and their understanding of them. (cited in Alexander 2000: 1288)

NOTES

1. The first edition of this text was published in 1735, but according to McCaskell, it said very little about human variation. The ideas discussed in this chapter were developed in later editions.
2. I am indebted to Wendy Pearson for drawing my attention to this text as well as to Goto (1994), and also for her insightful reading of *M*.

Butterfly developed in a lecture on race and sexuality presented at Macquarie University.

3. The obsession with purity mentioned here, is, claims Kevin Thomas Miles, central to Western metaphysics, and can be traced at least as far back as Hesiod's mythological description of human origins. See Miles (1997).
4. For a more detailed account of the connection between the regulation of racial purity and sexual hygiene, see Foucault (1980) pp. 115–31.
5. Pearson made this comment in the above-mentioned lecture.
6. De Lauretis discusses what she sees as three levels of fantasy at work in *M. Butterfly*: the diagetic fantasy, the film's fantasy, and the spectator's fantasy. In this chapter I will focus only on the first of these.
7. Puccini's opera *Madama Butterfly* tells the story of a Japanese woman who falls in love with an American officer. The American marries Butterfly, but then deserts her and returns to the USA where he marries a white woman. In despair Butterfly kills herself.
8. See de Lauretis (1999) pp. 309–12.
9. This claim is not only supported by the participants of the Black Queer Studies in the Millennium Conference held at the University of North Carolina in April 2000, but moreover, informed both the content of the conference, and the decision to use the modifier 'black' even though this may seem to some to be antithetical to the post-identity logic of Queer Theory. For a discussion of the conference, see Alexander (2000).
10. This sort of appropriation of black culture is, according to bell hooks, central to the resurgence of black nationalism, which, she argues, is often nothing like as essentialist or essentialising as particular white critics have suggested. See hooks (1992b).
11. For an insightful critique of nationalism in gay and lesbian and/or queer movements, see Duggan (1992). Anne McClintock (1993b) has also developed an important critique of the relation between dominant accounts of nation and heteronormative understandings of gender, sexuality, race, and the relations between them.
12. Isaac Julien's film *Looking For Langston* (1989) could be seen as a response to this insofar as it is an attempt to re-vision the Harlem Renaissance, in particular the homosexuality that was an integral (although all too often silenced) aspect of it.
13. Similar tensions surrounding and informing the experience of Jewishness, lesbianism, gayness, and/or transsexualism (and the relations between them) are discussed by Boyarin (1995), Burstin (1999), Goldflam (1999), and Scheman (1997). See also Gopinath's (1997) critique of the India Day Parade for a similar account of the tensions between national identity and sexual identity.

14. See the discussion of *Stonewall* in Chapter 2.

15. See the discussion of '1972', the second story in the film *If These Walls Could Talk 2*, in Chapter 2.

16. Similar claims have been made about Asian men who desire white men. Such men are sometimes critically referred to as bananas since they are allegedly 'yellow on the outside and white on the inside'.

17. This idea is also explored in the short film directed by Rodney Evans entitled *Two Encounters* (2000), and in relation to Anglo-Asian inter-racial relationships in the short film directed by Raymond Yueng entitled *Yellow Fever* (1998).

18. See Spelman (1988).

19. See Crenshaw (1991; 2000).

20. Jeffrey Eugenides' novel *Middlesex* (2002) could be said to (implicitly) use the notion of hybridity as a vehicle through which to explore an historically and culturally specific account of the relations between race, gender, and sexuality.

21. See, for example, Shrage's (1997) attempt to reconfigure not just the identities of two 'mixed-race' girls, but also the ways in which their white mother is ambiguously raced in and through her relation with her daughters.

22. In all sorts of interesting and insightful ways Shani Mootoo's novel *Cereus Blooms at Night* (1999) seems to explore the relation(s) between race, gender, sexuality, class, and so on, by drawing on post-colonial concepts such as hybridity and diaspora.

23. The diary was published in 1927 by Yale University Press, under the title *Journal of a Lady of Quality; Being the Narrative of a Journey from Scotland to the West Indies, North Carolina, and Portugal, in the Years 1774 to 1776*.

24. See Balibar (1994).

25. This perceptual oscillation is, argues Montag, repeated throughout the diary 'in which the familiar never ceases to be haunted by the strange, always internal to it' (1997: 286).

26. For critical analyses of whiteness, see Allison (1995); Dyer (1997); Hill (1997); Rasmussen *et al.*, (2001); Ware and Back (2001). Dorothy Allison has also written a novel entitled *Bastard Out of Carolina* (1993) which explores the intersections between race, sexuality, and 'white trash'. The novel was made into a film of the same name (1996), directed by Angelica Huston. For an analysis of Allison's work, see Sandell (1997).

5

Performance, Performativity, Parody, and Politics

MOST OFTEN, WE THINK OF a person's gestures, tastes, desires, and ways of being-in-the-world, as the expression of an innate, autonomous, and unique core, an 'I'. But according to many post-structuralist theorists, the 'individual' as it is conceived here, is a truth-effect of systems of power/knowledge that are culturally and historically specific rather than being something that exists in an essential sense. Likewise, it is a commonly held belief that gender is a natural attribute, an internal essence that manifests itself in characteristics such as (in the case of females) passivity, nurturance, maternal feelings, and so on. Feminists have countered this sort of essentialism by arguing that gender, like the notion of the individual, is a social construct. Drawing on, amongst other things, Foucault's work on subjectivity and sexuality, Simone de Beauvoir's account of gender as a learned set of attributes and actions,[1] Joan Rivière's notion of 'womanliness' as masquerade,[2] J. L. Austin's speech-act theory,[3] and Derrida's deconstruction of speech-act theory,[4] Judith Butler has developed an account of gender (and of identity more generally) as performative. In this chapter we will examine Butler's analysis of the relationship between actions, desires, gestures, and identity, the various ways in which her account of performativity has been taken up by other theorists, and the political implications of these theses.

As discussed in previous chapters, Queer Theory, as a deconstructive strategy, aims to denaturalise heteronormative understandings of sex, gender, sexuality, sociality, and the relations between them. Identity politics, on the other hand, could be said to be based on the assumption that sexual inclinations, practices, and desires are the expression of a person's core identity.

Consequently, as we've seen, identity politics has been accused of being complicit in the structures of meaning that it aims to challenge. As Butler puts it, 'identity categories tend to be instruments of regulatory regimes, whether as the normalizing categories of oppressive structures, or as the rallying points for a liberatory contestation of that very oppression' (1990: 13–14). Given this, Butler's account of the performative character of gender (and identity more generally) queers, many have argued, not only hegemonic institutions, identities, and relations – what Butler refers to as a 'heterosexual matrix' – but also identity politics and the fundamental assumptions upon which it (in its various forms) has been founded.

In her seminal text, *Gender Trouble*, Judith Butler argues that gender is neither natural or innate, but rather, is a social construct which serves particular purposes and institutions. Gender, she says, is the performative effect of reiterative acts, that is, acts that can be, and are, repeated. These acts which are repeated in and through a highly rigid regulatory frame, 'congeal over time to produce the appearance of a substance, of a natural sort of being' (1990: 33). In other words, rather than being expressions of an innate (gender) identity, acts and gestures which are learned and are repeated over time create the illusion of an innate and stable (gender) core. These acts

are *performative* in the sense that the essence or identity that they otherwise purport to express are *fabrications* manufactured and sustained through corporeal signs and discursive means. That the gendered body is performative suggests that it has no ontological status apart from the various acts which constitute its reality. (Ibid.: 136)

As we can see, Butler, following in the footsteps of Nietzsche,[5] is critical of the (humanist) distinction between the subject and action, the belief that the subject is the cause of action (rather than something that is constituted in and through it), and more particularly, of the kind of moralism that this distinction gives rise to – a moralism that upholds institutions such as the law.

According to Rosalyn Diprose (1995) – who shares with Butler and Nietzsche the belief that the subject is an effect rather than the cause of action – morality and the law are built upon the premise that an internal core self not only exists, but is the cause of, and is responsible for, (its) actions. Indeed, as Diprose goes on to note, we are all caught up in this kind of logic: none of us can honestly say that we never read the gestures, the actions, the appearance of

82

others as the expression of who we presume them to be. Let's imagine for a moment that we see two women passionately kissing. It is fairly likely that we will assume that they are lesbians (if, of course, we are familiar with this concept) and that their actions and desires are an expression of who they are, of their identity. Whilst we may not necessarily articulate it in this way to ourselves, we nevertheless make this (or some other) assumption at some level. We may even be unaware of the assumption we've made until something happens to challenge that assumption. As we saw in the previous chapter, such assumptions are regularly made in regards to race: we classify people in racial terms, and often only recognise this when the assumption that one has made is called into question – for example, when the light-skinned Aboriginal person who one has presumed to be white speaks of his or her Aboriginality.

If actions, gestures, and desires are seen as the expression of an innate self, it becomes possible not only to interpret others, but also to evaluate, and categorise them. And connected to this supposed capacity to know the other, is the possibility of self-knowledge. Let's return for a moment to the two women who are passionately kissing. If we unquestioningly interpret their actions as an expression of their identity, it then becomes possible for us to evaluate their being on moral grounds. At the same time, we will articulate, at some level, a sense of our selves and our position in the world in relation to them. If we are women, we may identify with their actions, desires, and supposed identity and claim that we too are, for example, lesbians, or we may identify ourselves in opposition to them, supposing that since we do not act in the same way, nor do we desire to, then we are non-lesbian (that is, heterosexual). Furthermore, we can, in a variety of ways, validate or denigrate, punish or celebrate their actions (what we presume to be) their desires, their identity, and in turn, our own. In short then, the notion of an autonomous, unified, coherent, and knowable self, as the source and cause of action, sustains liberal humanist principles which inform morality, the law, notions of responsibility, contract, and so on.

In her reading of Butler's work, Moya Lloyd explains that ontologies of gender – that is, commonly held beliefs regarding the essence of gender – establish what counts as intelligible, what kinds of identities can exist (1999: 196).[6] Identities are culturally and historically specific which means that their intelligibility is context-specific, as is the value accorded to particular identities.

Gender norms, as the examples discussed above demonstrate, are, as Butler says, 'regulatory fictions' (1990: 141). Ontologies of gender are integral to the production of these fictions that regulate ways of being and ways of knowing, and to the representation of these fictions as truths. As Butler puts it:

Gender is . . . a construction that regularly conceals its genesis; the tacit collective agreement to perform, produce, and sustain discrete and polar genders as cultural fictions is obscured by the credibility of those productions – and the punishments that attend not agreeing to believe in them. (Ibid.: 140)

The punishment or stigmatisation of so-called 'unnatural' actions and identities is everywhere apparent in our society, and functions to reaffirm or naturalise that which is held to be 'normal'. And we are all both agents and effects of disciplinary regimes. For example, most of us would feel uncomfortable if one of our class-mates turned up to a lecture naked. Some of us would shun him or her, someone would inevitably complain, some would laugh nervously, some would applaud, some may even react violently. Whatever the range of responses, it nevertheless would not be too long before that person was asked to leave, and it would perhaps be suggested that he or she would benefit from talking to someone about his or her (aberrant) desire to 'expose him or herself in public'. Both the actions undertaken by the student, and the desire that precipitated them, would be read as symptomatic of his or her subjectivity. He or she would be interpreted, evaluated, and categorised, and in and through this process the sense of self that each of us has would also be reconstituted.

Homophobia and 'gay-bashing' are other examples of the polic-ing of identity and of punishment for what is seen by some as 'unnatural', as are the often violent right-to-life protests held outside abortion clinics, and Fred Nile's[7] annual prayers for torrential rain on Sydney Gay and Lesbian Mardi Gras parade day. In each case, the construction of the other as 'unnatural' or aberrant functions to reaffirm the identity of the one who cringes, complains, protests, or attacks the other, as 'normal' or 'natural'. In short, identity functions as a regulatory and regulating fiction. Or, as Butler puts it:

The illusion of an interior and organizing gender core is discursively maintained for the purposes of the regulation of sexuality within the obligatory frame of heterosexuality. If the 'cause' of desire, gesture, and act can be localized within the 'self' of the actor, then the political regulations and disciplinary practices which produce that ostensibly coherent gender are effectively displaced from view. (Ibid.: 136)

One important conclusion that can be drawn from Butler's claim that 'genders are truth-effects of a discourse of primary and stable identity' (Ibid.: 136) that functions to conceal its own mechanisms, is that sexual categories such as heterosexuality and homosexuality are also cultural fictions, and if there is not an inner core, there can be no such thing, as Lloyd notes, as straight or queer, at least not in any essential sense – a claim we will deal with in more detail in Chapter 7. Therefore, one could say that rather than simply describing and managing identities, systems of power/knowledge constitute and regulate the sexual field, producing specific identities in order to serve particular ends, most notably, reproductive heterosexuality. It is crucial that we recognise this, says Butler (Ibid.: 136), because 'the displacement of a political and discursive origin of gender identity onto a psychological "core" precludes an analysis of' culturally and historically specific systems of power/knowledge and the subjectivities that they engender.

Having outlined the difference between an essentialist and a performative account of actions, desires, and so on, and touched briefly upon some of the implications of each, let us now turn to the issue of repetition which is central to Butler's model of performativity. As discussed earlier, Butler claims that gender is a tenuous identity constituted in and through 'the stylized repetition of acts' (Ibid.: 140). It is tenuous because gender is not the expression of a seamless internal identity, the essential ground of action. Rather, the gendered self is 'structured by repeated acts that seek to approximate the *ideal* of a substantial ground of identity, but which, in their occasional *dis*continuity, reveal the . . . groundlessness of this "ground"' (Ibid.: 141). In other words, whilst 'it is not in a single act of constitution or invention that the subject is brought into being, but through [the] re-citation and repetition' (Lloyd 1999: 197) of actions that are always public or shared, it is impossible for the reiteration of an action to occur in identical ways.[8] This impossibility is, at least in part, a consequence of the fact that identity is performatively constituted in and through relations with others and with a world, thus all action is contextual, uncertain, dispersed, inter-subjective, in-process, and so on. And in *Gender Trouble* it is the arbitrary relation between acts and the associated failure to repeat that at once 'exposes the phantasmatic effect of abiding identity as a politically tenuous construction' (Butler 1990: 141), and opens up the possibility of other ways of being.

This is perhaps most apparent in Butler's queering of the heteronormative model of identity in which gender follows from sex, and desire follows from gender. Since this model of identity, which is integral to the heterosexual matrix, is founded on a stable and dichotomous notion of gender, then Butler's account of performativity cuts to its very heart, and allows for the recognition of gender *dis*continuities that in fact 'run rampant in heterosexual, bisexual, and gay and lesbian contexts' (Ibid.: 136). The example of discontinuity between sex, gender and sexuality that Butler focuses on is, of course, drag.

For Butler, drawing on the work of Esther Newton,[9] drag subverts the expressive model of gender and the notion of a true gender identity because *'in imitating gender, drag implicitly reveals the imitative structure of gender itself – as well as its contingency'* (Ibid.: 137, emphasis in original). Drag, she says, suggests a dissonance between sex and performance, sex and gender, and gender and performance, because the so-called sex of the performer is not the same as the gender being performed. Gender, then, is nothing but a parody. But, rather than being a parody of an original, drag, as Butler sees it, parodies the very notion of an original, revealing that the supposed 'original' that the performer 'copies' 'is an imitation without an origin' (Ibid.: 138): gender is always already the embodiment and bodying forth of a set of culturally shared gestures, actions, and so on, and these shared gestures have no identifiable origin. Thus one could argue that drag queers the essentialised or naturalised notions of gender, sexuality, and the subject that are integral to hegemonic discourses and institutions. This is not, however, to claim that drag, as a parodic style somehow exists outside of the heterosexual matrix, or could be situated in complete opposition to it. Rather, these parodic styles and the gender codes associated with them are clearly drawn from hegemonic culture, but are denaturalised or queered in and through their parodic repetition. Parody then, it seems, is, in Butler's account, inherently subversive in that it demonstrates the plasticity and groundlessness of identity.

It is this aspect of Butler's account of performativity that was so quickly and so eagerly taken up by cultural critics and performers. Even Butler seemed surprised by this, stating, in her essay 'Critically Queer', that 'there were probably no more than five paragraphs in *Gender Trouble* devoted to drag [yet] readers have often cited the description of drag as if it were the "example" which explains the meaning of performativity' (1993b: 23). That drag came all too often to be unquestioningly associated with subversion is apparent in the proliferation of essays published in the early 1990s that seem to promote a sort of politics of parody.[10] In the majority of works that have followed in Butler's wake, drag (as the parodic enactment of gender) is represented as something one can choose to do: the imputation is that one can be whatever type of gender one wants to be, and can perform gender in whatever way one fancies. This is what you might call a voluntarist model of identity because it assumes that it is possible to freely and consciously create one's own identity. Whilst in many ways this voluntarist account of gender performance is in direct contrast with Butler's notion of performativity, Lloyd claims that it is also, at least in part, a consequence of the ambiguity of Butler's own account of the distinction between performance and performativity in *Gender Trouble*.

Before we turn to the question of the relationship between performance and performativity, I want to briefly outline some of the potential problems with the voluntarist model of identity. In her critical analysis of Bell *et al*.'s representation of the gay male skinhead as a subversive hyper-masculine identity that denaturalises the normative association between extreme 'manliness' and heterosexuality, Lloyd raises the question of whether or not this performance really is transgressive, and if so, under what conditions, and in what circumstances. For Bell and his co-authors, the degree to which a performance can be said to be transgressive is dependent upon the author's intention (Bell *et al*., 1994: 34), and the gay male skinhead, they imply, like the lipstick lesbian, unquestionably has political savvy. He intentionally inhabits, according to Bell *et al*., an identity that is associated with heterosexuality and is acceptable within the heterosexual matrix, but he inhabits it in much the same way as a virus, invisible to the eye of all but those with the 'right' kind of knowledge, inhabits a host body. Thus the gay skinhead who passes and yet whose parodic performance is 'visible' to others like him, 'creates a queer space in a heterosexual world' (Ibid.: 37), transforming or subverting that world and the mechanisms that support it.

Whilst this model of parodic political performance may be appealing in that it seems to offer the individual an unlimited

87

degree of agency, it is, for this very reason, problematic. What the analysis developed by Bell *et al.*, ignores is the context in which such a performance takes place, the response of others to this performance, and the ways in which these factors effect the performance and its (political) potential. The article as a whole also seems to completely bypass Butler's claim that the core self as the origin of action is in fact an illusion which is 'discursively maintained for the purposes of the regulation of sexuality within the obligatory frame of heterosexuality' (1990: 136).

Lloyd's critique of the figure of the transgressive gay male skinhead proceeds via a number of important questions. She asks who exactly it is that supposedly finds the image of the skinhead acceptable, and in what sense. Surely, she reasons, different people have different responses to this image depending on their own embodied history, their race, class, gender, religion, political affiliations, and so on. Historically skinheads have, Lloyd reminds us, been associated with fascism, neo-Nazism, homophobia, and racism, and thus the figure of the gay skinhead as a parody of straight hyper-masculinity may well 'occlude black people in general, but black gay men in particular' (1999: 200). And, as Lisa Walker (1995) points out in her response to the article, overlooking racial difference in this sense renders the thesis and the activism proposed by Bell *et al.*, dangerous, exclusory, and of course, race-blind. What Lloyd's analysis shows is that it is only possible to claim that a particular parodic performance is unambiguously and consistently transgressive if one decontextualises it and ignores 'the material and symbolic structures within which [such a performance] is embedded' (1999: 200).

If we take the critiques made by Lloyd and Walker seriously, it becomes apparent that whilst identity is mutable, the signifiers in and through which identity is performatively constituted, are never free-floating and radically open. Nevertheless, theorists such as Bell *et al.*, assume that since gender is performative then it is radically free; that one can perform whatever identity one chooses in whatever ways one chooses to. The assumption is

that gender is a choice, or that gender is a role, or that gender is a construction that one puts on, as one puts on clothes in the morning, that there is a 'one' who is prior to this gender, a one who goes to the wardrobe of gender and decides with deliberation which gender it will be today. (Butler 1993b: 21)

In other words, the voluntarist notion of performance is not only reliant on a naïve notion of unconstrained choice, but presupposes a subject who comes before, and makes, the choice. Butler's account of performativity, on the other hand, problematises the very notion of subjective agency in and through its deconstruction of the humanist subject. Performativity, as Butler understands it, is the pre-condition of the subject, the discursive vehicle through which ontological effects are produced. There is not first an 'I' who performs, rather, the 'I' is constituted in and through performative processes. Or as I put it earlier, the self is constituted in and through action rather than being the origin and cause of action.

Those who take a voluntarist position ignore Butler's claim that styles of being are 'never fully self-styled, for styles have a history, and those histories condition and limit the possibilities' of performativity (1990: 139) as Lloyd's analysis of the figure of the gay male skinhead has shown. In *Bodies That Matter*, which followed *Gender Trouble*, Butler responds to the voluntarist (mis)appropriation of her thesis by stating that 'performativity is neither free play nor theatrical self-presentation; nor can it be simply equated with performance' (1993a: 95). Butler's position could be said to be anti-voluntarist, particularly in *Bodies That Matter*, insofar as she emphasises that performativity is not something the subject does, but is a process through which the subject is constituted, and that gender is not something that can be put on or taken off at will. This distinction between voluntarism and anti-voluntarism is most often understood by commentators[11] as the difference between performance and performativity respectively.

So, let us turn then to the question of the relationship between performance and performativity. In his analysis of *Gender Trouble* and *Paris Is Burning*, Phillip Brian Harper suggests that performance could be thought of as a kind of theatrical production, whereas Butler's notion of performativity should be understood as a mode of discursive production (1999: 38–9). The crucial difference between the concepts, at least as Harper sees it, has to do with the notion of subjective agency that the former concept embraces, and the latter precludes. Similarly, in 'Critically Queer', Butler defines performance as a 'bounded act' whereas performativity *'consists in a reiteration of norms which precede, constrain, and exceed the performer and in that sense cannot be taken as the fabrication of the performer's "will" or "choice"'* (1993b: 24, emphasis in original). Whilst it is obvious that what Butler is referring to when she uses the term performativity is the reiteration of discursive norms in and through which identity is constituted, what she means when she claims that performance is a 'bounded act' is less clear. Lloyd offers the following helpful explanation of Butler's claim. She says that for Butler a performance is theatrical and 'bounded' in that it draws on, mimics, and often exaggerates existing signifiers and codes, rather than being an original (self-) creation. 'It is a process of *re*-signification and not signification *ab initio*' (Lloyd 1999: 202). But, as Lloyd goes on to note, this seems to suggest that insofar as a performance consist of reciting gestures, signs, images, and so on, that are drawn from a shared cultural reservoir that comes before and exceeds the performer, then a performance 'is itself performative' (Ibid.: 202). If this is the case, then a particular drag performance is inevitably constitutive rather than simply being theatrical, or wholly voluntary, which suggests that the distinction posited by Harper (between theatrical production and discursive production) turns out to be no distinction at all, or at least not an easily discernible one.

Lloyd also questions the notion of (drag) performance as parody, as a hyperbolic and excessive form of mimicry that illuminates the unnaturalness, the theatricality, of identity generally. This sort of mimicry is often posited in opposition to 'masquerade' – a performance in and through which one 'passes', and which therefore does not call into question hegemonic notions of identity. At one level this distinction may seem to be valid enough, and yet Lloyd 'troubles' it when she asks what makes something excessive, to whom, and in what circumstances. In other words, she raises the question of what makes a parody a parody, and whether or not a parody is a parody if it is not read as such. Again, the figure of the gay male skinhead illustrates the problems associated with the idea that a performance is unambiguously parodic.

Having mapped the supposed distinction between performance and performativity as it is (ambiguously) formulated in *Gender Trouble*, Lloyd turns to Butler's later attempt to explain the subject's investment in parodic practices whilst avoiding the voluntarist trap into which many of those who have drawn on her work on drag have fallen. In *Bodies That Matter*, drawing more heavily on psychoanalysis than she did in *Gender Trouble*, Butler critiques the notion of subjective agency via the idea that the subject whose psyche is split is never fully self-transparent, but rather, is governed, at least in part, by inaccessible unconscious mechanisms and drives. Given this, drag cannot be regarded as the expression of a performer's will as it is in the analysis of the gay male skinhead posited by Bell *et al.* In fact, as Lloyd's reading of Butler makes clear, quite the opposite is the case. What is performed, says the Butler of *Bodies That Matter*, '*works to conceal, if not to disavow, what remains opaque, unconscious, un-performable*' (1993a: 24, emphasis in original). What Butler means by this is that (male to female) drag is not a conscious expression of intent, but rather, should be understood, as Lloyd explains, as the melancholic enactment of the (unconscious) attachment to and repudiation of femininity. 'What drag symbolizes, for Butler, is that all gender identities are themselves a mélange of such disavowals and identifications' (Lloyd 1999: 203).

Whilst this analysis may be useful in that it explains both the limits of subjective agency and why it is that heterosexual ideals are impossible to attain in any absolute sense, Lloyd is nevertheless concerned that Butler's account of unconscious identifications and disavowals makes it impossible to decide what kinds of performances or actions might be politically effective. She asks: 'What distinguishes (if indeed anything can) a parodic performance based upon disavowed identification from a parodic performance emanating from a critical strategy of transgression?' (Ibid.: 204). And again, we could return to the figure of the gay male skinhead and argue that the performance could equally as well be understood in either way. On the one hand, it could be, and has been, read as subversive, and on the other, it could be, and has been, read as reinforcing particular hegemonic values and identities.

Perhaps ultimately, then, there is no way to decide what a particular performance will mean since first, it will signify many (often contradictory) things to many people, and, second, as Lloyd points out, 'all performances are imbricated in hegemonic power relations even as they contest them' (Ibid.: 206). This makes the formulation of political strategies particularly difficult, but the question is, does it render any conscious attempt at subversion impossible? According to Butler, the only thing that makes a performance subversive is that it is 'the kind of effect that resists calculation' (1993b: 29). What she means by this is that it is the very nature of signification (as multiplicitous, inter-subjective, and constitutive), and the subject's inability to control signification, that make subversion at once possible and unpredictable. We cannot, she argues, determine the effects of an action prior to its performance, nor can we calculate (in any absolute sense) its out-comes even after it has occurred. Some may argue that this sort of thinking tends to lead us into a political dead-end: that it encourages a kind of nihilism or fatalism that makes any (political) action deluded, pointless, or accidental.

It is here that Lloyd's critique of Butler's work offers the reader an alternative road to take. Lloyd states that, '[e]ven if we accept that there are incalculable effects to all (or most) statements or activities, this does not mean that we need to concede that there are *no* calculable effects' (1999: 207). In fact, Lloyd claims that it is possible to gauge the likely outcomes of particular actions if one examines the ways in which similar activities performed in similar contexts have functioned in the past. She stresses that this will not necessarily guarantee success, but it will make political action viable, if somewhat unpredictable. For Lloyd, then, the issue is not simply 'what parodic intervention signifies but also where, when, and to whom it signifies in the ways that it does' (Ibid.: 208), since these factors invariably effect, or are integral to, the performance and what it could be said to signify.

As this discussion of performativity has shown, all performances, and all attempts at subversion will be ambiguous and open to mul-tiple meanings. And whilst it may not be possible to formulate a final, all-encompassing interpretation of a particular performance, it is nevertheless necessary to be able to compare and evaluate var-ious forms of action in terms of their supposed (political) efficacy. Erica Rand's (1995) discussion of the case of the Barbie slasher who mutilated twenty-four Barbie dolls by slashing their breasts and crotches before leaving them in public places, could be said to illustrate this claim. According to Rand, the Ohio police responded to the mutilated Barbies by calling in the FBI because they feared that this violence at best symbolised a violation of femininity, and at worst, may spill over into actual violence against young women. The slashings and the events that surrounded them disturbed Rand for a number of reasons but perhaps primarily because,

even when slashers clearly signal that their intended target is the ide-ology that Barbie represents, the result is still the representation of violence against women that circulates in a culture in which too many people consider violence against women acceptable partly because of how frequently it circulates in representation. (Ibid.: 170)

What Rand is pointing to here is the fact that the (historical, cul-tural, and political) context in which an action occurs inevitably colours one's reading of that action. Her account of the slashings shows that actions do not simply signify what their author intends them to. Rather, both the other, and the world more generally, plays a significant role not only in the process of meaning making or queering, but also in the concomitant identities that are constituted in and through such action. Let me explain this by turning to Rosalyn Diprose's critique of Butler's account of performativity.

Diprose claims that Butler's thesis lends itself to misreadings that reduce the notion of performativity to a voluntarist notion of performance because, for the most part, there are only two terms in her account; namely, the performing body and the law. As she sees it, 'there is a third term forgotten in this haste to liberate ourselves from the law' (Ibid.: 13), and this term is the other. The other, as Diprose explains, is integral to the self and thus subjectivity is necessarily non-unified and 'ambiguous because body performance is never singular' (Ibid.: 13). Diprose draws on the work of Maurice Merleau-Ponty and Foucault in order to explore why and how it is that identity is ambiguous and open to change, and also why it is that it is simultaneously limited in its potential rather than radically free, as writers such as Bell *et al.*, seem to suggest.

As discussed in Chapter 3, Foucault claims that our relationship to our embodied being is (trans)formed in and through the discourses and discursive practices that make up systems of power/knowledge. These systems (ways of knowing, and ways of being) codify and constitute the body-subject, its movements, gestures and so on, in culturally and historically specific ways, and in accordance with hegemonic values and practices. Similarly, for Merleau-Ponty, the body-subject or self is constituted in and through action, and actions or behaviours are understood as shared socio-cultural practices. It is because we share a common social world through which we develop habits, modes of movement, and gestures that have a common meaning that Merleau-Ponty claims that body-identity is fundamentally inter-subjective. The body-subject, he explains, is constituted by mimesis and transitivism: by identification with and against others, and by the imitation of gestures, actions, and so on.[12] As Diprose puts it, one's bodily-being (or one's identity) 'is built on the invasion of the self by the gestures of others, who, by referring to other others, are already social beings' (1994: 120). In other words, the other is the medium through which the body-subject achieves an awareness of itself as self. One's experience of oneself a something or other – as a human, female, white, teenager, mother, sadist, beautiful, and so on – can only be achieved in and through the conceptual systems we share with others and the world that we find ourselves in. So, my relationship to my self – my awareness of my self as an 'I' – is formed in a socio-political context; the 'I' is constituted in and through its relations with others and with a world. For example, my sense of self as a writer is constituted in and through my relation with you, my readers, and with a world which recognises such concepts, relations, practices, and identities.

So, if subjectivity is inter-subjective and is effected in and through habitual acts, to what extent is it possible for the subject to transform him or her self? Whilst this question may be impossible to answer in any definitive way, it is nevertheless worth seriously considering if and when we feel the urge to turn to individualist accounts of freedom through self-definition. If we agree with Merleau-Ponty's notion of the body-subject as always already 'in situation', as enmeshed in a world of others, of culture, of history, and so on, then we must also recognise that any project of self-(trans)formation is necessarily limited, is already conditioned by the world, and thus is never autonomous. This tension, which again could be said to exemplify the difference between performance and performativity, is nicely illustrated in Jenny Livingstone's (1991) film *Paris Is Burning*.

Paris Is Burning is a documentary that focuses on the 'ball circuit' and its centrality to the lives of poor gay men and trans-genderists of colour in New York in the late 1980s. The balls are spectacular competitions in which competitors walk in the category of their choice (for example, 'Executive Realness', 'Butch Queen First Time in Drag at a Ball', 'Town and Country', and so on), mimicking supermodels and beauty pageant contestants. Like the latter, many competitors represent a 'community' or a 'house' as it is known. These houses are described by their members as families for those who do not have families, and as street gangs who fight it out on the runway. Each house is headed by a 'mother' and a 'father' whose so-called sex has nothing to do with the role that they play. There are, for example, what one might think of as 'feminine' mothers such as Angie Xtravaganza, and lean, mous-tached, fighting-machine or vogueing mothers such as Willi Ninja. Each member adopts as their last name, the name of the house. The film focuses both on the events that take place in the ballrooms and in the lead-up to the balls, and on the participants themselves. In and through interviews with the contestants and would-be contestants the viewer is exposed to certain aspects of their lives, their hopes, fears, aspirations, and frustrations.

Perhaps because of the fact that both were released in the same year, *Paris Is Burning* and *Gender Trouble* have often been yoked together. The intimation is that the (drag) ball competitors exemplify the Butlerian notion of parody as a form of subversion of hegemonic norms, values, and identities. The fact that in *Bodies That Matter* Butler uses the film to critically analyse the overly simplified equation of drag with conscious self-fashioning, at once furthers and problematises the connection between the texts, or at least the way in which this connection, and the concepts that inform it, has been understood.

On the film's initial reception the drag performances were read by many as 'personality overhauls' that illustrated the 'subversive edge' of the balls and the 'mutability of identity' more generally (Farber, cited in Harper 1999: 34). Walking and vogueing were considered to be radical political acts intentionally undertaken by 'post-gendered' agents in an attempt to transform and/or queer themselves and the world. In one sense many of the participants interviewed seem to reinforce this notion of identity as a commodity, as something that can be bought or self-fashioned. For example, Octavia St Laurent who wants to be a supermodel or 'a rich somebody' says that whenever she looks at the way wealthy people live she finds herself saying '"I have to have that", because I never felt comfortable being poor, I just don't, or even middle-class doesn't suit me'. Similarly, Venus Xtravaganza dreams of the day when she will become all that she desires: the day she is married (as a post-operative woman) to the man she loves, in a church, dressed in white. Venus too, wants to be a 'spoiled rich girl who gets what they want when they want it and doesn't have to really struggle with finances'. But simply wanting such commodities, relationships, identities, does not make them yours, as the film shows: neither Octavia nor Venus can transform themselves to fit their ideals. And even if they could, how transgressive would such a process of self-transformation be given that Venus' desire to acquire a vagina and thus become a 'real' woman is, some would argue, symptomatic of, and in keeping with, the heterosexual matrix. One of the problems with this individualistic notion of self-fashioning is that often, rather than being subversive, it feeds into the entrepreneurial myth that each of us is equally capable of becoming the 'self-made (wo)man' and that if we don't, the failure is entirely our own.[13] As discussed earlier, this sort of thinking precludes any analysis of the social mechanisms that give life to particular (non-egalitarian) identities and ways of being.

In the chapter of *Bodies That Matter* entitled 'Gender is Burning: Questions of Appropriation and Subversion', Butler claims that 'Venus and *Paris Is Burning* more generally, call into question whether parodying the dominant norms is enough to displace them', or whether parody can also be 'the very vehicle for a recon-solidation of hegemonic norms' (1993a: 125). bell hooks is of the opinion that drag ball performances, at least as they are repre-sented or framed in *Paris Is Burning*, tend much more toward the latter than the former.[14] In particular, hooks is disturbed by the fact that (Livingstone's representation of) the performances recon-solidate racist and colonialist norms, identities, values, and forms of social relations. For example, she argues that the ideal of femininity embraced by Venus, Octavia, and others, 'is totally per-sonified by whiteness' (Ibid.: 147), but that this tendency is not explained by a critical examination of 'whiteness' and the ways in which it functions. The film, she says, sets itself up as simply docu-menting, in a neutral way:

the way in which black people . . . worship at the throne of whiteness, even when such worship demands that we live in perpetual self-hate, steal, lie, go hungry, and even die in its pursuit . . . [It] affirm[s] that colonized, victimized, exploited, black folks are all too willing to be complicit in perpetuating the fantasy that ruling-class white culture is the quintessential site of unrestricted joy, freedom, power, and pleasure. (Ibid.: 149)

hooks' point is that the documentary is not neutral or objective. Rather, in failing to explore the question of why and how it is that some black gay men and transgenderists seem to willingly embrace a hegemonic system that continues to oppress and exploit them, the film uncritically universalises the beliefs, values, and aspirations of a small but powerful cultural elite: it makes them seem desirable, inevitable or simply 'true'.

If, indeed, the drag performances that take place on the ball circuit are radical expressions of subversion, the film, hooks claims, turns them into a harmless exotic spectacle for the titillation of the white, middle-class, so-called liberal-minded viewer.[15] hooks' critique reminds us of Lloyd's warning that it is dangerous to decontextualise a particular performance and to presume that its meaning is unambiguous and shared by all. We could also draw on Diprose's claim that the role of the other is integral to the constitution of meaning and identity, in order to explain why it might be that *Paris Is Burning* is not, and cannot be, a neutral account of the drag ball circuit, a sort of hole-in-the-wall through which we can grasp the truth of the other. Merleau-Ponty's notion of mimesis and transitivism would also help to explain how and why it is that we embody and body-forth hegemonic culture in ways that are both subversive and reaffirming. We could also return to the discussion of the ways in which identity is policed, and the rewards and punishments associated with particular performances. Combined, these theoretical insights may equip us to elaborate upon Butler's statement that '*Paris Is Burning* documents neither an efficacious insurrection nor a painful resubordination, but an unstable coexistence of both' (1993a: 137), to understand why it is that identity is never radically open nor entirely self-created, and yet why and how it is that resistance and change is possible. Armed with such analytic tools, we may also feel the confidence and the necessity to compare and judge potential political strategies and to evaluate the unexpected and uncontrollable outcomes of particular actions and performances.

NOTES

1. De Beauvoir (1973)
2. Rivière (1986)
3. Austin (1962)
4. Derrida (1991)
5. See Nietzsche (1989) for a critique of the tendency to 'separate lightning from its flash and take the latter for an action'. '[T]here is no "being" behind the doing' says Nietzsche, '"the doer" is merely a fiction added to the deed' (Ibid.: 45).
6. For a more detailed account of how it is that bodies come to matter, that is how they materialise, and how they acquire meaning, see Butler (1993a) and Costera Meijer and Prins (1998).
7. Rev. Fred Nile is a New South Wales Senator, founder of the Christian Democratic Party, and national co-ordinator and NSW director of the Australian Federation of Festival of Light Community Standards Organisations. Nile is responsible for introducing the following bills or motions to NSW state parliament and/or the Legislative Council: The Gay Mardi Gras Prohibition Motion; the

Anti-Discrimination (Homosexual Vilification) Repeal Bill; the Pre Surgery (HIV/AIDS Tests) Bill; the Pornographic Publications/Video Sales and Display (Prohibition) Bill; and the Unborn Child Protection Bill, amongst others.

8. As Lacan's (1977) notion of the 'ideal I', and Kristeva's (1982) analysis of the 'proper body' have made clear, the attainment of absolute coherence, or of what Lacan calls the Phallus, is impossible, and it is this impossibility or inability to live up to the symbolic law, that keeps meaning and identity open or in-process.

9. Newton (1972)

10. See, for example, Davis' (1999) reading of the French performance artist Orlan; Gabb's (1998) analysis of the work of Del LaGrace Volcano; Bell *et al.*'s (1994) account of lipstick lesbian and gay male skinheads; and Morkham's (1995) reading of *The Crying Game*.

11. See, for example, Jagose (1996), Harper (1999), and Schrift (1995).

12. See Merleau-Ponty (1962; 1964).

13. For further elaboration of this idea see Hennessey (1995), Sandell (1994), and Fraser (1999).

14. Similarly, Prosser (1998a) reads Venus' murder as symptomatic of the triumph of the heterosexual matrix.

15. Champagne (1995) offers a much more 'positive' reading of the ways in which *Paris Is Burning* could be said to offer a critical account of racism as a form of economic exploitation.

6

Transsexual Empires and Transgender Warriors

DURING THE 1980S CRITICAL THEORISTS became increasingly fascinated with the notion of ambiguity and, in particular, with bodies, genders, sexualities, and practices which appeared to defy traditional forms of categorisation. This focus on ambiguity continues in Queer Theory's concern with transsexual or transgendered bodies which, it is often claimed transgress, and thus help to dismantle, binary oppositions such as male/female, nature/culture, heterosexual/homosexual, and so on. In this chapter we will look at some of the ways in which transsexualism and transgenderism have been understood and experienced and what kinds of politics such understandings have made possible.

Although the terms transsexual and transgender have been coined only relatively recently, a variety of forms of gender ambiguity can be found throughout history and in a huge range of cultural contexts.[1] Moreover, gender inversion, rather than being a new object of critical enquiry, was debated and written about by the early sexologists mentioned in Chapter 1. In fact, Prosser and Storr suggest that it was sexology that enabled the emergence of the terms and treatments that are available today (1998: 75). At the same time, Prosser argues that the recent shifts which have taken place in transgender theory and politics enable us to re-read the notion of inversion as it functions in sexology texts (1998b: 117). According to Prosser, the term inversion, at least as it was used by Krafft-Ebing, Ellis, Ulrichs, Westphal, and Hirschfeld, refers not to homosexuality (sexual inversion), but rather, to gender inversion, which may have little, or at times even nothing, to do with homosexuality.

This is apparent in Krafft-Ebing's *Psychopathia Sexualis* in which we find a discussion of what the author identifies as the four degrees of inversion. They are as follows. First degree: the 'simple

99

reversal of sexual feeling' which is attained when a person is attracted to someone of the same sex and yet simultaneously retains a measure of attraction for those of the opposite sex. Second degree: the masculinisation or feminisation ('eviration and defemination') of one's psyche and one's desire resulting in attraction only to those of the same sex. Third degree: 'stage of transition to change of sex delusion'. What this refers to is a state in which 'physical sensation is also transformed in the sense of *transmutatio sexus* [change of sex]' (cited in Bland and Doan 1998: 79). Fourth degree: '*metamorphisis sexualis paranoica* [Delusion of Sexual Change]'. This final stage consists of a transformation or inversion of sex. As Prosser states, in current terminology these degrees of inversion would be referred to as bisexuality, homosexuality, trans-sexualism, and intersexuality, respectively. If this is the case, same-sex desire 'constitutes only one of four (and the second least extreme) symptoms of inversion' (Prosser 1998b: 120).

Similarly, in *Studies in the Psychology of Sex*, Havelock Ellis origi-nally used the term *sexo-aesthetic inversion* to describe gender ambi-guity, but later decided that the term inversion was problematic due to its association with homosexuality. He thus coined the term *eonism* which is derived from the figure of the Chevalier d'Eon de Beaumont, an eighteenth-century French nobleman who was said by many to be female-bodied. Again, in 1910 Magnus Hirschfeld developed an account of four 'types' of gender ambiguity that can-not simply be reduced to, or explained in terms of, homosexuality. Hirschfeld's thesis rests on the claim that there are four things that differentiate the sexes, namely, sex organs, secondary sexual char-acteristics, the sex drive or inclination, and what he refers to as 'other emotional characteristics' (cited in Bland and Doan 1998: 97). The 'absolute' woman according to this model, would be someone who has a vagina, ovaries and other reproductive organs associat-ed with female biology, secondary characteristics such as a 'wom-anly pelvis', not much body hair, a high voice, and so on, who is sexually passive and desires to be the object of male desire, and whose passions and emotions fit with those deemed 'feminine'. Interestingly, Hirschfeld states that 'these kinds of absolute repre-sentatives of their sex, are . . . only abstractions, invented extremes' (in Ibid.: 97). In reality, he claims, such creatures do not exist. Rather, every person contains, at least to a small degree, elements of the 'other' sex.

Further along the continuum, Hirschfeld identifies what he

refers to as 'sexual intermediaries', that is, people in whom a significant degree of discontinuity between the elements or gender characteristics outlined above is apparent. Consequently, it is possible, Hirschfeld claims, to classify gender ambiguous people in relation to the four categories. The first group consists of those with ambiguous sexual organs such as intersexed people. The second group is made up of people whose secondary sexual characteristics are supposedly at odds with their sex organs. For example, 'men with womanly mammary tissue . . . and women without such; women with manly hair such as manly beards . . . men with womanly pelvis (sic) . . . men with womanly bone and muscular structure . . . women with manly movements' (in Ibid.: 98).

Under the third heading we find 'persons divergent with regard to their sex drive'. What Hirschfeld means by this is passive men and sexually aggressive women, men who are attracted to butch-looking women, women who are sexually attracted to both 'feminine' men and 'masculine' women (bisexuals), those who desire people of the same sex (homosexuals), and so on. Finally, in group four we find 'men whose feminine emotions and feelings are reflected in their manner of love . . . their gestures . . . their sensitivity . . . [M]en who more or less dress themselves as women and live totally as such' (in Ibid.: 99), and vice versa. In short, Hirschfeld's work, like Krafft-Ebing's, identifies a range of forms of gender inversion, only a small portion of which (one in four) is consistent with sexual inversion or homosexuality.

One of the most interesting things about Hirschfeld's analysis is that he does not equate – as many of us are likely to – the donning of 'female' attire (by a man) with homosexuality. In fact, Hirschfeld argues that in most cases of transvestism – a term he coined to refer to 'the erotic drive to cross dress' – there is no evidence whatsoever of same-sex desire. One could argue that, on the one hand, the term transvestite allowed Hirschfeld to identify one particular example of gender inversion (to give it a 'special scientific stamp', as he put it) that is not necessarily coextensive with, or symptomatic of, sexual inversion. On the other hand, however, Hirschfeld was not entirely happy with the term since it seemed to him to refer only to the external side of the phenomenon, that is, to clothing (in Ibid.: 104). From his case studies he was led to believe that what he called transvestism also included, at least in some cases, something 'deeper', a desire or drive to sexually metamorphose.

101

Prosser reads Hirschfeld's dissatisfaction as symptomatic of the fact that 'his category of transvestite includes the transsexual' (1998b: 121) – a conceptual category or identity which at the time did not exist. Bullough and Bullough take a similar position, suggesting that of the seventeen cases of transvestism discussed by Hirschfeld, 'four might have become transsexuals had they lived at a later time' (cited in Prosser 1998b: 122). Thus for Prosser, Hirschfeld's work is evidence of the fact that sexology with its focus on gender (rather than sexuality) played a pivotal role in 'the discursive emergence of the transsexual' (Ibid.: 121).

The term transsexual, or more particularly, *psychopathia transsexualis*, was first used by David O. Cauldwell in 1949. In an article of the same name, Cauldwell, obviously alluding to Krafft-Ebing's *Psychopathia Sexualis*, describes the desire to live as a member of 'the sex to which [one] does not belong' (2001: 1) as a pathology or psychological disease which it may be possible to 'cure' but which it is ultimately better to somehow prevent. The category (transsexual) was subsequently depathologised, at least to some extent,[2] by Harry Benjamin, an American endocrinologist, who in the 1960s and 1970s played a crucial role in the development of sex-reassignment procedures and the establishment of gender identity clinics. For Benjamin, transsexualism is understood as a medical condition that can be cured in and through surgery. It is not a psychological illness, nor can it be equated with homosexuality.

In *The Transsexual Phenomenon* (1966) Benjamin posits an important difference between transvestism and transsexualism which hinges on the status of the sexual organs. He claims that 'true transsexuals', unlike cross-dressers, feel that 'their sex organs, the primary . . . as well as the secondary . . . are disgusting deformities that must be changed by the surgeon's knife' (Ibid.: 13–14). Whilst this distinction is important in that it enables us to think about the differences (as well as the similarities) between specific forms of gender ambiguity, it has nevertheless resulted in a number of problematic assumptions and practices that I will outline in due course. For the moment, however, I want to briefly explore the possibility that what we would now call transsexualism could have existed long before the term itself was coined.

Whilst Christine Jorgensen is most often cited as the first person to have undergone sex reassignment surgery in 1952, Zachary Nataf suggests that 'surgical intervention in sex conversion began to appear at the end of the nineteenth century' (1996: 10). The earliest known case, he says, occurred in 1882 and involved the masculinisation of the genitals of Sophie Hedwig who then became known officially as Herman Karl. What such an intervention in fact involved is unclear and Nataf notes that details regarding the case are, at best, sketchy. In 1933 Niels Hoyers published an account of the Danish painter Einar Wegener's experience of various surgical interventions aimed at enabling her[3] to live as her 'true' self – as Lili Elbe. Whilst some of the procedures attained a degree of success Lili died soon after an operation to construct a vagina.[4]

Both Nataf and Prosser also discuss the case of the British author and doctor Michael (née Laura) Dillon who in 1939 took advantage of very recent developments in the field of endocrinology and self-administered testosterone therapy. Dillon went on to have a double mastectomy and by 1945 (after thirteen operations over a six-year period) became 'the first FTM (female to male) transsexual to have full sex reassignment surgery' (Nataf 1996: 11). However, since the term transsexual was as yet unavailable, Dillon, and others like him, were forced to understand or articulate their identities using other, perhaps less appropriate, terms. As Prosser states, from the early 1900s homosexuality had begun to gradually replace inversion in medical literature, and concomitantly psychoanalysis began to gain precedence over sexology. What this meant was that a complex range of gender inversions now became equated with or collapsed into a fairly homogenous account of sexual inversion. As a result of such shifts, argues Prosser, Dillon and others were forced to articulate their transsexualism 'under the rubric of homosexuality' (1998b: 126). Nevertheless, as Prosser notes, Dillon's dissatisfaction with the available terminology is apparent in his book *Self: A Study in Ethics and Endocrinology* (1946) in which he attempts to differentiate between the homosexual who 'imitates and acquires' the traits and desires of the so-called opposite sex, and another type of being (the as-yet-unnamed transsexual) who 'seems to develop naturally along the lines of the other sex' (Dillon, cited in Prosser 1998b: 126), and who has always felt as if she or he were in fact a member of the so-called opposite sex. This nameless being is not represented in Dillon's text as someone who is in need of psychotherapy (which was the recommended clinical response at the time to homosexuality), but rather, as a person in need of physical alteration so that his or her body fits his or her mind – a claim Benjamin would reiterate a decade or so later. As Dillon puts it: 'Surely where the mind cannot be made to fit the body, the body should be made to fit, approximately at any rate, the mind' (cited in Ibid.: 126).

Again, this attempt on the part of Dillon, and later Benjamin, to articulate an ambiguous form of identity that does not fundamentally consist of a desire for persons of the same sex, could be said to be double-edged in terms of its effects. On the upside, it makes visible significantly different forms of non-normative embodiment that require quite different responses, but on the downside, it tends to forge what in time comes to be an almost inextricable link between transsexualism and surgery. Such an association is something that most of us presume and many definitions of the term transsexual reinforce it. For example, in the glossary of *Lesbians Talk Transgender*, transsexual is defined as 'anyone who [1] wants to have or [2] has had, a sex-change operation, including [3] non-surgical transsexuals' (Nataf 1996: 63).[5] This definition raises the question of exactly what a 'sex change operation' is, and what effects it produces. If it is not the case that one can entirely change sex through a single operation then what would we call a person who, for example, undergoes a mastectomy (breast removal), but chooses not to opt for phalloplasty (the construction of a penis)? We will return to this dilemma regarding definitions later in the chapter.

If we accept the idea that surgery is an essential aspect of transsexualism – and this is something that many transgender theorists have argued against – it is then necessary to ask who has been granted access to reassignment procedures, and under what conditions. In the ground-breaking paper 'The Empire Strikes Back: A Posttranssexual Manifesto' (1991), Sandy Stone claims that gaining access to surgical procedures is a difficult and often devastating experience. Those desiring surgery or hormone therapy must meet various requirements, and basically prove that they are in the 'wrong body', and that surgical intervention will 'rectify' this 'problem'. In the USA, for example, the Harry Benjamin International Gender Dysphoria Association Incorporated (HBIG-DA) has developed a set of standards that most physicians use in order to decide whether or not surgical and/or hormonal assistance is appropriate. Physical attractiveness, for example, is one factor that Judith Shapiro (1991) claims seems to feature significantly in clinical decisions about whether or not male to female reassignment surgery should take place. Stone makes a similar point when she describes the Stanford Clinic (established, along with a number of similar institutions, in the late 1960s in the USA by Benjamin and others), as a 'grooming clinic' or 'charm school' (Ibid.: 290) that taught (MTF) transsexuals how to perform femininity in so-called appropriate ways.

Perhaps the primary criteria for access to surgery (presuming of course, that one could gain access to the clinic in the first place),[6] was, and to some extent still is, the sense of being in the 'wrong body'.[7] In fact, Stone argues that '"wrong body" has come, virtually by default, to *define* the syndrome' (1991: 297). This image of the transsexual as a man in a woman's body, or a woman in a man's body is common in transsexual autobiographies, and is epitomised in the following description of entrapment from Jan Morris' auto-biography *Conundrum*. The post-operative Morris says:

if I were trapped in that cage [a male body] again nothing would keep me from my goal . . . I would search the earth for surgeons, I would bribe barbers or abortionists, I would take a knife and do it to myself. (1974: 169)

Not only does this impassioned statement illustrate the sense of being in the wrong body, it also seems to support Benjamin's claim that 'in the absence of surgery, transsexuals will engage in self-mutilation or suicide' (Califia 1997: 59). One could presume from this that transsexuals feel nothing but disgust for their 'biological' bodies, and in fact such feelings are read as indicators of transsex-ualism by many medical practitioners. Associated with this assumed self-loathing is the belief that (pre-operative) transsexuals cannot experience erotic pleasure from their genitals. Stone explains that in the heydays of gender dysphoria clinics such as Stanford, transsexuals who wished to be accepted for surgery would not dare to admit that they ever experienced genital sexual pleasure or that they masturbated, since such desires and pleasures would invariably lead to the charge of 'role inappropriateness' and would result in disqualification from the programme.

As Stone, Shapiro, and others note, prior to the emergence of (alternative) transgender discourses and activism, it was deemed appropriate and even necessary for pre-operative transsexuals to demonstrate a fetishistic obsession with genitals: to be rid of the ones they had, and to obtain the ones they wanted. This kind of relationship with one's genitals may sometimes seem strange to those who are not required to express such feelings, but as Shapiro points out 'transsexuals are . . . simply conforming to their culture's

criteria for gender assignment' (1991: 260). It is this sort of conformity though that has led to the accusation that far from
challenging gender norms, transsexuals reinforce them. Sheila
Jeffreys takes this position, stating that transsexuals are 'more
loyalists than rebels. They demonstrate the extraordinary power
of heterosexuality as a political system and are involved in the
constant reproduction of its basic dynamic, masculinity/femininity'
(1998: 89). Similarly, Thomas Kando says:

unlike militant homophiles, enlightened therapists, and liberated
women, transsexuals endorse such traditional values as heterosexuality,
domestic roles for women, the double standard of sexual morality, the
traditional division of tasks and responsibilities, and the discreditation
of deviant sexuality. Unlike various liberated groups, transsexuals are
reactionary . . . they are the Uncle Toms of the sexual revolution. With
these individuals, the dialectic of social change comes full circle and
the position of greatest deviance becomes that of greatest conformity.
(1973: 145)

It may be worth briefly raising the question here of whether or
not it is the intention or the desire of most transsexuals to challenge
patriarchy and heteronormative notions of gender, and whether or
not it is right of us to suppose that transsexuals should desire to
undertake such tasks. For many transsexuals it may well be the case
that a crucial aspect of their survival is their capacity to 'pass'.
Passing means being accepted as the gender one presents oneself
as. It means not being denied a job, laughed at, beaten up, or even
killed because one is 'weird'. This is a point raised by Ki Namaste
(1996) in her critique of the tendency amongst contemporary
critics to naïvely celebrate the subversive potential of transgender
or transsexualism whilst ignoring the material difficulties and
discriminations faced by transpeople on an everyday basis. Nevertheless, whilst the desire to pass may well be understandable,
passing, or becoming invisible as a transsexual also has its downside. According to Stone, passing necessarily involves forgetting
one's past or at least denying aspects of it that do not fit neatly
with one's gender of choice. Passing involves telling a story, living
an identity, that is supposedly seamless and unambiguous. As Stone
notes, a 'transsexual who passes is obeying the . . . imperative:
"Genres are not to be mixed. I will not mix genres"' (1991: 299).
And here genre refers, at least in part, to gender: genders must not
be mixed, one must be either a man or a woman.

Of course, not mixing genders essentially means performing

gender in a totally unambiguous way: it means being a perfectly feminine woman or a perfectly masculine man – a creature which Hirschfeld claims does not exist. And being a perfectly feminine woman or a perfectly masculine man necessarily involves reiterating heterosexual gender norms. So, for example, in Benjamin's scheme of things a 'successful' MTF transsexual would, for example, pass as a woman, marry a man who is older and wealthier than her, take on appropriate 'wifely' duties, and even keep her secret past well hidden.[8] The embodiment of these sorts of norms and desires is nowhere more apparent that in the case of Venus Xtravaganza whom we discussed briefly in the previous chapter. However, rather than simply accusing transsexuals of being dupes or unthinking agents of heteronormativity, it may be more productive to think about the ways in which transsexuals, like everyone else, are both agents and effects of the world in which they live. Non-transsexuals also perform gender roles and identities in ways that are both conformist and transgressive. In fact, Shapiro claims that 'transsexuals make explicit for us the usually tacit processes of gender attribution ... [T]hey make us realise that we are all passing' (1991: 257).

It is clear that for the most part, the medical establishment (and the values and beliefs that inform its practice) is intolerant of, and works to annihilate or 'rectify' ambiguity of any kind. In this sense, sex reassignment surgery and/or hormone therapy could be said to play a normalising, corrective role, at least as far as the medical profession is concerned. As Susan Stryker puts it, the medical profession's 'cultural politics are aligned with a deeply conservative attempt to stabilize gendered identity in the service of the naturalized heterosexual order' (1994: 242). Despite this, those who have undergone surgery and/or hormone therapy do not necessarily conceive of themselves as passive victims of an evil order who have unwittingly become tools of that order. Stryker adds:

None of this, however, precludes medically constructed transsexual bodies from being viable sites of subjectivity. Nor does it guarantee the compliance of subjects thus embodied with the agenda that resulted in a transsexual means of embodiment. As we rise up from the operating tables of our rebirth, we transsexuals are something more, and something other, than the creatures our makers intended us to be. (Ibid.: 242)

Whilst at the beginning of this chapter it may have seemed that defining the term transsexual would be a pretty straightforward task, what we have seen thus far is that transsexualism has been interpreted, evaluated, and constructed in a range of often conflicting ways, by both transsexuals and non-transsexuals. For example, transsexualism and homosexuality have sometimes been lumped together – perhaps inadvertently – under the term 'inversion" and, at other times, the two have been represented as unconnected modes of being. Furthermore, some people have argued that transsexualism is not just the same thing as homosexuality, but that transsexuals are homosexuals who are in denial. For example, Leslie Lothstein, an American writer who has been accused by many of transphobia, says:

the clearest motivation for transsexualism in both sexes has always been a despised homosexuality which caused men and women to believe they could not love their own sex without mutilating their bodies and professing to a new sexual identity which would make them really 'heterosexual'. (cited in Jeffreys 1998: 81)

On the other hand, there are transsexuals such as Mario Martino (1977) (a FTM) who are adamant that they are (and were prior to surgery) heterosexual men who love heterosexual women. Then, again, there are MTF transsexuals like Katherine Cummings (1993) who are sexually attracted to women and identify as lesbians. It is this latter group, transsexual lesbians, or more particularly transsexual lesbian feminists that Janice Raymond sees as epitomising patriarchy's attempt to appropriate or even annihilate 'real' women.

In her infamous book *The Transsexual Empire* (1979) Raymond, a self-proclaimed radical feminist, says:

the male-to-constructed-female who claims to be a lesbian-feminist attempts to possess women . . . under the guise of challenging rather than conforming to the role and behaviour of stereotyped femininity [as is the case with the non-lesbian, non-feminist MTF]. (1998: 306)

Basically Raymond, whom Califia so aptly describes as 'the Cassandra the goddesses of fundamentalist feminism have appointed to warn the rest of us against taking this Trojan horse [the transsexual lesbian feminist] into our gates' (1997: 92), conjures up a dystopian scenario, a transsexual empire, 'reminiscent of *The Invasion of the Body Snatchers*' (Shapiro 1991: 259). Here we find 'she-males' (MTFs) – as Raymond, refusing to recognise the possibility of transition, calls them – going to unbelievable lengths to possess women's bodies and, more particularly, the spirituality and sexuality of lesbian feminist women. The problem (as Raymond sees it), is that 'male-to-constructed-female' lesbian feminists do not renounce their masculinity. Evidence of this can be found, she says, in the fact that they are dominating, obtrusive, and desire to be in the limelight and in positions of power. Mary Daly, whom Raymond cites, goes one step further and argues that since MTF lesbian feminists have not suffered to the same extent as 'ordinary' women have under patriarchy, then they are likely to appear stronger, more confident, and self-assured than 'female' lesbian feminists. The fear is that this may well lead to a situation in which MTFs look like better candidates for lesbian feminism than 'real' women do. However, Raymond is quick to add that such an appearance is misleading since the MTF lesbian feminist 'can only *play the part*' (1998: 308) of the lesbian feminist, she (or he as Raymond would put it) can never really be one.

Far from supporting lesbian feminism, what in fact the MTF lesbian feminist does is appropriate 'women's minds, convictions of feminism, and sexuality' (Ibid.: 308), penetrate the most sacred of women's spiritual, sexual, and physical spaces, and ultimately, commit rape. As Raymond notes:

Rape . . . is a masculinist violation of bodily integrity. All transsexuals rape women's bodies by reducing the real female form to an artefact, appropriating this body for themselves. However, the transsexually constructed lesbian-feminist violates women's sexuality and spirit as well. (Ibid.: 308)

Now one may well argue that since the post-operative MTF lesbian feminist has been castrated – not only physically, but also symbolically – she is unlikely to have the sort of power that Raymond and Daly seem to unquestioningly accord her, the kind of power to violate that is associated with rape. However, Raymond counters this sort of claim by arguing that castration does not constitute what we might call de-phallicisation. In fact, quite the opposite is the case, at least as Raymond, following Daly sees it. Raymond says:

Because [MTF] transsexuals have lost their physical 'members' does not mean that they have lost their ability to penetrate women – women's mind, women's sexuality. Transsexuals merely cut off the most obvious means of invading women so that they seem non-invasive. However, as Mary Daly has remarked in the case of the transsexually constructed lesbian-feminists their whole presence becomes a 'member' invading women's presence and dividing us once more from each other. (Ibid.: 309)

The phenomenon of 'men without members' is not, we are told, a new thing, and Raymond suggests that feminists would do well to examine the role that such people have played in other patriarchal cultures. Here she cites the figure of the eunuch, the memberless man whom other more powerful men have used to keep women in (their) place, that is, in the house, in the bedroom, in the harem. But whilst eunuchs were attached to women's spaces, even and especially those barred to other men, they were apparently also (and as a result) accorded great status. Similarly, MTF lesbian-feminists have, according to Raymond, gained access to women's spaces closed to other men, and consequently can, and do, 'rise in the Kingdom of the Fathers' (Ibid.: 310), since they serve the state well in the ways outlined above. On this rather lofty note I feel compelled to quote Califia who says 'with such fervour as this, the Roman Catholic Church put Galileo under lifetime house arrest for saying the Earth moved around the sun' (1997: 92).

Obviously Raymond's position is not one that is shared by all lesbians and/or feminists, although it is important to note that it has engendered and continues to inform debates about whether or not MTFs should be granted access to women-only spaces. A number of objections have been raised over the years in response to Raymond's book, and also to the work of feminists such as Daly and Jeffreys who, for the most part, share Raymond's position. One of the main problems that has been noted is Raymond's unquestioned acceptance of the euphemism 'once a man always a man' – regardless of what kind of surgical procedures and/or hormone treatments one undergoes. This is apparent in her use of the term 'male-to-*constructed*-female' and her insistence on the pronoun 'he' when referring to a MTF transsexual. One could argue then, as Califia does, that 'Raymond is a true-blue gender essentialist' (Ibid.: 93). If this is the case, then Raymond's position seems to be at odds with the anti-essentialist attempts to understand gender and embodiment that the majority of feminists have been formulating for the last three or four decades.

One could also argue that Raymond's disregard for, or silencing of, the experience and/or identity of transsexuals has an 'othering' effect that is anathematic not only to transsexual/transgender politics, but also to feminism. Raymond never allows transsexuals to speak, nor does she recognise that the term transsexual inevitably includes a homogenous range of people from diverse racial groups,[9] age groups, family groups, classes, who have different, and often conflicting sexualities, political beliefs, religious commitments, social positions, physical capacities, aspirations, desires, problems, and so on. This tendency in Raymond's work has been read by some as symptomatic of both transphobia and of a fear of difference more generally.

Another possible criticism that could be made of Raymond's thesis is that her explanation of why some people (men in Raymond's terms) would go to such extreme lengths to gain access to women's bodies and spaces, seems unconvincing. Raymond seems to offer two reasons. First, because this is one way to 'rise in the Kingdoms of the Fathers', and, second, because 'of the recognition of the power that women have, by virtue of female biology' (Raymond, cited in Califia 1997: 94). The first explanation seems particularly questionable given that there are all sorts of other, simpler, less painful, and more socially acceptable ways for men to gain social status. Moreover, it is debatable whether in fact MTFs are regarded by patriarchs and heteronormative institutions in the way that Raymond claims they are. Some would argue that as a result of being seen to have chosen an 'inferior' social position (the position of woman) the MTF, rather like the male homosexual, is reviled and punished by individuals and institutions that value the masculine principle.

In relation to the second explanation, Califia claims that the MTF's supposed attempt to possess what Raymond describes as 'female creative energies' associated with, but not reducible to, birthing, reads like a biological-cum-mystical myth of womb envy. Moreover, she argues that it is problematic, particularly for feminists, to equate the essence of woman with procreative capacities, even tangentially. One reason being that woman who do not or cannot give birth are then, by implication, relegated to the realm of non-woman. If this is not the case, says Califia, if the non-fertile (whether by choice or 'accident') woman nevertheless partakes of the mystical essence Raymond refers to, then why can't the MTF transsexual? And what of the intersexed person?

Raymond's response to the gender dissatisfaction experienced by transsexuals is to claim that this is not the result of an illness or disorder, but rather, is caused by patriarchy. Furthermore, she says that such feelings – although expressed using different

111

terminology – are also experienced by feminists. In a nutshell, then, the 'problem', as Raymond sees it, is not transsexualism (which is a mis-diagnosis), but 'sex-role oppression', and the 'cure' will not be found in reassignment surgery and/or hormone treatment, but in a (lesbian) feminist revolution, which ironically, as Califia notes, the MTF transsexual will not be welcome to participate in.

These kinds of debates over transsexualism and its relationship to both the medical profession and to radical politics, gave rise in the late 1980s to the notion of transgender. This term was originally coined by those who did not feel that the term cross-dresser was appropriate, given their commitment to full-time gender bending, but who did not desire to undergo sex reassignment surgery and thus did not seem to 'qualify' as transsexuals. It is now used to refer to a wide range of gender-ambiguous identities including cross-dressers, drag queens and kings, intersexed people, hermaphrodykes, people who modify their bodies in a variety of ways and to varying degrees with or without hormones and/or surgery, butch dykes, fairies, she-males, bi-gendered individuals, those who see themselves as belonging to a 'third sex', androgynes, transsexuals, cyborgs, queers, and so on. In a sense, the term transgender provides an identity category and a sense of belonging to all those who have been excluded from gender identity programmes and denied access to surgery, and to all those who have felt marginalised by heteronormative values and institutions more generally. This collective sense of transgender could be said to inform and be informed by queer politics and the celebration of ambiguous and non-unified subject positions. It also allows people to identify as something other than a man or a woman, and, as Califia notes, 'question[s] the binary gender system that generates these labels' (1997: 225).

By the mid-1990s the popularisation of postmodern ideas, the shift away from a civil rights approach to queer politics, the emergence of a larger and more visible FTM contingent and of transgender studies, combined with a number of other important factors to 'produce a change in the tone of transgender activism and its agenda' (Ibid.: 223). Whilst transgender people and organisations continued (and still, by necessity, do) to lobby for greater access to surgery, policies which would enable changes to be made to official documents such as birth certificates, the right to marry, the right to adopt children, and so on, a more outspoken and 'in your face' kind of approach became increasingly popular amongst those who, like Stone, felt it imperative to expand the bounds of culturally intelligible gender, and to speak in their own voices rather than 'passing' into silence and invisibility.

In most accounts of transactivism, at least as it developed in the USA, two events are cited as central: Camp Trans, and the Brandon Teena case. The first of these involves an annual protest by the activist group Transexual Menace that first took place in 1994 outside of the Michigan Womyn's Music Festival, an event for 'womyn-born-womyn' only. Transsexual Menace challenged the organiser's concept of 'woman' and eventually gained the right for transsexual women to attend the festival.[10] The second event which galvanised transactivists was the 1993 murder of a young gender-ambiguous person named Brandon Teena (or Teena Brandon) and the ensuing trial of those held responsible. A week before the murder the twenty-one-year-old Brandon had been abducted and raped by John Lotter and Marvin Thomas Nissen who were eventually charged with the murder of Brandon and two others. No doubt, these events and the lead-up to them would not have received international press coverage, nor have been the subject of heated debates, if it were not for the fact that they revolved around a gender-ambiguous person. It is even less likely that a film (*Boys Don't Cry*) would have been made.

One of the interesting things about this tragic case is the competing ways in which the figure or corpse of Brandon has been classified, interpreted, judged, and fought over. As in *Boys Don't Cry*, prior to his (or her) murder, Brandon wore what we would usually think of as men's clothes, bound his (or her) breasts, used a prosthetic penis, had sexual relationships with women whilst claiming not to be a lesbian, and used names usually presumed to be male (Billy, Brandon, Charles). Nevertheless, according to C. Jacob Hale, at the hospital Brandon attended after the rape, the hospital chart was amended to read 'Teena Brandon/F' once it was 'discovered' that Brandon had a vagina rather than a penis (1998a: 311–12). The sheriff of Richardson County (Charles Laux) who dealt with the rape report was less convinced of Brandon's female status, callously referring to Brandon as 'it'. At least in *Boys Don't Cry*, Brandon, when questioned by the authorities in connection with warrants for petty offences claims that he (or she) is experiencing a sexual identity crisis, although exactly what this means or entails is unclear. As Hale notes:

a state of crisis over identity, sexual and otherwise, characterizes not only 'Brandon's' brief life but also the media attention devoted to this murdered youth. Much of this crisis finds its focal point in the necessity of being named. (Ibid.: 312)

As we have seen already, Brandon was classified as a female, an 'it', a non-lesbian, and someone whose sense of self was in 'crisis': he (or she) has been referred to as Brandon Teena and as Teena Brandon, as 'he' and as 'she'. So, which of these identities is the 'true' one?

Rather than attempting to define Brandon, it might be more useful to ask what the effects of naming are, who particular names serve, how and why. For transpeople, gays and lesbians, and in fact anyone who has been othered by dominant discourses and institutions, the importance of naming is abundantly clear, and in particular, the necessity to resist categories that are imposed by others and that are detrimental to the self. Transactivists are sensitive, as Hale notes, to the ways in which transgender or transsexual subjectivity can be rendered invisible in and through the use of names and pronouns (1998a: 312–14). For example, calling the gender-ambiguous person who was raped and murdered by Lotter and Nissen, Teena Brandon, or referring to Brandon as 'she' or 'her', covers over any sense of ambiguity, or denies the chosen gender of the subject concerned as is apparent, for example, in Raymond's use of the pronoun 'he' when discussing MTFs.

Given this, it is not surprising that self-naming is a right held dear by transgender activists such as the following contributor to *TNT: The Transsexual News Telegraph* who states, 'It is Brandon Teena (never, not ever Teena Brandon) . . . He (not Her, not ever Her because We decide who We are)' (cited in Hale 1998a: 313). Taking the same stance, Transexual Menace protested against Donna Minkowitz's (1994) article in *Village Voice* entitled 'Love Hurts: Brandon Teena Was a Woman Who Lived and Loved as a Man: She Was Killed for Carrying It Off', arguing that Brandon was not really a woman who masqueraded as a man, and that Brandon's murder was not a case of misogyny. Rather, they claimed that Brandon was a transgender man (or even an M2M)[11] whose murder is an example of the most extreme kind of transphobic violence.

So, in short, there are those who refer to Brandon as 'he', those who use the pronoun 'she' to describe the murdered youth, and those who are not sure what to say or not to say. So where would we situate *Boys Don't Cry* in all this? Does the film portray Brandon as a girl masquerading as a boy, as a boy who just happens to have a cleavage that we, along with Lana get a glimpse of, or as indeterminate? There are probably all sorts of responses to this question and it would be interesting to consider why we read the character of Brandon in the ways that we do, what sort of filmic devices and conventions encourage or discourage particular readings, and how, what effect the choice of an actress like Hilary Swank (who plays the part of Brandon) might have on our responses to the story, the character, and the issues of transgender and transphobia. Rather than engage in this sort of analysis here, I want to briefly mention a common tendency amongst students when discussing the figure of Brandon. Whilst most students in the Queer Theory course that I teach are happy enough to refer to Brandon as 'he', there nevertheless comes a point, or more particularly two points, at which this becomes extremely difficult. The two moments in the film that create a dis-ease with the use of the male pronoun are the rape scene, and the scene in which Brandon begins to menstruate. At this point in the seminar discussion almost everyone begins – more or less unconsciously – referring to Brandon as 'she': 'when she is raped', 'when she gets her period'. What this illustrates is the degree to which bodily being is culturally intelligible only within very strict gender parameters. For most people, the notion of a man who menstruates is even more unfamiliar (and therefore unintelligible) than a giant caterpillar who smokes a hookah. But if, as Judith Halberstam argues, gender is a fiction which we all live in varying ways, then it must also be possible to rewrite bodily being, to 'rewrite the cultural fiction that divides a sex from a transsex, a gender from a transgender' (1994: 226).

If we fail to deal with unfamiliar modes of embodiment by rendering them intelligible in terms of existing gender categories – that is, by 'proving' that, for example, Brandon really was a man or a woman – then we reinforce the idea that subjectivity is singular, unified, unambiguous, and knowable. We also, as Hale points out, overlook or deny our own complicity in the construction of the other – a construction that is informed by one's own norms, political investments, embodied history, sexuality, and so on, and not necessarily those of the person concerned. Thus one could argue that any naming of Brandon, no matter how well intentioned, appropriates the transgendered body by explaining away or veiling over any ambiguous or incongruous elements that might disturb the coherent image that we desire.

Hale claims that locating Brandon solely in terms of any one identity category constitutes 'a refusal to acknowledge that this person was a *border zone dweller*: someone whose embodied self existed in a netherworld constituted by the margins of multiple overlapping identity categories' (1998a: 318). Such a position involves recognising that identity categories are never discrete or self-contained. Rather, the supposed boundaries between them are permeable, undecidable, constantly shape-shifting. Perhaps then we might understand transgender as an attempt to move beyond dichotomies, to embrace the figure and the logic of the 'border zone dweller', or 'monster' in Susan Stryker's (1994) terms.

Whilst this may seem like a simple enough solution to the divisiveness caused by the debates surrounding transsexualism and, to some extent, transgender, it nevertheless can lead to quite different (and possibly contradictory) theoretical and political positions and forms of activism. For example, Kate Bornstein in suggesting that the word transgender be used inclusively to mean 'transgressively gendered' advocates a kind of queer utopia, 'one great big happy family under one great big happy name' (1994: 134) in which unity takes precedence over, or blissfully ignores, diversity. As we saw in Chapter 3, this sort of notion of inclusiveness ignores the fact that different sub-groups within a group have different histories and different goals and agendas. As Rita Felski puts it, transgender's 'elevation to the status of universal signifier . . . subverts established distinctions . . . but at the risk of homogenizing differences that matter politically' (cited in Prosser 1997: 321). It is for this reason that, for example, Hale (1998b) develops an analysis of the differences between FTMs and non-transsexual men, and more specifically of their relationships to feminist theory and practice; Halberstam (1994; 1998) examines the continuities and dis-continuities between FTMs and butch lesbians; Cromwell (1999) considers the relationship between female-bodied individuals who, in the past, lived as men for socio-economic reasons, for (homo)sexual reasons, or because they identified as men; and Roen (2001) explores why it is that transgender issues 'might require different subversive strategies, and different theoretical workings, according to the racial positioning of the transpeople concerned' (Ibid.: 261). What all this points to is the need to recognise that

Many bodies are gender strange to some degree or another, and it is time to complicate on the one hand the transsexual models that assign gender deviance only to transsexual bodies and gender normativity to

116

all other bodies, and on the other hand, the heteronormative models that see transsexuality as the solution to gender deviance and homosexuality as a pathological perversion. (Halberstam 1998: 153–4)

NOTES

1. See, for example, Krafft-Ebing's (1965) account of the case history of Count Sandor; Havelock Ellis' (1908) discussion of Miss D., and the Chevalier d'Eon de Beaumont; the story of Herculine Barbin edited by Foucault (1980); Shapiro's (1991) discussion of the *berdache* of North America, the *xanith* of Oman, and woman–woman marriage in various parts of Africa; Donoghue's (1993) account of 'female hermaphrodites' and 'female husbands'; and Epstein's (1990) analysis of the figures of the hermaphrodite and the transvestite in European history.
2. Nevertheless, whilst Benjamin's theory and treatment of transsexualism were widely accepted, transsexualism was added to the *Diagnostic and Statistical Manual (DSM) III* of the American Psychiatric Association in 1974 – the same year that homosexuality was removed from the list of psychosexual disorders.
3. As far as is possible I have chosen to use the pronoun preferred by the person under discussion.
4. For a fictional account of Einar/Lili's life, see Ebershoff (1999).
5. One of the problems that results from the association of transsexualism and surgery, is that divisive hierarchies then form between and amongst transsexuals. See, for example, Denny (1995).
6. Obviously not everyone had equal access to such institutions. Factors such as race, class, age, criminal history, religion, and so on, would all impact on an individual's experience of transsexualism or gender ambiguity and on his or her (capacity to) access discourses, information, and institutions surrounding and informing sex reassignment.
7. Cromwell (1998), like many other contemporary transgender theorists, argues that '"wrong body" is an inadequate description of an individual's experience of their body not being part of their "self"' (Ibid.: 127). He suggests that rather than accepting such a notion, we instead ask 'for whom is the body "wrong", . . . for whom is surgery "corrective"' (Ibid.: 127) and isn't this sense of 'wrongness' in fact the result of sexed/gendered ideologies that mandate what it is that constitutes 'femaleness', and 'maleness' (as the only possible modes of being)?
8. See, for example, Benjamin (1966) pp. 125–6.
9. For an interesting account of the ways in which race effects the experience of transsexualism, or 'gender liminality', as she calls it, see Roen (2001).

10. For a more detailed account of Camp Trans, see Califia (1997), and Wilchins (1997) who also discusses other activist events organised by Transexual Menace.
11. According to Califia (1997), M2M (male-to-male) is a relatively new term that 'disputes the idea that transgendered men were ever women' (Ibid.: 232).

7

Queering 'Straight' Sex

AS MANY COMMENTATORS HAVE pointed out, despite the considerable amount of research on 'sexuality', heterosexuality remains, for the most part, relatively unquestioned.[1] It is, as Kitzinger and Wilkinson put it, 'always a silent term' (1993: 3). Heterosexuality has, in contemporary Western culture at least, attained the status of the natural, the taken for granted. This is evidenced not only in the dearth of critical analyses of heterosexuality, but also more literally in the 1970 edition of *The Shorter Oxford English Dictionary* which defines 'heterosexual' as 'pertaining to or characterised by the *normal* relation of the sexes' (cited in Overall 1999: 295). By the 1985 edition, however, the definition of 'heterosexual' had changed to that which 'involv[es], [is] related to, or characterised by a sexual propensity for the opposite sex' (Vol. 2: 2634).

So, according to this second definition, heterosexuality describes or names a desire for, or sexual contact with, someone whose sex/gender is different from, and opposed to one's own. This particular definition of heterosexuality is informed by, and informs, a dichotomous understanding of sex/gender, and here sex/gender is, at least implicitly, represented as something that just is, something innate, natural, unquestionable, or – in the terms of the earlier definition – normal.

However, presuming or tacitly accepting that heterosexuality is 'natural' or 'normal' does not simply make it so. In fact, if, as Foucault and others have argued, sexuality is a discursive construct that takes culturally and historically specific forms,[2] then heterosexuality is no more normal or natural than any other form of sexual relations. So why do most people accept, to varying degrees, cultural myths regarding the naturalness of heterosexuality? Richard Dyer offers the following explanations:

opposite-sex sexual relations are seemingly practised by the majority of the population; such relations feature almost to the exclusion of all others in contemporary and historical texts; these relations are affirmed both explicitly and implicitly by major institutions such as religion and the law; and same-sex sexual relations have been represented as the means by which human procreation is made possible. (1997: 264)

Nevertheless, cultural critics, particularly feminists, have argued that heterosexuality is not simply a natural, universal, and trans-historical phenomenon, but rather, is a culturally constructed institution[3] that most often functions to the detriment of women.[4] Hence the need for a rigorous critical analysis of heterosexuality, and of what Kitzinger and Wilkinson refer to as the 'unexamined heterocentricity' (1993: 2) of everyday life.

Perhaps one of the most influential examples of such an undertaking is Adrienne Rich's landmark essay 'Compulsory Heterosexuality and Lesbian Existence' (1980). Here Rich recounts the many and varied ways in which women are coerced into heterosexuality, including the privileges and punishments associated with conformity and deviance. She argues that 'compulsory heterosexuality' is an institution (rather than a natural inclination or a choice) that plays a central role in the implementation and perpetuation of male domination. In short, 'compulsory heterosexuality' is the tool *par excellence* of patriarchy. However, whilst, on the one hand, 'compulsory heterosexuality' functions to reaffirm patriarchal values and relations, it simultaneously undermines the mythic naturalness of heterosexuality since by its very nature – its drive to cajole, coerce, convince – it reveals, Rich argues, what it tries so hard to deny; that is, that heterosexuality is not only illusory, but also and as a consequence, is 'an identity permanently at risk' (Butler 1991: 24). 'Compulsory heterosexuality is, to borrow from Butler again, 'continually haunted by [its] own inefficacy; hence the anxiously repeated effort to install and augment [its] jurisdiction' (1993a: 237).

According to Rich, 'compulsory heterosexuality' not only coerces women into heterosexuality and the gender norms associated with it, it also blinds them to the mechanics of their own oppression and delimits the possibility of alternative modes of being such as lesbianism. However, Rich's notion of lesbianism does not simply refer to sexual relations between women. Since Rich's aim is, in part, to identify instances of 'nascent undefined feminism' in which 'women-loving women have been nay-sayers to male possession and control of women' (Rich, in Schwarz 1979: 6), she introduces the concept of a lesbian continuum. This term embraces 'many... forms of primary intensity between and among women, including the sharing of a rich inner life, the bonding against male tyranny, the giving and receiving of practical and political support' (Rich 1980: 648). In short, for Rich, the 'lesbian continuum' represents a transhistorical and transcultural form of resistance to patriarchy and/or to 'compulsory heterosexuality'.

A number of criticisms have been made of Rich's article in the twenty odd years since its publication.[5] These include the claim that Rich implies that all heterosexual relations are coercive and work to further patriarchy; that the notion of the 'lesbian continuum' suggests that lesbianism is in essence political and that all lesbians therefore resist patriarchy; that this notion of 'political lesbianism' is highly problematic (for all the reasons outlined in Chapter 2); that the model denies heterosexual women (political) agency; that Rich fails to comment on the ways in which 'compulsory heterosexuality' oppresses gay men and other sexual minorities; and that her account is transhistorical and transcultural and therefore ignores differences between women. The notion of heterosexuality as an institution, rather than simply an act which takes place between a man and a woman, nevertheless continues to have critical currency. This is not of course to suggest that all critiques of heterosexuality (as an institution) share the same theoretical and political framework. As we shall see, there are many, often contradictory and competing, ways to 'denaturalise' heterosexuality, to make it strange, or to 'queer' it.

In the same year that Rich's article was published so too was Monique Wittig's 'The Straight Mind'. The title of Wittig's essay refers to what she identifies as 'the obligatory social relationship between "man" and "woman"' (1980: 107) and the system that supports and is supported by these ways of being and of knowing. Like Rich, Wittig argues that heterosexuality as an institution is so embedded in our culture, that it has become almost invisible. The 'straight mind' (and the discourses and practices that constitute it) 'envelops itself in myths, resorts to enigma, proceeds by accumulating metaphors, and its function is to poeticize the obligatory character of the "you-will-be-straight-or-you-will-not-be"' (Ibid.: 107). In other words, Wittig argues that the 'straight mind' is everywhere, that it dominates our current conceptual system and thus 'prevents us from speaking unless we speak in [its] terms' (Ibid.: 106). Given this, it is politically essential, Wittig claims, to abandon current categories and systems of thought, to rid ourselves of concepts such as 'man' and 'woman', since in continuing to speak of ourselves in these terms 'we are instrumental in maintaining heterosexuality' (Ibid.: 108).

Wittig also shares Rich's desire to articulate the possibility of resistance to such a system, and she too associates resistance with lesbianism. However, unlike Rich for whom lesbianism connotes (at least politically) woman-identified experience, Wittig makes what might seem to some to be an incongruous claim, that is, that 'lesbians are not women' (Ibid.: 110). This is because 'woman' only has meaning in heterosexual conceptual and economic systems, and since lesbianism is tantamount to a form of resistance to this system, its very being must somehow exist outside of, or apart from, such a system.

One may well ask, then, what a lesbian is, whence lesbianism comes, and how it manages to exist in an all-pervasive system in which it cannot speak its name and thus, one would logically conclude, cannot be conceived (of). As Judith Butler[6] has pointed out, Wittig's analysis of the 'straight mind' offers only two political options, namely radical conformity or radical revolution. What informs this either/or choice is the belief that all heterosexual relations function unambiguously, and by definition, in the service of a unified and monolithic regime (the 'straight mind'), and that lesbianism exists outside such a matrix and is radically untainted by it. Thus Wittig's logic is problematic, some would claim, first, because the radical opposition that she posits between straight and lesbian 'replicates the kind of disjunctive binarism that she herself characterizes as the divisive philosophical gesture of the straight mind' (Butler 1990: 121), second, because it denies the existence or the possibility of forms of subversion or resistance that take place within the heterosexual matrix and are in fact inseparable from it, and, third, because it fails to explain how it is that lesbianism (as Wittig defines it) exists at all.

Like Rich and Wittig, many other feminist writers have embraced the idea that heterosexuality is unquestionably oppressive for women, that it is one of, if not *the*, main way(s) in which patriarchy maintains itself, and that it is therefore antithetical to feminism. This is perhaps most apparent in the work of radical feminists such as Catherine MacKinnon, Andrea Dworkin and Sheila Jeffreys. For example, in *Feminism Unmodified: Discourses on Life and Law*, MacKinnon argues that 'the male supremacist definition of female sexuality [constructs it] as a lust for self-annihilation' (1987: 172) and that this is most explicitly apparent in pornography. But MacKinnon's thesis is not simply that pornography can and often does cause harm to women, but more importantly, that so-called 'normal' heterosexuality is always already pornographic, that is, non-egalitarian, oppressive, violent, and central to the subordination of women.

Andrea Dworkin, who also equates heterosexuality with intercourse and with male domination and violence, takes this position to its logical extreme calling for the rejection of (heterosexual) intercourse itself. Like the Leeds Revolutionary Feminists discussed in Chapter 2, Dworkin claims that since intercourse is immune to reform, then there must be no more penetration. She states that 'in a world of male power – penile power – fucking is the essential sexual experience of power and potency and possession; fucking by mortal men, regular guys' (1987: 124). In a particularly disturbing description of intercourse which, at first glance one may well mistake for a description of rape, Dworkin says, '[h]e has to push in past boundaries . . . The thrusting is persistent invasion. She is opened up, split down the centre. She is occupied – physically, internally, in her privacy' (Ibid.: 122).

Here heterosexual sex (read intercourse) is in essence a battlefield on which only the male can ever be the victor. On Dworkin and MacKinnon's view of heterosexuality, then, founded as it is on essentialised or essentialising notions of masculinity and femininity, activity and passivity, power and powerlessness, penetrator and penetrated, fucker and fuckee, sexual ethics is, as Moira Gatens points out, 'always already foredoomed' (1996: 78). There can be no consideration of the possibility that such representations of heterosexuality are (historically and culturally specific) discursive constructs, and that whilst they constitute lived embodiment in very real material ways, they are by no means immutable truths. But, if as Foucault claims, sexuality is a truth-effect of systems of power/knowledge, then Dworkin and MacKinnon's accounts of heterosexuality and of gender could be said to be complicit in the construction and reaffirmation of female embodiment as passive, penetrable, and powerless, and male embodiment as active, impenetrable, and powerful. Thus, it could be argued that rather than attempting to deconstruct the battlefield where the struggle for signifying supremacy is forever re-enacted, and where in the end, victory is equated with activity and defeat with passivity, Dworkin and MacKinnon re-enact the battle, essentialise the same old script, and thereby ensure – albeit inadvertantly – that the male is always the victor.

Like Rich, Wittig, MacKinnon, and Dworkin, Sheila Jeffreys is of the opinion that heterosexuality maintains the social and sexual power of men over women. Furthermore, along with Dworkin and MacKinnon, she argues that heterosexuality eroticises and natu-ralises dominance and submission. But for Jeffreys, heterosexuality is not simply tantamount to intercourse (at least not primarily), nor is it the sole domain of those we usually think of as heterosexuals. What concerns Jeffreys is what she refers to as 'heterosexual desire' by which she does 'not mean desire for the opposite sex, but a desire that is organised around eroticised dominance and sub-mission' (1998: 76); a desire in which one participant is 'othered'. Consequently, it is possible, Jeffreys argues, for gays and lesbians to experience heterosexual desire, and thus to reproduce gender norms and inequitable social relations. Examples of this, she claims, include butch/femme role-playing, sadomasochism, transgender practices,[7] and in fact any form of desire or practice that appears to eroticise 'race, class, or age differences' (Ibid.: 76–7). Inversely, it is also possible for same-sex couples to experience what Jeffreys calls 'homosexual desire', that is, 'desire based upon sameness instead of difference of power, desire which is about mutuality' (Ibid.: 77), although, given the ways in which the structural relations between men and women are currently organised, this, suggests Jeffreys, seems relatively unlikely.

For Jeffreys the eradication of heterosexual desire (of relations of domination and submission), as the fundamental aim of femi-nist politics does not necessarily involve legislating against sexual relations between men and women, but rather is possible only in and through the abolition of gender – a position shared, to some extent, by Wittig. But what would such a task entail? How could it be realised? Or, to put a slightly different slant on the question, is 'equality' attainable or desirable given that it necessarily involves the denial of difference(s)?[8]

The equation of heterosexuality with male domination and patriarchy is commonplace in second wave feminist writings and politics, and continues to resonate still. Doris DeHardt's words epitomise such an equation and highlight the ensuing tension between heterosexuality and feminism. Feminist heterosexual relationships, she says, are, 'like military intelligence, an oxymoron' (cited in Kitzinger and Wilkinson 1993: 20). In their editorial introduction to *Heterosexuality: A Feminism and Psychology Reader* Kitzinger and Wilkinson also seem to be critical of heterosexual feminism, although their odium is couched in less virulent terms. According to these (self-declared lesbian) authors, lesbianism, unlike heterosexuality, 'is an intrinsically politicized identity' (Ibid.: 7). Heterosexuality, they claim, does not and cannot have this kind of status because it is consistent with dominant group membership and with the beliefs, values, and institutions that support and are supported by that group. So, if heterosexuality cannot be claimed by heterosexual feminists as a political identity, where does this leave those whose very being appears to be a contradiction in terms?

Kitzinger and Wilkinson's discussion of the responses they received from heterosexual feminists to their call for papers, sheds some light on this dilemma. According to Kitzinger and Wilkinson, the responses included laughter, fear and hostility, puzzlement, attempts at disavowal, and most common of all, guilt.[9] However, some of the (potential) contributors took what might be loosely described as a postmodern position on the question of (their presumed) heterosexuality, suggesting that identity categories are debilitating, essentialising, and/or logically flawed. But despite the claim that they 'are acutely aware of the need for the continued development of more rigorous and sophisticated analyses of heterosexuality' (Ibid.: 25) Kitzinger and Wilkinson represent these responses less as an opportunity to open up spaces in which to rethink heterosexuality, and more as examples of disavowal, or at least political naïvety. They say:

In a perhaps understandable desire to dissolve their (unpoliticized) 'heterosexual' identities, choosing continua over categories, heterosexual feminists sometimes fail to appreciate the importance of the label 'lesbian' to those who claim it. It may be liberating for heterosexual feminists to know that they can be other than heterosexual, to cast off that label and escape from the 'prison' of categorical heterosexual identity . . . but for lesbian feminists, things are different. Every lesbian *knows* that she should be, is expected to be, and perhaps has been, or could be, other than lesbian. Affirming our lesbianism is a liberatory feminist act. When we say we are lesbian, it is not . . . because we cannot appreciate 'fluidity', 'flux', or 'change' in our lives;

but because while acknowledging the contradictions, we are making a political statement. (1993: 7–8)

It could be argued that, insofar as they set up a hierarchical binary relation between heterosexuality and lesbianism, Kitzinger and Wilkinson simply reaffirm what some would call phallocentric logic. One might even go as far as to claim that their editorial illustrates in a none too flattering way Carol Vance's statement that '[t]here is a very fine line between talking about sex and setting norms' (cited in Segal 1994: 223). Indeed, Lynne Segal seems to suggest that Kitzinger and Wilkinson do more damage than good when it comes to the task of rethinking heterosexuality. This is because they totally ignore the notion of (heterosexual female) pleasure, put undue emphasis on heterosexual women's doubts, anxieties, and feelings of guilt, and, in a sense, paint a 'condescending and self-righteous' (Ibid.: 216) picture of victims (heterosexual women) and victors (lesbians) which, rather than opening up, in fact closes down, the possibility of rethinking heterosexuality and its relation to feminism.

Christine Overall is one of many contemporary feminist theorists whose aim is to envisage a more compatible relationship between heterosexuality and feminism. Overall's focus is, in part, on the question of choice, and she argues that '[b]eyond the claim that heterosexuality is innate . . . and the claim that heterosexuality is coerced . . . there is a third possibility: that heterosexuality is or can be chosen, even – or especially! – by a feminist' (1999: 303). Overall does not dismiss the theory that heterosexuality is coerced, in fact, she argues that since this is by and large the case, then making a conscious and informed choice to participate in heterosexual practices 'without concomitant[ly] endors[ing] the heterosexual institution' (Ibid.: 305) could be regarded as a form of feminist praxis. Whilst such a choice is obviously possible, perhaps more needs to be said about its expediency, about whether or not it ought to be made by a feminist. Overall outlines a number of reasons why the choice to participate in heterosexual practices should, or at least could, be considered a legitimate option for feminists. First, such a choice involves giving credence to the distinction between the institution of heterosexuality and specific heterosexual relations and practices. Second, and connected to the first point, such a choice would mean acknowledging a distinction between 'the institution of manhood' (Ibid.: 307) and individual men. Third, such a choice is informed by and informs the belief that since heterosexuality is socially constructed it is therefore open to change. Fourth, such a choice allows heterosexual women to see themselves as something other than victims or dupes: in short, it gives them personal and political agency. Fifth, insofar as the choice is made by individuals, it will be lived and experienced in a variety of different ways and thus will illustrate (and perhaps even further) the heterogeneity of heterosexuality.

In many ways Overall's thesis appears to fulfil the conditions set out in the following statement made by Segal:

All feminists could, and strategically should, participate in attempting to subvert the meanings of 'heterosexuality', rather than simply trying to abolish or silence its practice . . . The challenge all feminists face, on top of the need to keep chipping away at men's continuing social power . . . is to acknowledge that there are many 'heterosexualities' . . . We need to explore them, both to affirm those which are based on safety, trust, and affection . . . and which therefore empower women, and also to wonder . . . how to strengthen women to handle those which are not. (1994: 260–1)

Whilst Overall's thesis may seem appealing in a common sense sort of way, and may fulfil Segal's call to acknowledge that there are many heterosexualities,[10] it nevertheless seems to side-step, rather than developing a critical analysis of, the concept of 'choice'. In failing to explain how choices are, or can be, made Overall's proposal leaves itself open to the claim that what might look like or be experienced as a choice is, nevertheless, nothing more than 'something that has [been] imposed, managed, organized, propagandized, and maintained by force' (Rich 1980: 634). Alternately, one could argue that choice, as Overall represents it, is problematic insofar as it is founded upon the notion of individual autonomy, the belief that the self is a unified and self-transparent entity independent (to some extent) of the systems and institutions that seek to govern it, and the idea that all subjects have equal access to such decisions (and the possibility of making them) despite their material differences.[11]

Like Overall, Segal – who finds the 'dual depiction of feminism as anti-heterosexual pleasure and heterosexual pleasure as anti-woman' (1997: 77) both dangerous and demoralising – is committed to the project of rethinking heterosexuality in all its complexities. But rather than simply encouraging (heterosexual) women to choose to participate in heterosexual practices on their own terms, Segal invites (straight) women to play an active role in subverting heterosexual norms by 'queering':

traditional understandings of gender and sexuality, questioning the ways in which women's bodies have been coded as uniquely 'passive', 'receptive', or 'vulnerable' . . . [and] look[ing] at male heterosexual desire (and how their bodies become 'receptive' and 'vulnerable) since the two are inextricably linked. (Ibid.: 88)

In short, Segal is concerned with lived embodiment and how it is experienced in gender (and other) specific ways. What this means is that whilst Segal is not interested in essentialising the hierarchies, privileges, and constraints that exist in contemporary culture, particularly in regard to gender, she is committed to the acknowledgment and analysis of the material conditions of heterosexuality in all its ambiguity, and in its many and varied forms.

In *Straight Sex: Rethinking the Politics of Pleasure* (1997), Segal suggests that such an undertaking would benefit from a Foucauldian analysis of the historically and culturally specific ways in which bodies are constituted, regulated, encoded, made to signify, marked as 'masculine', 'feminine', 'heterosexual', homosexual', and so on. She also proposes that whilst psychoanalytic theory has, for the most part at least, failed to question phallic authority, it nevertheless provides us with a comprehensive account of the psychic investments, tensions, and repressions associated with desire and with the assuming of sexed identity. Consequently, Segal combines insights and methodologies from both of these sources in her brief but interesting critique of scientific discourses and the construction of sexual difference (primarily) in terms of reproductive biology. In her engagement with a number of scientific texts, Segal finds, perhaps unsurprisingly, the equation of the female body with passivity, receptivity, penetrability, and the male body with activity, directness, determination, impenetrability, and so on.

But as Segal points out, these representations, as sexist and stupid as they may seem, are not something we can simply refuse. This is because they are never entirely separate from us. Rather, these discourses inscribe or (trans)form our very being, we embody them, they are an integral part of who we are and how we experience and understand ourselves (our bodily being) and the world. Or, as Elizabeth Grosz puts it '[m]asculinity and femininity are not simply social categories as it were externally or arbitrarily imposed on the subject's sex. Masculine and feminine are necessarily related to the structure of the lived experience and meaning of bodies' (1990: 73–4).

For Segal, and many of her contemporaries,[12] focusing on the materiality of sexed being does not mean relying on a notion of the biological body, in fact, quite the opposite is the case. Since, following Foucault, Segal claims that the body is always already a discursive entity – it does not simply exist as such, or at least, can not be 'known' outside of or apart from the grids of intelligibility that exist in our culture – then the aim of feminist theory is not to replace patriarchal myths with untainted biological truths, but rather, to recode, resignify, or reinscribe bodily being.

In her book *Imaginary Bodies* (1996), Moira Gatens says that if one wants to understand sexed embodiment then one needs a concept of what she calls 'the imaginary body'. Gatens uses this term to refer to the psychical image of the body which, as Lacan has explained,[13] (in)forms one's bodily being-in-the-world; that is, one's motility, one's desire, one's sense of self, and of others , and so on. She also argues that:

[t]he imaginary body is socially and historically specific in that it is constructed by: a shared language; the shared psychical significance and privileging of various zones of the body (for example, the mouth, the anus, the genitals); and common institutional practices and discourses . . . which act on and through the body. (Ibid.: 12)

This notion of the imaginary body or bodily imago is central to Catherine Waldby's attempt to queer heterosexuality and to reinscribe bodily being. Like Gatens, Waldby (1995) argues that the imaginary body inextricably 'links' corporeality with psychic life and plays an integral role in the production of culturally and historically specific modes of sexual difference and desire. Waldby also shares with Gatens the conviction that sexual difference is, for the most part, lived and experienced in hegemonic terms. In short, Waldby, like Segal, notes the predominance, in contemporary Western culture (and in feminist writing), of dichotomous images of the male body and the female body, of the penis and the vagina, of activity and passivity, of impenetrability and permeability.

What concerns Waldby is the tendency for the genital markers of sexual difference (the penis and the vagina and all that they connote) to 'render the kinds of power relations attendant upon them as natural and inevitable' (Ibid.: 268), since such a tendency can (and does) result, for example, in the belief that woman's natural receptivity means that non-consensual sexual penetration doesn't really count as an act of violence or violation. On the other hand, however, even the suggestion of penetration transgresses the

boundaries and threatens the hegemonic bodily imago of masculinity, and thus, in a very real sense, is experienced as an act of
violence or violation. This is evidenced, as Waldby points out, by
the very existence of 'homosexual advance defence' (HAD) which
has enabled men to argue that the supposed advances made by
another male are enough to justify an attack on, or even the murder
of, the protagonist. It is telling that something like 'heterosexual
advance defence' does not exist whereby women could be acquitted
of violence towards men on the grounds that their (physical and
psychical) integrity had been threatened by the advances made.
Although, as Waldby states, 'if such overtures counted as violence
against women, and women felt free to retaliate, the streets would
be littered with battered men' (Ibid.: 269) as they are in Diane
DiMassa's *Hothead Paisan: Homicidal Lesbian Terrorist* (1994) (see
Chapter 11).

Straight sex could well be interpreted as simply reaffirming the
hegemonic bodily imagos described above, and thus as consoli-
dating gender inequality. But unlike the radical feminist theorists
discussed earlier, Waldby argues that not only is this 'ideological
reading' (Ibid.: 269) not 'true' in any absolute sense, but more
important still, 'in closing off other interpretive possibilities such a
reading tends to work against its own best intentions . . . [to] shore
up exactly what it sets out to problematize' (Ibid.: 270). Waldby
proceeds to critique this ideological reading of straight sex on
two counts. First, she argues that it is not necessary to read
penis–vagina sex as a militarised invasion and occupation of a
passive female body. Instead one could imagine, for example, that
the vagina enfolds the penis, or even as Irigaray suggests in
Elemental Passions (1992) that the sexual encounter consists of
something other than two separate, autonomous, and supposedly
complementary bodies that come together. Second, and related
to the first point, Waldby proposes that (hetero)sexual practice,
and the bodily imagos that inform and are informed by it, can
be reinscribed precisely because, as Segal (1994), Bersani (1987),
Cornell (1991), Thomas (2000) and others have shown, sex is
inevitably intersubjective: sexual pleasure involves the transgression of the supposed boundaries between self and other, subject
and object, inside and outside, active and passive, power and
powerlessness. As Segal puts it, '[i]n consensual sex when bodies
meet, the epiphany of that meeting – its threat and excitement – is
surely that all the great dichotomies . . . slide away' (1997: 86).

Consequently she concludes that '[s]exual relations are perhaps the most fraught and troubling of all social relations precisely because, especially when heterosexual, they so often threaten rather than confirm gender polarity' (1994: 254–5). Obviously this 'threat' does not always simply induce feelings of excitement or pleasure, and homophobia and misogyny are all too common responses that cannot afford to be ignored when one is engaged in the task of rethinking heterosexuality.

In an attempt to counter the fear associated with the breakdown of boundaries and identities in and through erotic pleasure, Waldby asks that we consider the erotic cost of inhabiting the position of mastery that is so inextricably bound up with the hegemonic masculine imago. Such an undertaking is important because it not only shifts the focus away from masculine power and privilege but also enables those who have the most invested in this sort of imaginary to consider the possible benefits of other ways of being. Waldby suggests that the erotic costs include: almost exclusive focus on the phallic penis and an associated de-eroticisation of the rest of the body; fear of abandoning one's sovereign ego, one's power and status, and thus fear of erotic pleasure; anxiety and/or shame regarding penis size, impotency, and premature ejaculation; an injunction against passivity; prohibition against the pleasure of being looked at or objectified; and above all 'the injunction against what Sartre called "men's secret femininity", receptive anal eroticism' (1995: 271–2).

Whilst Waldby, like Jeffreys, is interested in reciprocity, her work is by no means an attempt to implement equality in and through the annihilation of difference. Nor, it seems, is Waldby's thesis inspired by what might be described as a politically correct stereotype of happy, healthy, humane, (hetero)sexual relations. Rather, what drives her analysis is 'the possibility of a reciprocity of destruction' which runs counter to both the (essentialised or essentialising) association of men with destruction and women with the destroyed, and the desire for what she sees as an anodyne form of egalitarian intimacy. What Waldby means by erotic destruction is 'both the temporary, ecstatic confusions wrought upon the everyday sense of self by sexual pleasure, and the more long-term consequences of this confusion when it works to constitute a relationship' (Ibid.: 266). She goes on to explain that:

[t]hese momentary suspensions, when linked together in the context of a particular relationship, work towards a . . . kind of ego destruc-

131

tion . . . [T]he ego in love relations in [not] destroyed in any absolute sense. Rather, each lover is refigured by the other, made to bear the mark of the other upon the self. (Ibid.: 266–7)

One site where this sort of reciprocal destruction and reconfiguration might possibly take place, suggests Waldby, is heterosexual male anal eroticism. This is because it is profoundly opposed to a phallic imago whose function is to vigilantly patrol the supposed boundaries and differences between the imaginary anatomies of sexual difference, and to reaffirm the social imaginaries that inform and are informed by them.

Whilst Waldby's approach to the queering of heterosexuality is both innovative and theoretically sophisticated, her positing of a form of anal eroticism as something which might possibly enable a reconfiguration of the heterosexual male body and thus of heterosexual relations more generally, is something that may not go down well with many readers, as I have witnessed in my undergraduate Queer Theory course. Of course, the level of discomfort experienced amongst students required to read Waldby's paper is, in itself, telling. But the problem remains that if an idea is simply too confronting, then it is likely to be quickly disregarded rather than seriously considered, or, as Waldby is well aware, it may even incite violent responses. Given this, it may be useful to briefly consider a slightly different approach to the task of queering heterosexuality; one which involves a consideration of the notion of heteronormativity, and of whether or not heterosexuality is (always) heteronormative.

Lauren Berlant and Michael Warner define heteronormativity as 'the institutions, structures of understanding, and practical orientations that make heterosexuality not only coherent – that is, organised as a sexuality – but also privileged' (1998: 565, n.2). They, like Segal and Waldby, point out that heteronormativity (or heterosexuality as an institution) is never absolutely coherent and stable and that its privileges take many, sometimes contradictory forms. Consequently, heteronormativity does not exist as a discrete and easily identifiable body of thought, of rules and regulations, but rather, informs – albeit ambiguously, in complex ways, and to varying degrees – all kinds of practices, institutions, conceptual systems, and social structures. Given this, it is possible to argue, as Berlant and Warner do, that some 'forms of sex between men and women might not be heteronormative' and that '[h]eteronormativity is thus a concept distinct from heterosexuality' (Ibid.: 565, n.2).

Calvin Thomas further suggests that '[h]eteronormative sex is teleologically narrativized sex: sex with a goal, a purpose, and a product' (2000: 33). The product that must be (re)produced, argues Thomas, is 'the person' and this can be understood in terms of 'the child', 'the ego', or both. Given this, one could propose that heteronormativity is anti-sexual insofar as its primary aim is in direct contradistinction with what Segal, Bersani, Waldby and others have claimed is the fundamental characteristic of sex, that is, the (at least momentary) loss or destruction of the self and boundaries that constitute it. Ironically, then, perhaps, as Thomas suggests,

people who fuck in the name of identity [and presumably this could include people who share the various ideological positions outlined by the Leeds Revolutionary Feminists, Andrea Dworkin, Catherine MacKinnon, Adrienne Rich, Kitzinger and Wilkinson, Sheila Jeffreys, and so on] who make an identity out of who they fuck, who fuck to reproduce 'the person', are fucking heteronormatively . . . even if 'the person' or 'identity' thereby reproduced is 'homosexual'. (2000: 33)

Another interesting example of an attempt to denaturalize or queer heterosexuality and its attendant privileges is the public art project 'Hey, hetero?', produced by Deborah Kelly and Tina Fiveash.[14] The project, which consists of six brightly coloured, highly stylised images, originally appeared in a range of illuminated public spaces in Sydney during the month-long 2001 Sydney Gay and Lesbian Mardi Gras Festival. The aim of the project was to invite viewers to consider the rituals, customs, costumes, privileges and rights associated with (white middle-class) heterosexuality, and to show that rather than being natural, heterosexuality is a cultural construct, a product that is represented as essential, and, like all commodities, is packaged and sold accordingly.

Indeed, one could well develop an Althusserian reading of this project and the ways in which it turns 'ideology and ideological state apparatuses'[15] (such as the advertising industry) on their heads. According to Althusser, capitalist society reproduces itself, its values, beliefs, and forms of knowledge, in and through the creation of subjects who are its agents and its effects. It achieves this by interpellation, that is, by calling out to us. The hailed individual, writes Althusser, 'will turn round. By this mere one-hundred-and-eighty-degree physical conversion, he becomes a *subject*' (1971: 163). Similarly, although to significantly different ends, Kelly and Fiveash's posters literally interpellate the (straight) viewer: they call out 'Hey, hetero!'. But rather than reinforcing dominant ideology, or heteronormativity if you like, these images, in effecting a 'one-hundred-and-eighty-degree physical conversion' queer the subject in/of heterosexuality and all that supports and is supported by it.

The six images in the series highlight the privileges associated with heterosexuality, illustrate the dangers of not conforming to socio-sexual norms, and engage with a range of current political debates and controversies. For example, 'Hey, hetero!, Have a baby . . . no national debate', is a response to the recent attempt by the Howard government in Australia to deny access to reproductive technologies to lesbians and single women, on the grounds that parents are (or at least should be) by definition heterosexual couples – hence the notion of the (ideal) family which consists of a man, a woman, and their off-spring. A critique of this ideal and all that it negates on the one hand and silences on the other (single parents, 'non-normative' groups of people who love and support one another, domestic violence, incest, and so on) can be found in 'Hey, hetero! When they say family they mean you'. Here we have 'the family': a youngish (but not too young), white, middle-class, able-bodied, gender conformist, married, hetero couple and their obviously well-planned child, immersed in and surrounded by what one might think of as 1950s-style white picket fence values. In and through the process of interpellation 'the family' (and/or heterosexuality as a hegemonic institution) is shown to be nothing more than 'a constant and repeated effort to imitate its own idealizations' (Butler 1993a: 125). The series also includes 'Hey, hetero!, Membership has privileges . . . accepted worldwide'; 'Hey, hetero!, Get Married . . . because you can'; 'Hey, hetero!, You can do it with your eyes closed . . . no one will hurt you'; and 'Hey, hetero!, Bashers target straights . . . in 0.05% of sexuality-motivated attacks'.

As we have seen, the denaturalisation or queering of heterosexuality can take many forms, can lead to different and often contradictory outcomes, and can produce as many questions as it does answers. Since queer need not be simply equated with same-sex relations, and sex between men and women need not necessarily be heteronormative, then queering what we usually think of as 'straight' sex can allow the possibility of moving away from stabilised notions of gender and sexuality as the assumed foundations of identity and social relations.

NOTES

1. See, for example, Dyer (1997); Overall (1999); Kitzinger and Wilkinson (1993).
2. See, for example, Katz (1996).
3. Overall (1999) offers the following definition of the heterosexual institution: 'the systematized set of social standards, customs, and expected practices which both regulate and restrict romantic and sexual relationships between persons of different sexes in late twentieth-century Western culture' (Ibid.: 297).
4. See, for example, Millett (1977).
5. See, for example, Ferguson *et al.* (1981).
6. For a more detailed critique, see Butler (1990: 120–8).
7. Obviously Jeffreys' interpretation of these practices is debatable. For an extended discussion of Jeffreys position on SM, see Jeffreys (1986). For a critique of this position on SM, see Neath (1987), Sullivan (1997).
8. For a critical analysis of the notion of 'equality' and its relation to feminism see Gatens (1991), Gatens (1996), particularly Chapter 5, 'Power, Bodies, Difference', and Diprose (1994).
9. For a different response to the difficult relationship between heterosexuality and feminism, see Foertsch (2000), who sees her position as a straight feminist, 'an oxymoron, an ontological impossibility... both supremely threatening and thrillingly liberating' (Ibid.: 52) since it has motivated her to develop a critique of the tendency to derive practice from identity (we do this because we are this) and to argue for a shift in focus from identity to activism, from being to doing.
10. For analyses of the ways in which race, class, and physical (dis)ability are integral to the experience of heterosexuality, see Kanneh (1993), Griffin (1993), and Appleby (1993).
11. For a feminist critique of the notion of 'choice', see Bordo (1993), Brush (1998), and Diprose (1994).
12. See, for example, Gatens (1988; 1996), Diprose (1994), Kirby (1991), and Grosz (1990; 1994b; 1995).
13. See Lacan (1953; 1977).
14. See http://www.abc.net.au/arts/visual/stories/s453374.htm
15. See Althusser (1971).

8

Community and its Discontents

WHAT DO WE MEAN WHEN we speak of community, and, more particularly, of the 'gay and lesbian community', the 'queer community', and so on? In this chapter we will consider the commonly held notion of community and the kinds of assumptions that inform it. We will also look at some of the problems or discontents which have arisen regarding the idea(l) and experience of community, and engage with a variety of recent writings that attempt to deconstruct or queer 'common-sense' understandings of community and the assumptions about subjectivity, social relations, and politics, on which they are based.

The Shorter Oxford English Dictionary defines community as

the quality of appertaining to all in common; common character, agreement, identity; social intercourse, communion; society, the social state; the commonality; a body of people organised into a political, municipal, or social unity; a body of persons living together and practising community of goods.

In short, what seems to characterise community is a sense of commonality: of a common identity, a common purpose, or a shared set of beliefs. What is implied in the definitions quoted above is that those who share an identity will have beliefs and practices in common, and vice versa. Moreover, this sense of commonality is often represented in idealised terms as an 'ecstatic sense of oneness' (Allison, cited in Young 1986: 10), a sense of harmony that may not occur naturally, but that could (and should) nevertheless characterise (political) communities such as the feminist community. Following on from this, community, as an ethical and political ideal, is often represented in opposition to individualism or liberalism.[1] This is apparent in the definition of community as 'a network of social relations marked by mutuality

136

and emotional bonds, shared understandings and a sense of obligation, affective and emotional ties, rather than by a perception of
individual self-interest' (cited in Phelan 1994: 77–8) proposed by
Thomas Bender. One thing that becomes clear from Bender's
definition of community is that a network of social relations
marked by mutuality or commonality seems likely to hold the
social good (the good of the community) in higher regard than
individual self-interest.

Before we critically analyse this concept of community in any
more detail it might be useful to ponder for a moment why it is
that people seem to be drawn to such a notion. Zygmunt Bauman's
response to this question would be that the word community 'feels
good'. This is because community is imagined, he says, as 'a
"warm" place, a cosy and comfortable place. It is like a roof under
which we shelter' (2001: 1). In opposition to 'the world outside'
which often seems dangerous, alien, or hostile, one assumes that in
one's community one is safe, that all the members of the community understand and support each other as Bender claims, and that
disagreements, far from being dangerous or destructive, enable
the community to develop and to improve itself. Here community
is represented as a source of strength, a safe place you share with
others like you, a 'home'.

Lisa Kahaleole Chang Hall notes that this search for 'home' is
apparent in the metaphor of the family that is frequently used by
social and political groups or movements. This is clear, Chang Hall
claims, in *Paris is Burning*, and can also be found in the feminist
notion of 'sisterhood', the Marxist image of the proletariat as
'brothers in arms', and in gay and lesbian anthems such as 'We Are
Family'. Robert Nisbet sees no problem with this conflation of
community and family when he states that the 'archetype, both historically and symbolically, of community, is the family, and in
almost every type of genuine community the nomenclature of
family is prominent' (cited in Phelan 1994: 83). However, Shane
Phelan asks, 'how many of us experienced a family or home that
was in fact what the rhetoric of community invokes as a model?'
(1994: 83). The answer, she says, is most likely none.

As many contemporary theorists and activists have pointed out,
this image of community is not only idealistic, but is problematic
for a range of reasons. Definitions of community, such as those
mentioned so far, tend to imply that community membership is a
straightforward issue. One reason for this might be the assumption

that certain kinds of people have, by nature, things in common. For Phelan this belief is central to what she calls the 'ascriptive model' of community. She states that, according to this model, common identity is based upon a primordial bond, a 'natural' basis for community. Race, for example, could be, and often is, seen as a 'natural' basis for community, as could gender or sexuality (if defined as biologically determined). On this model, the identity of the individual – the Caucasian person, the man, the lesbian, and so on – precedes the community that forms around it.

However, Phelan points out that this 'natural' basis for community does not necessarily guarantee community. Rather, according to a number of ascriptive theorists with whom Phelan engages, the 'natural' basis of community can only develop into 'full community' in and through social relations that foster a collective consciousness, a recognition of others as like ourselves (Ibid.: 78). Thus, one could argue that women do not necessarily constitute a 'full community' unless they actively form a community based on their common identity as women, for example, the feminist community. Feminism then, could be said to be an example of a 'full community' because it fosters the recognition of a 'natural' bond between women based on sex/gender. This sort of position is apparent in the writings of those feminists who lament the fact that women, despite their (supposed) primordial bond, fail to recognise or foster a community that would enable them to fight in solidarity against their oppressors (men) – with whom they may nevertheless share other 'natural' characteristics.

The problems with this position and the notion of community that informs, and is informed by it include, first, the assumption that all women are primarily the same, despite differences in race, class, ethnicity, religion, age, ability, sexuality, and so on, and, second, that one natural characteristic will take precedence over others. However, what has become increasingly apparent in feminism is that differences between, amongst, and within women are not simply surmountable by claiming that at a fundamental level we are all the same. In fact, rather than resulting in a unified and coherent community, such assumptions function to exclude multiplicity by ignoring the lived realities of women's lives, and in doing so cause all sort of rifts and divisions within so-called feminist communities.

As both Iris Marion Young and Chang Hall have noted, one of the things that members of (political) communities often experience is a sense of pressure to choose a single identity and thus to suppress any sense of difference that may be regarded as a potential breach of commonality. Lesbians of colour, for example, may feel that they have to form allegiances in and around sexuality rather than race, or that they have to choose one or the other – a tendency which, as the discussion of Barnard's work in Chapter 4 shows, will invariably lead to a politically debilitating inability to theorise the complex intersections between class, race, sexuality, gender, and so on. As Chang Hall notes, 'a lesbian identity that ignores cultural, racial, and class differences, [or] a racial identity that represses sexual differences and multiracial histories' makes solidarity impossible (1993: 222). In fact, she claims that 'assuming that 'unity' inherently exists, is a set-up for major explosions when all our [disavowed] differences surface with a vengeance' (Ibid.: 225) – a phenomenon which we have seen occurring again and again within, amongst, and between communities.

Community can equally well be thought of as something we consciously choose to join. Phelan uses the term 'nonascriptive' communities to refer to voluntary associations of individuals, which, she argues, are most often formed in order to create and maintain non-hegemonic or non-heteronormative identities and life-styles. Such communities often define themselves as opposed to, and autonomous from, 'mainstream' culture. Gay and lesbian communities, SM communities, transgender communities, and so on, could be seen as examples of nonascriptive communities if we presume that sexual practice is not the expression of an innate and essential identity.

It may seem that this model of community is opposed to the ascriptive model insofar as the focus on conscious choice implies that identity is more about group identification than about any primordial essence. In choosing our community, the implication is that the identity we achieve or recognise there is not previously given, for, as Phelan notes, if it were, we would not need to choose to join this community since we would always already be a part of it. Nevertheless, Phelan argues that the seeming opposition between 'natural communities' (ascriptive model) and 'created communities' (nonascriptive model) is not as clear-cut as it may first appear, and that the nonascriptive model of community naturalises identities even if it does not see them as essential. To put it simply, both models presume that identity is unambiguous regardless of whether or not it is natural or cultural: both imply that I can call myself, for example, a lesbian, that this identity is straightforward, and that sharing this identity with others will be unproblematic. But of course, in practice, this is never the case.

It follows that since identity is never straightforward or simple, then neither is community membership. Consequently, debates regarding who should be allowed membership of a particular community and access to community events, and on what basis such judgements could and should be made, are rife within and amongst gay, lesbian, transgender, queer, and feminist groups. The fairly recent controversies over whether or not male to female transsexuals should be allowed to participate in the Sydney Lesbian Space Project are just one example of how a supposed community can be fraught with contradictions which fracture any hope of communion. Similarly, disagreements have occurred over who should be allowed to be a member of the Sydney Gay and Lesbian Mardi Gras (SGLMG), who should be admitted to the parties organised by Mardi Gras, and on what grounds such decisions can and should be made.[2] The cases put forward for consideration nevertheless often continue to be framed in the same old terms. As one letter in the *Sydney Star Observer*[3] states: 'the parties – Sleaze Ball and Mardi Gras – are private celebrations for *our* community' (cited in Bollen 1996: 49). This sense that 'the parties are for *us*' is again apparent in the following cautionary message to SGLMG members contained in the twentieth SGLMG festival guide. 'Members: The Mardi Gras party is a gay and lesbian event. Before you invite your guests, think carefully: will they add or detract from our gay and lesbian paradise? Its our tribal gathering: are you sure they're a member of the tribe' (1998: 113).

Whilst the reasoning behind such statements may, on the one hand, be perfectly understandable, on the other, the question of who exactly the 'we' of these statements is, remains unclear and open to debate. If, for example, the reader of the letter in the 'community' newspaper, or the message in the SGLMG festival guide is a woman who sleeps with men but whose primary relations are with gay men and lesbians, who does voluntary work for gay and lesbian organisations, and who is involved in various forms of anti-homophobic political activism, reads this term community as including herself, what happens when someone else argues that in fact she is not a member of the community or tribe (because she has sexual relations with men and therefore is heterosexual) and thus should not be allowed to attend the SGLMG parties? Moreover, how can such rules and regulations be policed? How can ticket sellers tell whether or not the guests of the person buying the tickets (who is assumed to be gay, lesbian, or transgendered because she or he has been accorded membership to the SGLMG, of which, 'homosexuality' or 'transgender' is a prerequisite) are gay or lesbian or transgendered? What, in fact, does it mean to be gay or lesbian or transgendered, or even queer? Who decides, and on what basis?

As we saw in Chapter 2, the answer to this question is far from simple. For example, women who identify as (political) lesbians, but who do not have sexual relationships with other women, are not, in the eyes of some, considered to be 'true' lesbians. Similarly, if one considers the ongoing debates in a wide range of lesbian magazines it is clear that some women who have sex with both men and women sometimes regard themselves, and are sometimes regarded by others, as lesbians, whilst simultaneously it is the case that such women are not only not regarded as lesbians, but worse still, are seen as a threat to the unity and coherence of the lesbian community since they supposedly want a foot in both camps, communities, or tribes. Take, for example, the scene from *Go Fish* in which Daria (who has recently had sex with a man) is accosted by two figures who force her into an interrogatory space. 'In a pointed reversal of who poses a threat to a lone woman on the street at night, the captors and inquisitors are themselves lesbians . . . and almost all hold Daria in contempt for sleeping with a man and still calling herself a dyke' (Henderson 1999: 57). The impassioned policing of identity and community that takes place goes like this:

Woman 1: What do you think you're doing?
Woman 2: It makes me sick.
Daria: Does it make you sick, or does it scare you?
Woman 3: Just don't call yourself something that you're not.
Daria: If you're talking about me calling myself a lesbian, that's
          what I am.

. . .

Daria: I'm a lesbian who had sex with a man.
Woman 4: No such thing!
Daria: I had sex with one man. You know, if a gay man has sex
          with a woman, he was bored, drunk, lonely, whatever,
          and if a lesbian has sex with a man, her whole life
          choice becomes suspect. I think it's bullshit.

. . .

141

Woman 5: I don't think she's really a dyke.
Woman 6: I don't think she's strong enough to be a dyke.

Likewise, butch/femme couples or sadomasochists are sometimes accused of not being 'authentic' lesbians – or at least of uncritically embracing 'heterosexual desire' – since, according to Jeffreys, for example (1986; 1998), they reinforce patriarchal values and ways of being.

As Chang Hall explains, this difficulty with and debate over definitions is central to the disillusionment with community that many people feel. She says:

Because no one has been able to agree on a single definition of what constitutes a 'lesbian', it shouldn't be any surprise that the struggle to define or create a lesbian community has been so deeply problematic and painful.

. . . When we speak of the lesbian community we're almost always thinking of a very particular subset . . . of all the women who sexually relate solely or primarily to women . . . But even among these subsets, the notion of a singular, unified lesbian community is absurd. Even if every lesbian in the United States was white, middle-class, able-bodied, Christian-raised, and living in the urban environment, there would still be bar dykes, sports dykes, women who aren't into roles, radical politicos, butches, separatists, s/m leather girls, those who aren't lesbians but who are just in love with 'x', believers in the Lesbian Nation, femme tops, Young Republicans, assimilationists . . . piercing queens . . . and that's just for starters. (1993: 225)

We could complicate this even further by suggesting that the so-called lesbian identities that Chang Hall lists are never singular, and that the array of possible identities and complex combinations thereof is infinite. Given this, the assumption that community is based on commonality – common identity, a common political goal, or a set of commonly held beliefs and practices – makes for all sorts of problems, divisions, and exclusions because such a notion of community cannot really tolerate difference. An example of the tension that exists between commonality (or what, in effect, amounts to sameness) and difference, and one of the ways in which is it often (supposedly) overcome is apparent in the 1998 SGLMG commitment statement which reads:

Sydney Gay and Lesbian Mardi Gras Ltd is an organization formed out of the *diverse* gay and lesbian *communities* of Sydney to enable us to explore, express and promote the life of our *combined community* through a cultural focus. We affirm the pride, joy, dignity, and identity of our community and its people through events of celebration. (SGLMG festival guide 1998, my emphasis)

What we see here is both a recognition of difference ('diverse communities') and the invocation of an overarching singular and unified entity called 'our combined community'. So in effect what is implied in this statement is that whilst there are differences between and amongst gays and lesbians, fundamentally, gays and lesbians share a common (sexual) identity which serves to unite and unify. 'Our combined community' then, becomes the ideal(ised) destination towards which we must all work despite the fact that our separate visions of what 'our combined community' will look like will no doubt differ radically from one another. Given this, one wonders whether 'our combined community' is in fact the 'paradise' that many have envisaged it to be, or whether it is far from perfect, or perhaps even impossible?

Bauman and others have suggested that community as it is commonly imagined is, first, not available to us since it does not and cannot exist, and, second, is an idealised image of a state we desire to inhabit or to possess precisely because we cannot inhabit or possess it. In order to illustrate this claim, Bauman points out that community is almost always represented nostalgically as either a 'paradise lost' – something we once had and wish to return to – or a 'paradise to be found' or made, that is, something which will exist in the future even though it may never have existed in the past.[4] We can see these sorts of idea(l)s at work in various of the theoretical and political positions taken by gay and lesbian writers and activists discussed in earlier chapters. For example, liberationists assume that homosexuality or perhaps even a poly-morphous sexuality, has been repressed by normative society and that the goal of politics is to free this innate state or potential in everyone. Presumably this would then make way for a community of (at least sexually) free individuals. Assimilationists, like liberal feminists, have argued for inclusion in mainstream society, for the right to be seen as equal with, and fundamentally the same as, everyone else. Again, the assimilationist or liberal agenda is informed by a desire for sameness, or for community, if you like. This is sometimes represented as a state that could be returned to in and through social change, and sometimes as a state of affairs that has yet to be achieved but which can and will come into being if certain steps are taken. Queer Theory could also be said to some-times promote a sort of a narrative of progression, to imagine a

143

future in which fluidity, heterogeneity, and so on, exist unrestrained. On the other hand, critics of Queer Theory often represent it as an example of a more general postmodern malady, a sort of a homesickness, which results from the loss of identity, of community, of notions of progress, and of other modernist principles and practices.

So why is it that community cannot exist, and as a consequence we desire it and/or mourn it so desperately? There are a range of sometimes competing and contradictory reasons that have been put forward by cultural theorists. In *Civilization and its Discontents*, for example, Freud claims that the subject is always torn between self-interest (the egoistic urge) and the interests of the group (the altruistic urge). Bauman develops a similar line of argument, suggesting that communities demand, at least implicitly, obedience and loyalty in return for the sense of belonging that they promise to provide. The trade-off , as Bauman sees it, is if 'you want security . . . [you have to g]ive up your freedom, or at least a good chunk of it' (2001: 4).

As can be seen in the debates discussed both in this chapter and in Chapter 2, and in the scene from *Go Fish* mentioned earlier, being a secure member of a community necessarily entails policing the community and its boundaries, making sure that those who are on the inside really are members of your 'tribe' and that those who are not, remain outside. Drawing on Derrida's critique of the metaphysics of presence,[5] Young explains this dilemma as paradigmatic of, and endemic to, 'a logic of hierarchical opposition' (1986: 3). She argues that any attempt to define a unified (community) identity necessarily involves excluding elements that seem to contradict the desired totality. It is a case, she says, of separating 'the pure from the impure' (Ibid.: 3), and displacing the 'impure' onto the 'other', the outside. And, of course, if the unified identity of the community or the subject is to remain intact then the borders between self and other, inside and outside, must not be transgressed: 'the logic of identity seeks to keep those borders firmly drawn' (Ibid.: 3). However, Young, like Derrida, argues that in fact since the other is always already an aspect of the self, then absolute distinctions are logically impossible: discrete entities do not, and cannot, exist.

Bauman agrees that the logic of identity is central to the creation and maintenance of a sense of belonging, and thus belonging, he claims, will necessarily entail speaking the same 'language' as the other members of your community, embracing the same beliefs, participating in the same practices, and consistently policing one's behaviour, thoughts, desires, and so on. It will mean, as we have seen, excluding those who do not do these things, and continually patrolling the boundaries between those who do and those who do not. It will mean viewing every other individual or group as friend (a member of your community) or foe (not just not a member of the community, but more importantly, a potential enemy or threat to the community and all that it holds dear) (Bauman 2001: 3–4). Bauman, however, seems less disturbed by what Young identifies as the logic of identity and the fact that it is central to the ideal of community, and more with the idea that any attempt to achieve community will necessarily involve the giving up of one's freedom. In short, for Bauman, like Bender, there is a fundamental tension between personal freedom and belonging or community: community is tantamount to conformity, and therefore to the (at least potential) loss of individuality. In political philosophy more generally, there have been many and varied attempts made to overcome, or at least respond to, this tension, from Hobbes' notion of the body politic (the Leviathan),[6] to Rousseau's model of the social contract,[7] from Hegels' concept of Spirit ('the we that is I and the I that is we'),[8] to Rorty's attempts to imagine a 'contingent' community.[9]

But for Young, the aim is neither to reconcile community and individualism, nor to give one precedence over the other. This is because each is infused with the same logic or the logic of Sameness, and thus entails the denial of difference. Liberal individualism, she says, 'denies difference by positing the self as a solid, self-sufficient unity... Community, on the other hand, denies difference by positing fusion rather than separation as the social ideal' (1986: 7).

Another theorist who is troubled by the conception of a unified community, and its associated denial of difference is Linnell Secomb. In a paper entitled 'Queering Community', Secomb makes the point that whilst identities such as gay and lesbian have been challenged by poststructuralist critiques of subjectivity and debates that have taken place in Queer Theory, the notion of community as a collection of individuals nevertheless 'seems to have remained strangely immune to these debates' (1997: 10). To put it another way, Secomb, like Chang Hall, argues that one of the main problems with the ideal of community is that it is founded on the assumption that subjectivity or identity is 'singular and fixed, self-evident and mutually exclusive' (Chang Hall 1993: 221). For post-structuralist theorists like Secomb, subjectivity is constituted in and through relations with others and thus is never autonomous, singular, unified, or static, but rather, is relational, heterogenous, fractured, and in-process.

Accepting these ideas entails recognising that 'shared characteristics' 'exist as such only within a given community of understanding' (Phelan 1994: 81). For example, the category 'homosexual' is not an essential thing that somehow exists outside of or prior to culture; rather, it is a multifaceted mode of being (or diverse modes of being) that is culturally and historically specific. There is no such thing as a homosexual outside of a given system in which such a concept exists in all its complexities. Phelan's (poststructuralist) thesis is that identity does not simply pre-exist community since subjectivity is constituted in and through relations with others and with a world and is continually in-process. But for Phelan, recognising that identity is not essential does not necessarily mean that one must therefore abandon the concept of identity altogether. Indeed, Phelan argues that a notion of identity, however provisional, is necessary if collective action is to occur, thus she is drawn to Spivak's 'stategic essentialism', a term that describes the 'strategic' and temporary positing of a (non-essential) identity for a specific purpose. Similarly, she is loath to abandon community and suggests instead that we 'think of it as a process' (Ibid.: 87) which, like subjectivity, is always in a state of becoming and thus is open to, and requires, negotiation. Ultimately, then, Phelan's aim is not to find ways in which to make community happen, but nor does she want to abandon it as an impossibility. Rather, Phelan is concerned with analysing the communities (or at least the alliances) which she claims we do have, the ways in which we negotiate them, the strategic identities that (provisionally) form in and through them, and the benefits and costs involved.

Rather than focusing on strategic identities and the possibility of (temporary) consensus in and through rational negotiation, Secomb, drawing in part on the work of Jean-Luc Nancy, proposes 'an interpretation of community as an expression of difference and diversity that is made manifest through disagreement and disunity' (2000: 134) – a notion that is supported by the continual negotiations and criss-crossing multiplicitous and shifting cultural positions at work throughout *Go Fish*. This 'fractured community', claims Secomb, is opposed to, and disruptive of, the logic of identity that Young critiques insofar as it engenders and is engendered by heterogeneity. So, if we return to the interrogation scene in *Go Fish*, what matters is not so much what a lesbian is, but the film's refusal to answer the question and its associated illustration of the fact that irresolution, conflict, difference – or more particularly *différance* – is the generative dynamic that renders affiliations both possible and continually shape-shifting.

Central to Secomb's thesis is a model of being as always already in-common, that is, as always already social. Unlike those theorists who posit a distinction and a tension between the individual and community, Secomb, following Nancy, argues that 'singularity'[10] and community are inextricably bound, they are mutually constitutive but are not reducible to one another. For Secomb. like Nancy, community is a matter of 'being-with'. What this means is that there is not first of all being (or individuals), and then being-with (community or society), but rather, being is always already a being-with, the subject is always already a part of the social, the world of others – and vice versa. Perhaps, to put it more simply, one could say that subjectivity is always already inter-subjective: 'a single being is a contradiction in terms' (Nancy 2000: 12).

So, for Secomb and Nancy community is not 'a communion that fuses the *egos* into an *Ego* or a higher *We*' (Nancy 1991: 15). But this is not to suggest that since there is no such thing as an autonomous individual ('a single being') that humanity is therefore a mass of indistinguishable beings. Rather, being is always 'singular plural'. Nancy uses the term 'compearance' to refer to the idea of the 'appearing together' (the being-with) of the singularity (or subject as we might prefer to call it) and the social (others). For Nancy, this inter-relation is fundamental or primordial: community is 'simply the real position of existence' (Nancy, cited in Phelan 1994: 81), 'an experience that makes us be' (Nancy 1991: 68).

Being-in-common (or being-with), as it is outlined here, has nothing to do with the characteristics that people do or do not share, and community does not (and cannot) refer to an identifiable institution, a particular population, or a project of fusion.[11] Rather, community as Nancy understands it, is what undoes the logic of identity, and far from being an object that can be known, community is nothing but this undoing, or, as Secomb puts it, fracturing. In Nancy's terms, rather than making politics and political activism possible, the (essentialist or essentialising) logic of identity that Young is also critical of constitutes 'the closure of politics' – a point with which Phelan seemingly disagrees, at least in part. For Nancy, the political is the art of being-with, and the ideal of community disavows being-with (or the political) in favour of identity and thus is a (futile and misguided) attempt to distance ourselves from the insecurity and instability, the flux and hetero-geneity of being-with. Given this:

[t]he political, if this word may serve to designate not the organization of society but the disposition of community as such, the destination of its sharing . . . need neither find, nor regain, nor effect a communion taken to be lost or still to come . . . [T]he political . . . must inscribe the sharing of community . . . 'Political' would mean a community order-ing itself to the *unworking* of its communication, or destined to this *unworking*. (Nancy 1991: 40)

So, to summarise, for Nancy community as a being-with desta-bilises the logic of identity in and through the invocation of multi-plicity, heterogeneity, or *différance*, or, to put it more simply, in and through the transgression of boundaries, identities, categories. Thus community is an unworking of the humanist model of identity and sociality. Community, in this sense, rather than deny-ing or covering over differences in the service of unity, is the experience of the impossibility of communion, the experience of radical difference. Community is, as Secomb puts it, 'a being-together animated by resistance, discord, and disagreement' (2000: 147): it is an unworking which fractures the humanist myth of oneness and allows for the recognition of irreconcilable but productive differences, and the debates generated in and through these.[12] In a sense, then, one could claim that this notion of com-munity as a fracturing or undoing shares resonances with the way we have been thinking about queer as a deconstructive strategy that denaturalises heteronormative identities, relations, and insti-tutions. Consequently, on this model, queer community is less a collection of individuals who share a common sexual orientation (queer), and more a fracturing process that enables difference and diversity and the radical unknowability of such.

I want to end this chapter by briefly summarising Jacques Derrida's work on community[13] which shares resonances with Nancy's work, but which also, some have argued, differs in sig-nificant ways.[14] What particularly bothers Derrida is the fact that the identitarian logic central to the commonly held notion of community involves a necessarily inhospitable (even hostile) response to the other. As we have seen, a firm sense of identity (whether it be individual identity or group identity) can only be formed in and through the exclusion of difference and increasingly vigilant forms of border patrol. As a consequence of the deep-seated and seemingly inextricable connection between community and hostility toward difference, Derrida focuses instead on the notion of hospitality.

According to Derrida, etymologically speaking, the word hospitality means, on the one hand, the benevolent welcoming of the stranger, and on the other, the power of the one who welcomes to remain in a position of mastery over both the premises or group into which the stranger is welcomed, and, by association, over the stranger himself or herself.[15] In short, this term is internally duplicitous, it carries within itself the seeds of its own undoing, as, one might argue, does the term community for Nancy. Rather than trying to cover over or explain away this tension, Derrida focuses on the ways in which such an aporia keeps hospitality open, alive, dynamic. Hospitality here is not a thing, an object that can be known or achieved, but rather, as John Caputo puts it, is 'an enigmatic "experience" in which I set out for the stranger, the other, for the unknown where I cannot go' (1997: 112). In short, hospitality is an impossible (but nevertheless necessary) action that consists of pushing against the limits of what one knows, moving into a beyond that one cannot anticipate or control. This is not to suggest that hospitality is something the already constituted subject decides to do or not to do. As *Go Fish* demonstrates, one's being-in-the-world is always marked, molded, formed and transformed in and through encounters with others and with a world – encounters that are beyond one's own volition and are central to one's sense of self. For example, one can only identify as a 'lesbian' if such an identity category exists. But as the debates about Daria's lesbian credentials show, identity is never simply a question of self-authorship. Since identity is not essential (and therefore a non-issue) identity categories are open to debate, and in and through conceptual conflicts identities are continuously fracturing, multiplying, metamorphosing. Identity, one could argue, is always already haunted by the other, by that which is not 'I'. Or, to put it another way, identity is social, unstable, continually in process, and, to some extent, is both necessary and impossible. And it is the aporetic structure of subjectivity and social relations that, according to Derrida, disallows the unification, solidification and immobilisation of being, that disallows, we might say, community.

NOTES

1. For a more detailed account of this so-called opposition, see Young (1986). For a critique of this opposition, or at least of the claim that it is central to the (wrongheaded) radical individualism of Enlightenment thinkers such as Rousseau, Hobbes, and Smith, see Werhane (1996).
2. For a more detailed discussion of this debate see Bollen (1996); and SGLMG (1995).
3. This is the name of an established Sydney-based gay and lesbian newspaper.
4. Bollen (1996) also makes this point.
5. For an alternative account of Derrida's response to the ideal of community, see Cornell (1992).
6. See Hobbes (1997).
7. See Rousseau (1968).
8. See Hegel (1977).
9. See Rorty (1989).
10. This is a term that Nancy uses to refer to the human existence. He does not uses terms such as 'individual', 'subject', or 'citizen' because of the connotations associated with them.
11. For Joe Sartelle (1992), on the other hand, community is a project; it is something we have to make in and through shared practices and commitments.
12. Secomb supports this notion of community in and through an interesting and persuasive reading of current relations between indigenous and non-indigenous Australians.
13. See Derrida (2001) and Deutscher.
14. See, for example, Bernasconi (1993).
15. For a more detailed account of the etymology of the term and its effect on Derrida's work, see Caputo (1997) pp. 110–13.

9

Sadomasochism as Resistance?

WHAT IS SADOMASOCHISM? FOR MANY, sadism and masochism are different, but connected practices. Sadism, which *The Shorter Oxford English Dictionary* defines as 'a form of sexual perversion marked by a love of cruelty' is named after the Marquis de Sade (1740–1814), author of *120 Days of Sodom, Justine*, and *Philosophy in the Bedroom*. Masochism, defined in the same text as 'a form of sexual perversion in which one finds pleasure in abuse and cruelty from one's associate', is named after Leopold von Sacher-Masoch (1836–95) author of *Venus in Furs*, and *The Master Masochist*. It was Richard von Krafft-Ebing who first categorised and named these practices in *Psychopathia Sexualis* in which he stated in reference to the latter: 'I feel justified in calling this sexual anomaly "Masochism", because the author Sacher-Masoch frequently made this perversion, which up to his time was quite unknown to the scientific world as such, the substratum of his writings' (1965: 87). Presumably the same logic informed his naming of sadism.

Following Krafft-Ebing's coinage and classification of sadism and masochism as sexual perversions in 1886, Freud refers to sadism and masochism as 'sexual aberrations' in the first of his *Three Essays on the Theory of Sexuality* (1905). Sadism and masochism, he claims, like transvestism, voyeurism, exhibitionism, and fetishism, are sexual aberrations insofar as they involve a deviation from the 'normal' sexual aim, that is, heterosexual coitus and/or reproduction. He later expanded on these ideas in 'Instincts and their Vicissitudes' (1915), 'A Child is Being Beaten' (1919), 'Beyond the Pleasure Principle' (1920), and 'The Economic Problem of Masochism' (1924).

From the outset, sadism and masochism have, for the most part, been represented or constituted according to two dominant paradigms. On the one hand, for writers such as Sade and Sacher-Masoch, sadistic and/or masochistic practices function to repudiate supposedly universal moral truths and the subjectivity(s) to which they give rise. Therefore, those who have followed in the footsteps of Sade and Sacher-Masoch have argued that sadism and/or masochism can be seen as potentially positive forms of subversion. For writers such as Krafft-Ebing, Havelock Ellis, and Freud, on the other hand, sadism and masochism are more properly forms of psychopathology for which it may be deemed necessary to develop treatments or cures. These polarised positions – or at least versions of them – are still apparent in contemporary writings on what has now come, by and large, to be known as sadomasochism – a term which implies the inextricability of sadism and masochism. The recognition of such a connection is not new although the ways in which it has been configured vary considerably. In 1905 Freud stated that:

masochism is nothing more than an extension of sadism turned round upon the subject's own self . . . [A] person who feels pleasure in producing pain in someone else in a sexual relationship is also capable of enjoying as pleasure any pain which he may himself derive from sexual relations. A sadist is always at the same time a masochist. (1977b: 48, 50)

For many commentators, however, sadism and masochism may well be connected, but this does not mean to say that they are simply conflatable. For Krafft-Ebing masochism is the polar opposite of sadism and thus whilst the terms may be related, they are by no means reducible to one another. Ted Polhemus claims that sadomasochism is more accurately represented by 'S/M' than by 'S&M', since the latter seems to imply the existence of two separate (albeit complementary) types or practices, whereas the former indicates reciprocity and 'symbiotic interdependency' (Polhemus and Randall 1994: 113). There are a number of other ways to conceptualise the relation between sadism and masochism, as we shall see in due course.

Before we examine the debates surrounding and informing sadomasochism let us first of all think about what is usually meant by the term. This term has been used to cover a range of practices some of which are not explicitly sexual – although, of course, in the psychoanalytic imaginary all pleasure is associated with sexual pleasure. Sadomasochism can include spanking, biting, bruising, slapping, burning, cutting, fantasies, various forms of restraint or bondage, domination and submission, discipline, the use of sex-toys, uniforms, and so on. According to Juicy Lucy, whose position on S/M is obviously closer to Sade's and Sacher-Masoch's than Krafft-Ebing's or Freud's, S/M is 'passionate, erotic, growthful, consensual, sometimes fearful, exorcism, reclamation, joyful, intense, boundary-breaking, trust building, loving, unbelievably great sex, often funny, creative, spiritual, integrating, a development of inner power as strength' (cited in Bersani 1995: 19–20). S/M is not, at least as Lucy sees it, abusive or non-consensual; it does not involve 'rape, beatings, violence, cruelty, power-over, force, coercion' (cited in Ibid.: 19–20) despite (some) feminist claims to the contrary.

Sadomasochistic practices take place between people of all ages, ethnic backgrounds, classes, occupations, body types, and sexes/genders. S/M is not a specifically gay or lesbian phenomenon, although, as we shall see, many contemporary theorists claim that it can be said, for various reasons, to be queer (at least potentially). S/M is most often described, at least by its proponents, as a form of play or a game that involves the assigning of roles. Various terms are used to describe these roles. For example, a 'top' or 'dominant' is a person who controls the action, determining what is going to happen, where, when, and how, whereas a 'bottom' or 'submissive' follows the top's lead. This structure is loose, as Laura Antoniou, the editor of *Some Women* (1995) puts it, because of the vast array of choices available within these categories or positions. For example, a 'top' may be a Mistress, ordering her 'bottom', or her 'slave', to perform erotic tasks, to pleasure her. Alternatively, a 'top' might be the partner who does the tying-up, the spanking, the disciplining, the giving of pleasure/pain. 'Tops' may even be on the receiving end of painful attention from their 'bottoms' if they so choose. The key element, at least as Antoniou sees it, is who is guiding the action (1995: 58). Similarly, a 'bottom' may enjoy pain, or humiliation, or bondage/restraint, or all of these things, or none of these things, or different combinations of these thing depending on circumstance and personal history.

According to some writers and practitioners, these positions are reversible. Such an idea is apparent, as we have seen, in Freud's work. Likewise, in an interview published under the title 'Sex, Power, and the Politics of Identity', Foucault states: '[T]he S&M game is very interesting because . . . it is always fluid. Of course, there are roles, but everybody knows very well that those roles can be reversed' (1997: 169). For Foucault then, unlike Freud, the roles are simply roles, that is, ways of being that are intentionally donned for particular purposes and at specific times. S/M practices therefore should not, Foucault argues, be conceived of as the expression of an essential identity. This is in line with his critique (discussed in Chapter 3) of the individualising effects of humanist discourses and discursive practices that surround and inform sexuality as it is currently understood and experienced.

However, not everyone shares Foucault's position. In the BBC documentary *Pleasure and Pain*, we find quite a different account of S/M.[1] In the first story, entitled 'Submission', the viewer is introduced to John, a submissive, and his partner Sable whose role as dominant makes her feel '10ft tall ... in command'. From what we see of John and Sable's life together, these roles are not something that they simply don on the weekend, nor are they reversible. Rather, it appears that John and Sable live their polarised identities (in a range of ways) pretty much constantly. Whilst John is not always to be found suspended from the ceiling in a leather harness, tied to a crucifix clad only in the tiniest of leather briefs, or literally relegated to the doghouse, he nevertheless performs the role of submissive in almost every scene of the documentary – whilst washing the dishes, discussing films, going for walks, eating in restaurants, and so on.

It is only when John becomes Rosie that his/her 'role' changes. John puts it like this: 'I feel, as Rosie, I have more power. I can get what I want. As a man I'm very limited ... It's like she [Rosie] knows exactly what she's doing ... using every moment for her own pleasure.' In fact, when John becomes Rosie, s/he also becomes the 'top' in her/his sexual encounters with men. This is apparent in the scene in which Rosie tells the male 'friend' with whom she is dining that she has a black shiny plastic dress that he would love, and that she has worn on other occasions in which she has 'played the dominant part' and given a number of men 'a nice whipping'. It is inconceivable, however, that John would or could play this role as John. Likewise, the viewer cannot even begin to imagine Sable bound and gagged, whipped or humiliated.

Similarly, of the thirteen couples interviewed in *Rituals of Love: Sexual Experiments, Erotic Possibilities* (1994) only two are what you might call 'switchers'. Of the others, four couples have reversed roles occasionally, but not, it seems, with much success. The remaining five couples of the eleven who engage in what could be regarded explicitly as S/M are clearly uninterested in, or even turned off by, the thought of role reversal. Nevertheless, Ted Polhemus, the editor of *Rituals of Love*, stresses that

[not] everyone in the [S/M] scene falls easily or permanently into a submissive or dominant classification. Certainly there are those whose identity is fully linked with either the Mistress/Master or Slave prefix but there are also those who happily switch from Top to Bottom and back again, depending upon mood or situation. (1994: 73)

Perhaps we can conclude from Polhemus' statement that some people live their roles as an expression of what they believe to be their innate identities whereas others treat S/M as something more like a game in which it is possible to take up whatever position one chooses. The latter approach presupposes a level of flexibility, experimentation, malleability, and agency that is nothing like as apparent in the former. It suggests that S/M is a game in which the participants create their 'selves' at will. This sort of image of S/M is apparent in 'Sex, Power, and the Politics of Identity', in which Foucault claims that S/M could be understood as a subversive form of self-fashioning, or self-(trans)formation through the use of pleasure. This is similar to the thesis developed in *The History of Sexuality* Volume II: *The Use of Pleasure* (1987), in which he argues that the ancient Greeks did not read pleasure in the same way that we read desire: that is, hermeneutically. In an interview in a 1981 edition of *Mec* magazine Foucault makes an important distinction between desire and pleasure, which informs both his work on ancient Greek ethics and on S/M as a strategic form of self-(trans)formation through the use of pleasure. He says:

I [Foucault] am advancing this term [pleasure] because it seems to me that it escapes the medical and naturalistic connotations inherent in the notion of desire. That term [desire] has been used as a tool . . . a calibration in terms of normality. Tell me what your desire is and I will tell you who you are, whether you are normal or not, and then I can qualify or disqualify your desire. The term pleasure on the other hand is virgin territory, almost devoid of meaning. There is no pathology of pleasure, no 'abnormal' pleasure. It is an event 'outside of the subject' or on the edge of the subject, within something that is neither body nor soul, which is neither inside nor outside, in short a notion which is neither ascribed nor ascribable. (Foucault, cited in Macey 1993: 365)

This distinction allows Foucault to argue that in the case of antiquity, self-(trans)formation through the practice of pleasure was not a hermeneutical introspective preoccupation, but, rather, a wide range of freely chosen occupations. For Foucault, the self which is (trans)formed through the practice of pleasure is not so much an innate essence or personal identity, but rather something which could be described as a 'strategic possibility'.[2] In other words, sexual practices or practices of pleasure are understood by Foucault, following the ancient Greeks, as practices of self-(trans) formation rather than as the expression of an innate identity.

David Halperin agrees with Foucault, suggesting that the pleasure produced by practices such as fisting, anonymous sex, bondage, and so on, functions – however briefly – to 'shatter identity, and dissolve the subject' (1995: 95). This is because such practices work against the logic of heteronormative sex – a practice that ultimately serves to reproduce selves (in the humanist sense). For example, as Halperin sees it, neither fisting nor bondage are a means to an end, that is, to orgasm, reproduction, and so on. Moreover, such practices are not fixated, he says, on the genitals (as heteronormative sex allegedly is), nor do they reaffirm sexual categorisations founded on object choice. In short, according to Halperin, such practices are non-reproductive, they open up a sort of polymorphous perversity, and they enable us to rethink pleasure and/or sexuality in terms of one's preference for 'certain acts, certain zones or sensations . . . a certain frequency . . . certain relations of age or power . . . a certain number or participants, and so on' (Sedgwick 1990: 8), rather than simply in terms of the gender of one's sexual object choice.

Foucault seems to take a similar line when, in 'Sex, Power, and the Politics of Identity', he says:

[SM is] a process of invention . . . it's the real creation of new possibilities of pleasure, which people had no idea about previously . . . I think it is a kind of . . . creative enterprise, which has, as one of its main features, what I call the *desexualization* of pleasure. The [psychoanalytic] idea that all bodily pleasure should always come from sexual pleasure, and the idea that sexual pleasure is the root of all our possible pleasure – I think *that's* something quite wrong. These practices are insisting that we can produce pleasure with very odd things, very strange parts of our bodies, in very unusual situations, and so on. (1997: 165–9)

For Foucault and Halperin, then, S/M is a strategic game, a political practice of queer pleasure that functions to denaturalise sexuality:[3] it is not the expression of an innate identity. But not everyone shares this view of S/M. For some proponents of S/M, as well as for some of its most virulent critics, S/M practices and pleasures are inextricably bound up with an inner core self. Sable, for example, says in *Pleasure and Pain*, 'I do not play out my role and neither does he [John]. It's got to be utterly real for both of us.' Similarly, Vein (one of the interviewees in *Rituals of Love*) responds to the question of whether S/M is a permanent part of her life, with 'Definitely, it's a part of me' (Polhemus and Randall 1994: 108).

This idea that S/M is the expression of an inner self is also structurally elaborated in *Pleasure and Pain* in which two out of three of the personal narratives are embedded in, or framed by, what one might call a logic of cause and effect. 'Submission' begins with a partial image of John's face accompanied by a description of his desire for 'extreme' forms of bondage. This is interrupted by a jump-cut to a haunting black and white scene in which a small schoolboy is being bullied by a group of children and is, eventually, knocked to the ground. Again, this is accompanied by the voice of John telling us how he was bullied, humiliated, and belittled at school to the point of extreme emotional exhaustion. The bullying scene becomes a primal scene that is returned to repeatedly throughout the narrative and functions, at least implicitly, to provide a cause for John's sexual submissiveness. Likewise, in a highly stylised scene in which her face is partially lit in a way that seems to connote interrogation or even torture, Sable tells of the internment of one of her parents in a WWII concentration camp, and a lifetime of suffering that ensued. This scene functions to 'throw light' on the 'tortured' psyche of Sable who is haunted by the fear that 'if you don't succeed you're going to be put down'.

In the second half of the documentary, in a story entitled 'Dominance', these sorts of filmic devices are again employed in order to explain why it is that David 'like[s] to be in control', doesn't like to be touched by women – since touching is equated with controlling – and enjoys restraining women but refuses to be restrained. In a disturbing bricolage of fast-moving images and cacophonous voices, slaps, and cries of terror, we become aware that as a small child David was abandoned by his mother. Consequently he 'felt very let down by that' and thus, he explains, 'couldn't trust anyone'. David's desire to restrain and control women, then, is configured – at least metonymically – as the result of infantile trauma and as a displaced attempt to retrospectively (re)gain mastery over the first woman he loved and lost.

Narratives such as these are not uncommon in our culture.

Indeed, as Polhemus notes, the submissive's desire, what drives him or her, is often explained in one of three ways. Either as a desire for a break – however brief – from the responsibilities of life,[4] as a craving for attention, or as a need to 'expunge deep-rooted guilt or self-loathing' (1994: 84–5). The second, and more particularly the third, of these explanations could be said to be applicable in the case of John, who, at one stage in the narrative says explicitly 'I feel in some ways that it [S/M] may be a way of punishing myself.'

Similarly, although of course to very different ends, critics of S/M have interpreted the participation in such practices as symptomatic of guilt, self-loathing and/or the internalisation of abuse. For example, in *The Sexual Outlaw* (1979) John Rechy describes gay male S/M as a form of internalised homophobia. The gay male sadist, he says, 'is transferring his feelings of self-contempt for his own homosexuality onto the cowering "M", who turns himself willingly into what gayhaters have called him' (1979: 261). Thus he concludes that 'Gay S&M is the straight world's most despicable legacy' (Ibid.: 262). In a comparable critique of lesbian S/M Diana Russell states that 'sadomasochism among lesbians involves . . . the internalization of a homophobic heterosexual view of lesbians' (1982: 176), and thus is anti-lesbian, anti-woman, and anti-feminist.

What the statements made by Rechy and Russell, and even by John, Sable, and David, seem to imply is that the distinction between pleasure and desire made by Foucault is somewhat tenuous. People obviously can and do read the (S/M) pleasures experienced by themselves and others as the expression of an inner self. To further illustrate this tendency we might turn to Sheila Jeffreys' (1994) critique of a range of practices (including tattooing and piercing) which she claims are sadomasochistic. For Jeffreys sadomasochistic icons such as piercings are in fact 'forms of self-injury that abuse non-survivors . . . sometimes employ' (Ibid.: 21), they are 'stigmata of body abuse' (1994: 21). In effect, then, Jeffreys reads these bodies and/or bodily pleasures as a form of what we might call 'corporeal confession', and concludes that they signify an unhealthy tendency to internalise abuse and turn it against oneself. Thus S/M as a form of self-abuse is read by Jeffreys as both the internalisation and the perpetuation of patriarchal violence. It is, to modify Rechy's statement slightly, patriarchy's 'most despicable legacy', particularly when it is employed by lesbians.

What is important about Jeffreys' article is not so much her definition of S/M, but rather, the fact that it shows that it is possible to read pleasure hermeneutically, that is, as the expression of an innate self. Moreover, in interpreting sadomasochistic pleasure(s) as symptomatic of a sort of a pathological state of being, Jeffreys' article throws into question Foucault's suggestion that pleasure is 'virgin territory' and that there is no pathology of pleasure. Further, insofar as Jeffreys reads the bodily pleasures of the sadomasochist as a form of corporeal confession, it becomes evident that identity can never be simply self-authored or self-(trans)formed as Foucault might put it.

In the article mentioned above, and in her work more generally, it is apparent that Jeffreys shares Diana Russell's belief that S/M and feminism are mutually exclusive. This is because S/M exemplifies what Jeffreys refers to as 'heterosexual desire', that is, a desire that is organised around eroticised dominance and submission' (1998: 76); a desire in which one participant is 'othered'. What most bothers Jeffreys, then, is the inequality that appears to be at the very heart of S/M. Perhaps one way to counter this kind of argument would be to deny that S/M is based on inequality, but this is a proposition that one rarely comes across in the writings of S/M proponents. Instead what we find are attempts to sever the association between inequality and abuse. Ted Polhemus' endeavor to do so involves positing a distinction between private and public, between what goes on in the 'bedroom' (or dungeon) and what goes on in the world. He says:

Obviously S/M is predicated upon a Sub/Dom...Bottom/Top dichotomy...[I]ts vocabulary is that of control, power, dominance, restraint, and inequality...[T]ake away the premise of inequality and you are left with the equivalent of a car without a motor...with 'vanilla sex'...[But S/M] is not...simply the actual inequalities of real-life ...extended into the sexual field...[S/M] is best understood as a sort of a game – an enclosed microcosm with its own rules and territory – and as such...*it is autonomous from real-life inequalities.* (1994: 73–4, my emphasis)

For Polhemus, then, the relation between S/M and 'real life' is one of absolute separation and thus the abuses that occur in and through the inequalities that exist in the world have nothing to do with the inequality that drives S/M (and vice versa). Lynda Hart, on the other hand, argues against such a separation. For Hart, the playing of a game, the acting out of 'roles' or 'theatre', as it is often understood, is not the *opposite of life* as it is sometimes posited. Nor does 'playing a role' take one out of the ideological circulation of the dominant culture. The way in which 'theatre' is used as an implied synonym for 'fantasy' ignores the complexities of both. (1998: 64)

In short, Hart claims that the S/M scene and the 'outside world', 'fantasy' and 'reality', are neither consonant, nor 'entirely disjunctive' (Hart and Dale 1997: 350). However, in making a claim such as this, Hart is not suggesting that there is a simple cause and effect relation between one's history and one's desires or sexual pleasures as is implied in the narratives of Sable, John, and David.

Pat Califia, one S/M's most well-known toast-mistresses, also acknowledges that sexuality is culturally shaped and that therefore it is impossible to posit an absolute distinction between the dichotomous logic that is a powerful part of S/M, and social relations more generally, informed as they are by a humanist ontology. However, given that all sexuality is socially constructed, it is difficult to imagine that some kinds of sexual relations are somehow untainted by, for example, patriarchy, as suggested by feminists such as Jeffreys and Russell. Indeed, Calfia vehemently opposes the suggestion that S/M 'is the result of institutionalized injustice to a greater extent than heterosexual marriage' (1996: 233).

Patrick D. Hopkins, who also recognises that sexuality and sociality are inextricably bound, has argued that S/M could be thought of as a simulation rather than a replication of patriarchal values and relations. Whilst replication implies the reproduction of patriarchal modes of behavior in an alternative context (the S/M scene), simulation, Hopkins claims, implies that S/M replays such behaviors in a significantly different context, thus, in a sense, re-inscribing them. He says:

SM participants do not rape, they do rape scenes ... do not enslave, they do slave scenes ... do not kidnap, they do capture and bondage scenes ... As with other kinds of ... simulations, there appear to be many similarities between the 'real' activity and the staged activity ... But similarity is not sufficient for replication. Core features of real patriarchal violence, coercive violence, are absent. (1994: 8)

Foucault takes a position comparable to Hopkins, describing S/M as something other than the simple reproduction of (heteronormative or patriarchal) power; as 'an acting out of power structures by a strategic game that is able to give sexual pleasure or bodily pleasure' (1997: 169). Similarly, in 'A Secret Side of Lesbian Sexuality', Califia states that 'in an SM context, the uniforms, roles

and dialogue become a parody of authority, a challenge to it'
(1983a: 135). And Robert Hopcke's claim that S/M is a politically
powerful practice for gay men, a poignant way to 'give a patriarchal, heterosexist society a stinging slap in the face by calling upon
the masculine power of men's connection to men to break the
boxes of immaturity and effeminacy into which gay men have been
put (1991: 71), draws on the assumption that the recontextualisa-
tion and/or parody of patriarchal or heteronormative values and
relations enables a subversive rewriting of such. The question is,
does it? How exactly, one might ask, does a man dominating a
woman in an S/M scene differ from a husband forcing his wife to
have sex in the context of the so-called 'real' world? And how does
the former undermine the latter, presuming, of course, that it does?

One response would be that in an S/M scene power is not
connected to privilege. What informs this claim is, first, the belief
that S/M roles are not the expression of a true self, and, second,
that they are reversible or at least not set in stone as social roles
seem to be. Califia claims that participants in an S/M scene choose
which role they want to play and thus exercise a level of freedom
unavailable in most other circumstances. Or as she puts it: 'If you
don't like being . . . a bottom switch your keys. Try doing that with
your biological sex or your race or your socioeconomic status'
(1996: 233). In effect, then, S/M could be said to provide an
opportunity for individuals to inhabit positions of 'privilege' from
which they are, in everyday life, excluded. But, as Leo Bersani has
noted:

> this doesn't mean that 'privilege' is contested; rather you get to enjoy
> its prerogatives even if you're not one of the privileged . . . Everyone
> gets a chance to put his or her boot in someone else's face – but why
> not question the value of putting on boots for that purpose in the first
> place? (1995: 18)

So, the question remains, does S/M queer heteronormativity by
challenging the hierarchical dichotomous system of evaluation on
which normative notions of identity and difference are founded, or
does it simply play around with or reverse normative hierarchies
and thus perpetuate conservative, dichotomous, and potentially
destructive modes of being?

Let us explore this question further by returning to the idea
that S/M roles are not an expression of one's inner self, but rather,
are fluid, non-essential, freely chosen, subject positions that
destabilise the humanist model of the subject and the logic of

cause and effect which informs, and is informed by, it. In the quotation from Robert Hopcke cited earlier, the author suggests that gay men have historically been associated, in the heteronormative imaginary at least, with femininity, and thus with subservience, penetrability, inferiority, and so on. S/M, he argues, is an 'unadulterated reclamation of masculinity' (1991: 71), and as such it obliterates (or at least reinscribes) the stereotype of the immature and effeminate 'sissy'. Given the possibility of role-reversal and the ensuing denaturalisation of the commonly assumed link between submission, femininity, and inferiority, even the man who is dominated, humiliated, or penetrated by his male S/M partner can no longer be regarded – according to the logic that informs Hopcke's thesis – as socially inferior to so-called 'real men'. Distinctions and oppositions no longer hold, which is not to say that they cannot be enacted (strategically).

This sort of slippery logic is apparent in a number of the interviews in *Rituals of Love*, and also in *Pleasure and Pain*. For example, in the latter, Sable says of John, the submissive partner in the top/bottom dyad, 'basically he's stronger than I am emotionally'. And, in the former in an interview with Franko B. (a top) and his partner Philip (a bottom) Franko says, 'although I'm the dominant one, Philip has more power because he's the one who allows me to do things to him' (Polhemus and Randall 1994: 91). Consequently, Polhemus asks whether it might in fact be valid to conclude that ultimately it is the submissive who inhabits the position of power since 'passivity and unlimited compliance mocks, rather than celebrates, authority, for it denies it its *raison d'être*' (Ibid.: 87). The final bullying scene in John's narrative seems to support this idea. Here John tells the viewer that when the bullying at school finally became unendurable he decided that he must somehow turn the situation around. The way he allegedly achieved this was by ignoring the taunts, the punches, that fact that his books were torn from his hands. In short, by refusing to acknowledge the power of the other children, remaining inert, John enacted what he refers to as a 'submissive rebellion'. In Polhemus' terms John's story demonstrates that the 'submissive possesses the power to define power as an absurdity' (Ibid.: 87).

Perhaps we could conclude from these statements made by Hopcke, Sable, John, Franko B, and Polhemus that S/M has the potential to reinscribe or re-evaluate submissiveness, and to disassociate it from all that is commonly held to be negative in

contemporary Western culture (for example, weakness, vulnera-
bility, emasculation, penetrability, inferiority, and so on). This is
because in S/M – as it is represented in the above-mentioned
accounts – the 'bottom' seems ultimately to be the 'top'.[5] What is
interesting, and perhaps telling, is that the emphasis here is on
autonomy, agency, intentionality, and self-definition, all of which
are characteristics of the humanist subject. Consequently, one
might argue that such an emphasis reaffirms heteronormative
values by sidestepping, rather than critically examining, the normative structural association between passivity, femininity, objec-
tivity, immaturity and inferiority. In short, even bottoms need not
be seen as embodying (at least in any essential way) these 'negative'
characteristics. So, does this mean that some of the discourses
proponents of S/M draw on, inadvertently constitute a revalorisa-
tion of characteristics conventionally associated with the masculine
(as the autonomous and active subject of pleasure whose identity
is self-defined)? And if so, would it be valid to conclude, as some
feminists have, that S/M is inherently masculinist or patriarchal?

In a collection of papers entitled *Against Sadomasochism* (1982)
Bat Ami Bar-On takes just such a position arguing that S/M
'embodies the same values as heterosexual practices of sexual
domination in general, and sexually violent practices like rape in
particular' (1982: 75). But surely, as proponents of S/M have
insisted, in cases of violence and rape the victim has been given
no choice in the matter, s/he has not consented and thus s/he has
been reduced to the object of another's wishes and denied her or
his personhood. In an S/M scene, however, the recipient of what
Bar-On and others have defined as violence has consented, and
herein lies the difference. But whilst this response may seem to
some to offer a convincing counter-argument to the claim that
S/M reiterates and perpetuates patriarchal violence, others remain
sceptical. Some feminists have argued, for example, that the
notion of consent has long been used to justify the unequal position of women, and that the fact that women often say that they
consent to certain patterns of male domination exemplifies how
deeply the internalisation and naturalisation of oppression go.
Diana Russell takes this position noting that '[m]any young
Brahmin women in the nineteenth century "voluntarily" jumped
into the funeral pyres of their dead husbands' (1982: 177). Given
that it is hard to believe that anyone would 'freely' choose to do
such a thing, Russell uses this example to illustrate her claim that

consent does not necessarily rule out the abuse of power, in fact, quite the opposite if, as in this case, women consent to die in (what may seems to white Western women to be) unimaginably horrific and painful ways. So, as Judy Bulter puts it, the fact that S/M 'requires consent does not mean that it has overcome heterosexual power dynamics' (1982: 172). But then again, are there any kinds of sexual relations that we can unambiguously claim are untainted or untouched by heteropatriarchy?

Even if we acknowledge that all sexual relations, practices, and identities are culturally constructed and are therefore implicated in heteronormativity, we may nevertheless want to argue that some relations and practices are more problematic than others because they seem much more likely to reaffirm conservative values than to queer them. Hilde Hein, for example, argues that because it endorses the degradation of human beings (even when such persons have consented) S/M promotes the idea – at least implicitly – that the abuse of human beings is acceptable.[6] Diana Russell also believes that even if the participants involved in a particular S/M scene are opposed to violence, torture, and so on, S/M imagery more generally fosters the (heteropatriarchal) idea that women really do enjoy 'rough' sex.

Many S/M proponents have been critical of the feminist focus on S/M, arguing that often such writers have no first-hand experience of S/M and therefore grossly misrepresent it. S/M, says Califia, has been distorted and disparaged by some feminists in much the same way that homosexuality has been by homophobes. One of the ways in which such distortion has been achieved is through the association of S/M with atrocities such as the genocide of the Jews by the Nazis. Sheila Jeffreys makes such a connection in a paper entitled 'Sado-Masochism: The Erotic Cult of Fascism' (1986) and substantiates the analogy by citing the existence of one British S/M dyke who allegedly wears swastikas and other such symbols associated with fascism. From this Jeffreys concludes that all British S/M lesbians support fascism, at least implicitly. But as Jeanne F. Neath – a British separatist lesbian feminist who practises S/M – points out in a response to this article by Jeffreys, 'there are different politics held by different S/M dykes' just as there are 'different politics held by different separatists or feminists' (1987: 96).

Neath's point is an interesting one because it highlights the ways in which advocates of S/M (like critics of S/M) are often constructed as an homogenous group whose beliefs, values, and lives are identical. In short, S/M practitioners are represented by anti-S/M writers as violent, abusive, self-loathing, fascists. On the other hand, those opposed to S/M are (often) represent by advocates of S/M as narrow-minded, puritanical, repressive, fascists. Furthermore, when these arguments take place between S/M feminists and/or lesbians and anti-S/M feminists and/or lesbians each side represents the other as non-feminist. Given this, one could argue that the S/M debates have, to date, functioned in accordance with what Irigaray has referred to as an Economy of the Same. As Lynda Hart notes: '[N]either side can claim a coherent identity without recourse to the other . . . The opposing sides are caught up in an endless cycle of naming and renaming that does not recognize the inherent contradiction of "epistmological resolution"' (1998: 60). In effect, each group sets the other up as its own opposite. So, for example, if the anti-S/M writer is feminist, then she constructs the S/M participants as non-feminists, and vice versa. Consequently, since difference is understood in terms of one valued term and its opposite, such debates (re)produce subjects in accordance with heteronormative logic. Hart, however, suggests that perhaps anti-S/M lesbian feminists and pro-S/M dykes 'are not one another's opposites but one another's doubles' (1998: 38). What she means by this is that each is an integral part of the other, but a part that has been (and must be) disavowed 'in order to sustain the fictive coherence of one's "self"' (1998: 38–9). As we saw in the previous chapter, any attempt to define a unified identity necessarily involves excluding elements that seem to contradict the desired totality. It is a case, as Young points out, of separating 'the pure from the impure' (1986: 3), and displacing the 'impure' onto the 'other', the outside. But, given that self and other never are entirely separate, an 'epistemological resolution' is a contradiction in terms, an impossibility, and, as a consequence, boundary patrolling becomes – at least metaphorically – a matter of life and death.

Rather than simply claiming that the S/M debates illustrate the violence that lies at the heart of identitarian logic and thus of subjectivity and social relations generally, Hart offers an historical account of the ways in which lesbianism has been socially constructed and the impact of this on lesbian S/M. Hart suggests that in response to the figure of the sexually voracious and potentially violent masculine lesbian constructed by sexologists and psychoanalysts, second-wave lesbian feminists tended to downplay the sexual side of lesbianism, and to focus on political and emotional intimacy or woman-centredness as it was sometimes referred to. This resulted, as we saw in Chapter 2, in the construction of politically correct sexual practices that were presumed to be an expression of the innate purity of 'true' lesbianism, and the exclusion or silencing of all those who dissented. Califia describes this state of affairs in the following tongue-in-cheek way:

As I understand it, after the wimmin's revolution, sex will consist of wimmin holding hands, taking their shirts off and dancing in a circle. Then we will all fall asleep at exactly the same moment. If we didn't all fall asleep, something else might happen – something male-identified, objectifying, pornographic, noisy and undignified. (cited in Hart 1998: 49)

Given that this (culturally and historically specific) notion of lesbianism as innate, 'pure', repressed by patriarchy, and therefore in need of liberation, was invested in and embodied by many second-wave lesbians and/or feminists (and still is by many who identify with this discourse), it seems understandable that alternative definitions of lesbianism can be and have been experienced as threatening. And insofar as S/M lesbians have, at least in Hart's opinion, emphasised the fluidity and maleability of identity, 'they threaten not only mainstream feminism's foundation but also its foundationalist fiction of a coherent identity, which may in fact come to the same thing' (1998: 66).[7]

The contextualisation and historicisation of anti-S/M feminism and/or lesbianism is not an attempt on Hart's behalf to justify such a position. Rather, by focusing on the mechanisms of identity formation, and the particular way in which they have functioned in and through the S/M debates, Hart brings to light the rhetorical violence that is at the heart of identitarian logic. In this way, Hart, who is supportive of lesbian S/M, avoids the pitfalls of claiming that S/M is in itself queer, and instead could be said to queer (to expose and thus denaturalise) the discursive mechanisms that have fuelled the debates surrounding and informing S/M and the identities associated with such practices. Hart thus demonstrates that identities do not exist prior to their enunciation, but rather, are produced in and through the construction and negation of the other. Such a model of identity as complex, inter-relational, and in-process could be said to accommodate a range of anti-identitarian projects, of which S/M may well be one since, in

Hart's opinion, S/M does violence to the fantasy of a unified and abiding self. As she puts it:

[T]o do 'violence' to one's 'object' [that is, in psychoanalytic terms, the desiring-fantasy of the one who desires] then is to break open, shatter, stretch, expand, seduce, coerce, force – if necessary – one's *own* ability to imagine alternatives to the rigid, limited, and impoverished sites of desire to which we have constrained ourselves. (1998: 68)

But since the notion of an epistemological resolution is antithetical to this way of thinking then perhaps it is not only unlikely, but, more importantly undesirable that a consensus be formed on the issue of S/M.

NOTES

1. *Pleasure and Pain* is part 2 of a series on masculinity entitled *From Wimps to Warriors* – a BBC production directed by Marc Munden and Penny Woolcock (1991).
2. In 'On the Genealogy of Ethics' (1991) Foucault states: '[T]he self is not given to us . . . [and] there is only one practical consequence: we have to create ourselves as a work of art' (Ibid.: 351).
3. For Foucault, the aim of queer politics is not to liberate our sexual selves but rather, to free ourselves from the notion of sexuality (as it has been constructed in Western modernity).
4. See, for example, Baumeister (1988).
5. See also Farr (1982) pp. 187–8.
6. See Hein (1982), especially p. 87.
7. See also Hart (1998) p. 60.

10

Fetishism(s) and the Politics of Perversion

IT'S NOT UNCOMMON NOWADAYS to hear someone describe their love of shoes, handbags, ties, seafood, or just about anything for that matter, as a fetish. However, traditionally, the term fetishism has been used to signify an attachment to an object that is much stronger than an inclination or a liking. Indeed, *The Shorter Oxford English Dictionary* defines fetishism as 'the worship of fetishes'. Now whilst many of us may, for example, be extremely fond of shoes, and may even buy them more often than we should, it's unlikely that most of us literally revere them. What makes a fetish a fetish, is, as *The Shorter Oxford English Dictionary* makes clear, the fact that it is 'irrationally reverenced', that it is invested with 'supernatural' powers.

The claim that a fetish is irrationally reverenced implies that fetishism involves the over-evaluation of something that is not culturally accepted as an object that 'naturally' deserves reverence. So, for example, amongst Christians the worship of God – or of objects that symbolise God – is not thought of as fetishistic because the assumption is that God naturally deserves to be revered, whereas shoes do not. In a context in which such beliefs are shared by the majority of people, the shoe fetishist's devotion to shoes will be constructed as 'unnatural' and thus as perverse, that is, as a turning away from what his or her culture holds to be the 'normal' path towards self-fulfilment and the attainment of culturally shared values and ways of being. Consequently, a number of contemporary theorists have argued that fetishism, insofar as it is – or has been constructed as – perverse, has the capacity to challenge or to queer sexual and social norms. In this chapter, then, we will begin by considering various understandings of fetishism and then move on to examine critical responses to these traditional accounts and the assumptions that inform them.

As Anne McClintock, William Pietz, and Lorraine Gamman and Merja Makinen have noted, in the fifteenth and sixteenth centuries Portuguese merchants and explorers trading along the West Coast of Africa used the word *feitiço* to describe the ritual objects used by African peoples. This term, derived as it is from the Latin *facticius*, denotes the artificiality of the objects employed by those presumed to be 'primitive' or 'savage' as amulets or means of enchantment. Far from being a neutral descriptor, the term, particularly as it continued to be used by European travellers and writers, implies the 'unnaturalness', the supernaturalness, of non-European rituals. In short, fetishism signified, according to colonialist discourses, a less developed evolutionary status (atavism), or an 'unnatural' regression to earlier forms of human being (infantilism), and was associated with 'pagan' religions and superstitions that were held to be barbarous, idolatrous, and a threat to the truth of Christianity and Western civilisation more generally. As Captain Camille Coquilhat put it in 1888:

The people of Upper Congo, given over to cannibalism, human sacrifice, judgments by poison, fetishism, wars of plunder, slavery, polygamy, polyandry, and deprived of all unity in government, science, writing, and medicine, are less advanced in civilization than the Celts were several centuries before Christ. (cited in Mirzoeff 1999: 135)

Consequently, various normalising strategies were implemented by colonialist forces to civilise the perversity of the savage, to correct his heathen beliefs and practices, and to return him to the path of 'truth' from which he had, for various reasons, strayed.

Nicholas Mirzoeff provides an interesting account of the role of fetishes (*minkisi*) in the struggles that took place between the colonialist forces and the Kongo peoples in the nineteenth century, especially in regions in which explicit and direct forms of resistance to colonial rule were not possible. When activated by specific rituals, these fetish figures, carved in the shape of humans or animals and often driven through with nails, were, Mirzoeff explains, 'able to invoke the powers of the dead against hostile forces, whether illness, spirits, or individuals' (1999: 148). Consequently, the *minkisi* enabled the indigenous people to experience a sense of active agency, to 'imagine themselves as subjects within the colonial system rather than merely its servants or objects' (Ibid.: 150). Of course, this meant that the *minkisi* represented a very real threat to the authority of the colonisers, and as a result, they were constructed as idolatrous, removed by force, and destroyed by missionaries and military men alike.

The *minkisi* were not, argues Pietz and Mirzoeff, a relic proper to archaic West African cultures and rituals. Rather, both authors claim that such fetishes derived their meaning and function in and through cross-cultural encounters, and thus constitute a kind of hybrid figure representative of the tensions and complexities of transculturalism. As McClintock notes, 'the fetish became the symbolic ground on which the riddle of value could be negotiated and contested' (1993a: 6). The fetish, she says, 'is the embodiment of social contradictions, which the individual cannot resolve at a personal level' (Ibid.: 6). What we see here, is that the fetish does not simply symbolise conflicting values, beliefs, desires, fears, and so on, in some sort of abstract way, but rather, becomes (over-) invested with meanings and powers that far exceed the object itself. What is also apparent, is that the fetish is the site at which the battle for identity and difference is played out, and this is an issue that we will return to throughout the chapter.

Gamman and Makinen, following in the footsteps of others writing on this topic, claim that fetishism has been conceptualised in the following three ways: anthropological fetishism, commodity fetishism, and sexual fetishism. The previous discussion of the *nkisi*,[1] and in particular its construction as evidence of primitivism and/or heathenism, is typical of what Gamman and Makinen refer to as anthropological fetishism. They suggest, however, that such an understanding of fetishism as the reverence of an object, and the investment of that object with extraordinary powers, could also be applied to an analysis of Western practices such as particular religious rituals, and the construction of pop and film idols.[2] Such an undertaking, they argue, may go some way towards addressing the ethnocentrism inherent in so much of the work that conflates fetishism with the figure of the racial/ethnic other.

The term commodity fetishism is associated with the writings of Karl Marx. In *Capital*,[3] Marx, who was critical of the depoliticising effects of religion which he believed distorted or veiled over the truth of the politico-economic structures of the time, claims that both religion and capitalism are forms of fetishism that function in and through (mis)recognition, disavowal, and substitution. What he means by this is that in a capitalist economy the value of the commodity is displaced from the labour that goes into producing it, onto the thing-itself, which is thereby 'irrationally reverenced'. In this way, the commodity hides what Marx believes to be the truth of social and economic relations. A commodity, says Marx, is 'a very queer thing, abounding in metaphysical subtleties and theological niceties' (in Tucker 1978: 319). Thus, for example, a wooden table, whilst continuing to 'be that ordinary everyday thing, wood', once it 'steps forth as a commodity... is changed into something transcendent' (Ibid.: 320). In short, the table takes on a life of its own and enters into relations with other things and with the world of human commerce: it is no longer a piece of wood shaped by the hand of a particular person, it becomes a thing-in-itself with its own essence, its own powers, its own functions.

Gamman and Makinen suggest that it was the work of Thorstein Veblen[4] that enabled a shift from the focus on production in Marx's account of commodity fetishism, to a consideration of consumption and the conferment of 'unnatural' value from an object to the person who consumes it. Veblen's thesis was taken a step further by Georg Lukács[5] in his account of the way in which subjectivity (and social relations) are constituted as an abstraction in and through the consumption of commodities. For Lukács there is no outside of commodity fetishism, or reification as he called it. There is, he writes, 'no natural form in which human relations can be cast, no way in which man can bring his physical and psychic "qualities" into play without their being subjected increasingly to this reifying process' (cited in Gamman and Makinen 1994: 31). In other words, commodity fetishism perverts (and/or fetishises) not only the commodity, but also the subject who consumes the object, and the forms of social relations that are engendered in and through such an all-encompassing economy. Here, life, in its entirety, becomes fetishistic.

The third account of fetishism, and the one that we will focus most closely on, is sexual fetishism. Probably the best-known theorist of sexual fetishism is Sigmund Freud, but before we turn to his somewhat infamous writings on the topic I want, first, to mention Paul Gebhard's model of the four stages of sexual fetishism, and, second, to touch very briefly upon the sort of medical discourses that no doubt had a profound effect on Freud's work. In a paper published in 1969 Gebhard divides what in Freud's works appears to be a continuum of fetishistic behaviour into four levels, the first of which involves only a slight preference for certain kinds of sexual practices and/or partners, and thus should not really be thought of as fetishism proper. The second level involves a strong preference for particular practices, and/or partners, and is described by Gebhard as the 'lowest intensity of fetishism'. Specific stimuli are essential for sexual arousal and performance on the third level which constitutes a 'moderate intensity of fetishism', whereas, on the fourth level particular stimuli take the place of a sexual partner, and this is thus described as 'high level fetishism' (cited in Gamman and Makinen 1994: 38). Like Gamman and Makinen, I believe Gebhard's model is useful in that it allows us to consider fetishism as a diverse range of practices and intensities, and to move away from the universalising and essentialising notion of fetishism as a singular pathology. In effect, then, it enables us to explore the historically and culturally specific ways in which we are all implicated in fetishistic practices, whether they be a love of high-heels, a voracious appetite for seafood, a preference for sex in public places, or a tendency to find car mechanics, or tall people with dark hair and brown eyes, sexually desirable. Keeping this in mind, let us now consider, in a very truncated fashion, what Robert Nye refers to as the 'medical origins of sexual fetishism'.

As we saw in Chapter 1, in the West during the nineteenth century there was a significant increase in the amount of time and energy devoted to the identification, classification, and interpretation of so-called sexual perversions. Although many of the perversions examined at this time may not necessarily have been labelled fetishistic, Foucault identifies fetishism as the 'model perversion' which, 'as early as 1877, served as the guiding thread for analyzing all the other deviations' (1980: 154). He supports this claim by explaining that during this period sex was conceived of as a biological function and as an instinct that could, for various reasons, become attached to 'unnatural' objects, that is, become perverted. Sexual perversions, then, were constituted as a turning away from what were considered to be the 'natural' aims and objects of sex. And fetishism, apparently more clearly than anything else, enabled sexologists and the like to 'perceive the way in which the instinct became fastened to an object in accordance with an individual's historical adherence to biological inadequacy' (Ibid.: 154). Freud's account of fetishism, as the result of the male child's recognition of his mother's castration and his disavowal of this in and through displacement, is one example of perverse sexual development, but, what Foucault's identification of fetishism as 'the model perversion' shows, is that Freud's thesis, which, in

1877 was yet to be formulated, was (in)formed by, and is paradigmatic of, a particular way of understanding sex and sexual perversions more generally. In other words, Freud's theory of fetishism did not emerge in a vacuum, but rather, should be understood as an effect of culturally and historically specific ideas concerning subjectivity, sexuality, and social relations.

In 1882 Jean-Martin Charcot and Valentin Magnan, two of the most influential French psychiatrists of the era, published a paper entitled 'Genital Inversions, and Other Sexual Perversions' in which they suggested that all forms of inversion and perversion are the effect of physical, psychic, and moral degeneracy – an idea that was shared, as discussed in Chapter 1, by Krafft-Ebing and others. These theorists drew connections between sexual perversity and moral and social decline. Sexual perversions, they claimed, rather then being the expression of an innate and corrupt essence, 'are the degrading consequences of a weakening of morals in a profoundly vitiated society' (Charcot and Magnan, cited in Nye 1993: 21). In 1887, Alfred Binet, a student of Charcot's, published a paper entitled 'Fetishism in Love' in which he too located the cause of this particular sexual perversion in cultural crisis and the exhaustion of moral codes and practices. In fact, Binet claimed that it is only in such contexts, when the individual is 'already in a weakened state' (cited in Nye 1993: 22), that s/he will seek out perverse pleasures.

Interestingly, Binet claimed that fetishism is an aspect of love relations generally, in that these involve the deification of the beloved. However, problems arise when one aspect or part of the loved one – for example, particular body parts, bodily fluids, or items of clothing – arouses feelings that under 'normal' circumstances are evoked by the loved one in his or her entirety. Thus, for Binet, fetishism, at least in its more extreme forms, involves a perversion of the 'natural' aim (heterosexual intercourse and reproduction) and object (a person of the opposite sex) of love relations. Binet also argued that inversion is a form of fetishism in that it too involves the perversion of 'natural' aims and objects. But, if, as Binet claimed, perversions are the result of the moral decline of a culture, all love is fetishistic to some degree, and inversion is just as fetishistic as an obsession with shoes, then why is it that not everyone is positioned in the same way in relation to fetishism? Whilst Binet agreed with Charcot, Magnan, Krafft-Ebing, and others, that some people have a heredity disposition towards particular forms of perversion, he also argued that a person's life experiences impact greatly on his or her sexual development. Consequently, Binet emphasised the importance of examining individual cases of fetishism since each, he believed, hearkens back to a specific accident in the fetishist's particular psychic history (Ibid.: 22).

What is important about Binet's account of fetishism, at least for the purposes of this chapter, is first, his emphasis on the need to consider the ways in which the individual's history may have shaped his or her psyche, and, second, the fact that for Binet, the normal and the perverse do not belong to qualitatively different registers: the difference between them is merely one of degree. This idea is also apparent in the work of Emile Laurent who in 1905 published a book entitled *Fétichistes et Érotomanes*, in which he posed the following question:

Have you ever contemplated at the National Museum of Naples the Venus Callipyge, that divine piece of marble which throws off sparks of life, grace, and love? Is it not the most beautiful, the most lifelike, the most voluptuous, the most desirable of antique Venuses? In the presence of that incomparable spectacle the fetishism of buttocks is self-explanatory, for it is highly unlikely that all admirers of the Venus Callipyge are sick. (cited in Ibid.: 23–4)

In his analysis of these and many other examples of the ways in which perversion was understood by sexologists in the nineteenth and early twentieth centuries, Nye, citing Lawrence Birkin, argues that such writers tended, on the one hand, to dissolve the distinction between the normal and the perverse, whilst on the other, they 'desperately sought to uphold such a distinction by understanding desire in its radically idiosyncratic form as "fetishes" or "perversions"' (Birken, cited in Ibid.: 27). This kind of ambivalence or tension is also apparent, as we shall see, in the work of Freud.

In 'The Sexual Aberrations', the first of his *Three Essays on the Theory of Sexuality* (1905), Freud identified two types of sexual aberration. The first consists of a deviation with respect to the sexual object, and thus includes inversion, bestiality, pedophilia, necrophilia, and so on, because in each case the object of desire is something other than a living adult human being of the opposite sex. The second type of sexual aberration involves deviations with regards to the sexual aim and thus includes voyeurism, sadism, masochism, exhibitionism, and so on, in which the aim is something other than heterosexual coitus and/or reproduction. Freud included fetishism in this second category on the grounds that its fundamental characteristic is the sexual deification or over-evaluation of a body part, or an inanimate object that then becomes essential for the achievement of orgasm. Indeed, this object, and the pleasure it induces, come to replace the 'natural' aim, 'the union of genitals in the act known as copulation' (Freud 1996: 82–3). Freud does state, however, that fetishism could just as easily be regarded as belonging to the first category of sexual aberrations, since it also involves a deviation from what is considered to be the 'normal' sexual object (a sexual partner of the so-called opposite sex). Either way, for Freud, fetishism constitutes a form of sexual perversion in that it consists of a turning away from what is 'natural' or 'normal'. At the same time, however, Freud notes the rudiments of perversion in 'normal' sexual practices such as kissing and touching which, whilst possibly leading to intercourse, nevertheless are experienced as pleasurable in themselves. What we find here, then, is evidence of the tension identified by Nye, between a reliance on, and reaffirmation of, heterosexual coitus as the norm, and simultaneously, evidence of a proliferation of potentially non-normative practices.

Four years after the publication of *Three Essays on Sexuality*, Freud presented a work in progress paper entitled 'On the Genesis of Fetishism' to the Vienna Psychoanalytic Society.[6] In this paper he links fetishism to the repression of the scopic drive – the drive to look – and to men as subjects of this drive. However, he goes on say:

Half of humanity must be classed among the clothes fetishists. All women, that is, are clothes fetishists . . . It is a question of the repression of the same drive [the scopic drive], this time, however, in the passive form of allowing oneself to be seen, which is repressed by the clothes, and on account of which clothes are raised to a fetish. (cited in Gamman and Makinen 1994: 41)

So, as Gamman and Makinen note, whilst Freud allows women a part in this perversion, it is nevertheless a passive one. In this account, women cannot actively lust after, or experience intense pleasure from, clothes, they can only displace the passive acceptance of themselves as objects to be looked at (by men) onto the garments which at once cover their naked bodies and draw attention to them. It is thus as the site of a tension, a contradiction, that clothing is 'raised to a fetish'.

Despite this association of women with fetishism, in his 1927

175

paper entitled 'Fetishism' Freud strongly suggests that this form of perversion is apparent only in men, and declares that 'the fetish is a substitute for the penis' (1977b: 351). Now, unless one is familiar with the Oedipal drama that informs psychoanalysis, this might seem like a strange claim to make given that supposedly men have penises and therefore should not need substitutes, whereas women do not and therefore presumably might – which may explain why some women choose men as the objects of their sexual aim. But this is not how the logic of psychoanalysis works. In fact Lacan, following Freud, firmly announces the 'absence of fetishism in women' (cited in McClintock 1993a: 2). Whence Naomi Schor's claim that 'female fetishism is, in the rhetoric of psychoanalysis, an oxymoron' (1986: 365). Whilst, on the one hand, it might appear to be a good thing that women are, for once, excluded from the position of the perverse, on the other, feminist theorists such as McClintock, Schor, Gamman and Makinen, and Elizabeth Grosz, are of the opinion that this is yet another example of the denial of female sexual agency, another scenario in which woman functions merely as 'a more or less obliging prop for the enactment of man's fantasies' (Irigaray 1985b: 25).

So, exactly why is it then that in the rhetoric of psychoanalysis fetishism is the exclusive domain of men? Unsurprisingly, the answer is to be found in the 'horror of nothing to see', in the gaping wound of woman's so-called castrated genitals, which, according to Freud, invokes in the male child traumatic feelings, since he fearfully imagines that this may one day become his fate also. But, perhaps in my impatience with this story I've missed out something important, and that is, the fact that for Freud, the fetish is not just a talismanic substitute for any old penis, but rather, 'for a particular and quite special penis that had been extremely important in early childhood but had later been lost' (1977b: 352). This 'special penis' is, of course, the mother's penis which the male child 'once believed in and . . . does not want to give up' (Ibid.: 352). What happens then, as Freud tells it, is that the little boy refuses to acknowledge the fact that his mother does not possess a penis. He cannot, or will not believe it, since he assumes that if she has been castrated then conceivably he too is (at least potentially) in danger of suffering the same fate. Why he reads the mother's body in this way, and why he fears that this particular aspect of her fate will become his, is somewhat unclear, but if we are to continue with the story we will need to suspend disbelief for just a little bit longer.

As luck should have it, 'Nature', as Freud explains, has endowed the boy with a narcissistic attachment to his penis, and it is this that enables him to rebel against that which is too traumatic to acknowledge (his mother's 'castration'). Despite the fact that the 'Throne and Altar are in danger' (Ibid.: 352), as Freud puts it in an interesting and telling analogy, the boy will not only survive, but will, if all goes well, become a man – even if a fetishistic one – rather than a homosexual. So what exactly does the little boy's rebellion against, and overcoming of, this trauma involve? In short, the answer to this question is that the progression of the boy's psycho-sexual development is achieved in and through disavowal and displacement.

The term disavowal, as least as Freud uses it, connotes a sense of ambivalence or ambiguity, an oscillation between opposing viewpoints, a tension if you like. What I mean by this is that in disavowing his mother's castration the boy does not simply maintain, in an unaltered form, the image that he had of her prior to seeing her 'mutilated' genitals. But nor does he completely accept the supposed fact of her castration. Rather, the boy retains the belief that woman, the mother, has a penis, and at the same time renounces it. As Freud states:

In the conflict between the weight of the unwelcome perception and the force of his counter-wish, a compromise has been reached . . . Yes, in his mind the woman *has* got a penis, in spite of everything; but the penis is no longer the same as it was before. Something else has taken its place, has been appointed its substitute as it were, and now inherits the interest which was formerly directed to its predecessor. (Ibid.: 353)

And this 'something else' is, of course, the fetish. As Elizabeth Grosz stresses, 'the fetish cannot simply be equivalent to the maternal or female penis because it both *affirms* and *denies* women's castration' (1995: 145). Thus the fetishist 'both knows and does not know simultaneously' (Gamman and Makinen 1994: 46): as John Ellis put it, '*I know* (the woman has no penis), *but* (she does through the fetish)' (cited in Mercer 1993: 316).

Fetishism thus involves a form of disavowal that necessarily incurs displacement. According to Freud, the child displaces his libidinal attachment to the (idea of the) mother's phallus onto the last object that he saw prior to his vision of her castrated genitals. This fetishistic object – the foot, shoe, an article of underwear, pubic hair, and so on – 'remains a token of triumph over the threat of castration and a protection against it . . . [and] endows women with the characteristic which makes them tolerable as sexual objects' (1977b: 353)! However, Freud notes that in and through this displacement of the child's interest from the mother's penis onto the substitute, there occurs 'an extraordinary increase' in interest, and hence the fetishistic substitute becomes over-determined or invested with 'supernatural' powers. The substitute is fetishistic, then, insofar as it is constituted in and through the 'unnatural' or perverse creation of an object that is irrationally reverenced. The fetish object, as both a *momento mori* and a talismanic form of protection, becomes the irrationally reverenced aim and object of the fetishist's sexual drives.

Perhaps we could conclude from all this that fetishism is not necessarily a bad thing despite the fact that it is allegedly a form of sexual perversion. In fact, insofar as the fetish renders women tolerable as sexual objects for men, then it seems that heterosexuality would be considerably less popular if fetishism, at least in its milder forms, did not exist. Moreover, as Freud tells it, even though the fetish may be recognised by its devotee as an abnormality, it is rarely experienced by the fetishist as 'the symptom of an ailment accompanied by suffering' (Ibid.: 351). However, the fetish is always – insofar as disavowal necessarily involves an oscillatory subject position: 'I know, but . . . ' – an object of affection and hostility for the fetishist. These emotions, says Freud, are 'mixed in unequal proportions in different cases' (Ibid.: 357). Thus whilst fetishism is (in)formed in and through its relation to a universal and transhistorical phenomenon – namely, woman's castration and its anxiety producing effects – it nevertheless manifests itself in a variety of ways depending on the individual's psychosomatic history.

Freud's story of the psycho-sexual development of the fetishist and his peculiar veneration of an object not ordinarily associated with sexual pleasure is illustrated in graphic and, some might say, disturbing ways in David Cronenberg's 1996 film *Crash*. The film begins with three separate but similarly passionless sex-scenes, followed by a car accident in which James Ballard – who is viewing porn and driving at the same time – is quite badly injured, and the driver of the other car is killed, although his wife, Dr Helen Remington, survives. Sometime after their release from hospital James and Helen meet again, are involved in another (minor) car accident, and end up having sex in his car – which is an exact replica of the car that was written off in the earlier accident in which

Helen's husband was killed – in the car park of the airport hospital where both had been patients. The camera then cuts to a sex-scene involving James and his wife Catherine, before jumping to a re-enactment of the fatal crash of James Dean being staged by Vaughan, a motorcycle accident 'victim' whose life project is to live, to experience, what he refers to as a 'benevolent psychopathology': that is, 'a liberation of the sexual energy of those who have died [in car crashes] with an intensity that is impossible in any other form'. To this particular end Vaughan orchestrates the re-enactment of famous fatal car crashes in which he plays a starring role, and, with the help of a police radio, rushes Weegee-like[7] to accident scenes where he takes photographs of mangled cars and broken bodies. James, Helen, and Catherine soon become inextricably bound up with Vaughan and his like-minded friends and fellow accident 'victims' Gabrielle and Seagrave, and for the entire duration of the film the viewer is presented with alternate images of car crashes, sex, and sometimes a combination of both, involving various members of this rather motley crew.

No doubt there are all sorts of ways in which *Crash* could be interpreted, but it seems to me that, in one sense at least, each of the characters in the film embodies the fetishist's inability to resolve the riddle of the value of life and death that each has encountered in his or her own specific experience of the ambiguous relation between the human body and modern technology. Consequently, each disavows what s/he cannot bear to acknowledge and displaces this tension onto the car or, more specifically, the car crash. As McClintock has explained, because the fetishist cannot resolve the particular contradiction with which he or she is faced, it is therefore 'displaced onto, and embodied in the fetish object, which is thus destined to recur with compulsive repetition' (1993a: 6). Thus, the characters in the film are driven to play out their perversions again and again, and nowhere is this more clear than in the closing scene in which James, who, in the car belonging to the now-deceased Vaughan, has run Catherine off the road, bends over the prostrate figure of his wife and responds to her assurance that she is alright with the words 'Perhaps next time darling, perhaps next time'. But there is more to *Crash* than the re-enactment (with monotonous regularity) of idiosyncratic perversions in the form of car crashes and sexual encounters. Rather, one could argue that the film's narrative structure performs the logic of fetishisation, thus invoking the viewer's complicity in the

179

(re)production of cultural fictions that (in)form identity and difference. This deadening repetition, combined with a scarcity of dialogue and a scopic dereliction (a 'horror of nothing to see') reminiscent of some of Cronenberg's earlier films,[8] leaves the viewer, like the fetishist, feeling that there is something missing. Exactly what this is, I know, but . . .

Before we move on to consider some critical responses to Freud's account of fetishism let me first of all make clear why it is that in the logic of psychoanalysis, female fetishism is an oxymoron,[9] despite the evidence to the contrary offered in *Crash*. On Freud's reckoning, female fetishism is not a possibility since there is no imperative for the girl to disavow the mother's castration. Rather, she is much more likely to passively accept it. This is because, unlike the boy, she cannot protect herself against castration given that it has always already occurred. Thus it makes no sense for her to disavow her mother's castration, although that does not mean of course, that she will not attempt to disavow her own, as Freud explains in his account of what he refers to as the 'masculinity complex'.

For Freud, the 'normal' path to femininity necessitates an acknowledgement of castration, the transfer of desire from the mother to the father, and the replacing of the 'active' clitoris (as the primary site of sexual pleasure) with the 'passive' vagina. The woman 'suffering' from the masculinity complex refuses to comply with these imperatives: she 'refuse[s] to accept the fact of being castrated, may harden herself in the conviction that she *does* possess a penis, and may subsequently be compelled to behave as though she were a man' (Freud 1925: 248). To put it simply, she refuses to become the passive, penetrated object of another's (man's) desire. As Grosz notes, Freud also suggests that 'although the masculinity complex may not necessarily imply lesbianism, nevertheless many lesbians can be classified under this label'. Such a claim is, of course, reminiscent of the view, outlined in Chapter 1, that lesbianism constitutes, and is constituted by, a form of masculinisation. Thus it seems that if we are to accept the (phallocentric) logic that is central to psychoanalysis we must arrive at the conclusion that women can be neither fetishists or lesbians without giving up their 'femininity' and becoming pseudo-men.

What each of the three types of fetishism discussed thus far have in common is that they involve disavowal and the displacement of a set of 'social contradictions which the individual cannot resolve at a personal level' (McClintock 1993a: 6), onto an object – a fetish – which, as a result becomes overdetermined. And as McClintock explains, 'by displacing power onto the fetish, then manipulating the fetish, the individual gains symbolic control over what might otherwise be terrifying ambiguities' (Ibid.: 6). In each case the logic of fetishism could be said to be informed by, and to inform, a humanist understanding of identity and difference, which, as we saw in Chapter 3, is itself inherently contradictory. For the remainder of the chapter we will consider the ways in which fetishism as the disavowal of radical difference functions in the (re)production of limiting idea(l)s regarding gender, sexuality, race, and the relations between them.

Let us begin with the psychoanalytic construction of sexual difference in terms of penis/lack (of penis) since this (in)difference[10] is central to both Freud's and Lacan's accounts of fetishism. In my Queer Theory classes I have found that the most common 'gut' response that students have to Freud's work on fetishism is disbelief, anger, and a refusal to take seriously the claim that women are castrated, and/or that little boys interpret their mother's bodies in this way. So, given that for most contemporary readers the idea that a woman is either castrated, or that her clitoris is really an atrophied and inferior penis (Freud 1977b: 357) is unbelievable, then why, one could ask, does this 'myth' continue to play such a central role in psychoanalytic accounts of sexual difference and so-called sexual perversions?

McClintock begins her analysis of this strange story of (in)difference by raising the question of why it is that in his hasty declaration that the fetish is a substitute for the mother's (missing) penis, Freud does not even contemplate the possibility that the fetish could equally well be understood as a substitute for the father's (absent) breasts. Obviously the answer to this question is that for Freud breasts do not hold much value, at least not in comparison to the mighty 'Throne and Altar' (Ibid.: 352), or the 'family jewels' as male genitalia is colloquially known. What this tellingly hierarchical evaluation of body parts seems to suggest, is that Freud himself over-invests the penis, and insofar as he irrationally reverences this rather mundane object, he constitutes it as a fetish. Or, as McClintock puts it, 'the logic by which Freud privileges the penis in the scenario of fetishism is fetishistic indeed' (1993a: 4).

What is actually disavowed in Freud's fetishistic account of fetishism is women's and/or gender difference and the anxiety-producing difference which he simultaneously 'knows and does not know', but which he cannot control, is displaced onto 'a single privileged fetish object, the penis' (Ibid.: 4). Likewise, what motivates the male child's (mis)recognition of his mother's difference and his ensuing displacement of the crisis of meaning and identity onto the fetish, is the fear of castration, and here 'castration' could be understood symbolically as the loss of self as autonomous, unified, omnipotent, omniscient, and so on. But why would the child and/or Freud fear difference? The answer to this question lies, perhaps, in Lacan's notion of the Mirror Stage which provides an account of the inherently ambiguous character of the ego.

Lacan argues that during the Mirror Stage the identification that the young child makes with the reflection of himself, is both affective and projective. It provides the child with a gestalt – a libidinally invested image of itself as a unified totality – which is significantly different to his experience of himself (as a 'body-in-bits-and-pieces'). The child's identification with this image impels it to long for a mythical past in which it was presumably symbiotically complete (at one with the mother), and, at the same time, to project itself into an ideal (but ironically impossible) future in which it will have complete mastery over itself and be completely separate from the mother (and from others more generally). Thus the child's recognition of its self is, for Lacan, a *mis*recognition in that it is both visually accurate and simultaneously delusory since it prefigures a unity, mastery, and autonomy that the child will always lack. In other words, one could say that the child takes as its own an (ideal) image which is other to itself and outside of its control, and at the same time, is central to its sense of self. What we have here then is an ideal, but inherently contradictory, image of the subject that parallels McClintock's description of the fetish as 'the embodiment of social contradictions which the individual cannot resolve at a personal level' (McClintock 1993a: 6). What must be disavowed if the male child is to take up the position of subject is both the difference within himself (the fact that he is not unified, coherent, and so on), and the other within himself (the intersubjective character of identity) since both inevitably pose a threat to the irrationally reverenced figure of the (humanist) subject.

Given that psychoanalysis appears imbued with a fear of difference, one may well wonder whether or not it is of any value to feminists and other contemporary critics, or whether we might be better off pursuing an alternative theoretical approach to fetishism. For McClintock, the fact that Freudian/Lacanian psychoanalysis is 'profoundly conservative and pessimistic' in its construction of woman as 'inherently and invariably subordinate' (Ibid.: 17), is, in itself, a reason to engage with, and to attempt to queer, such a discourse. More specifically, what motivates McClintock's research is her conviction that female fetishism does not simply exist, but is central to a roaring trade in a plethora of commodities, clubs, and magazines. Gammen and Makinen agree with McClintock citing the existence of a large number of case studies that attest to the fact that female fetishism is not merely the figment of a feminist imagination. McClintock's aim, however, is not to simply add women to Freud's and/or Lacan's theory. In fact, as she makes clear, to do so would be impossible. This is because female fetishism

radically challenges the magisterial centrality of the fictitious 'phallus' and the castration scene . . . [It] throws into disarray the . . . economy of one: the decree that there be only one trope of desire to which women must genuflect, rather than a myriad of competing desires subordinated by social violence and male decree. (Ibid.: 2)

Thus she concludes that the denial of female fetishism is less an accurate description of an ontological reality, than 'a theoretical necessity that serves systematically to disavow female agency on terms other than those prescribed by men' (Ibid.: 2). In short, the disavowal of female fetishism enables (and in fact is essential to) the (re)production of phallocentrism as the over-valuation of the male sex organ and all that it fetishistically stands in for. Consequently, claiming that female fetishism can and does exist is tantamount to unveiling the fact that woman's castration is 'a *hole* in men's signifying economy' (Irigaray 1985a: 50), a blind spot in the phallocentric conception of (in)difference. Female fetishism, then, queers phallocentric logic and the notions of gender and sexuality that it engenders.

In her paper 'Lesbian Fetishism?'[11] Elizabeth Grosz pursues the possibility of such a phenomenon to quite different ends. As she sees it, the lesbian – the woman 'suffering' from a masculinity complex – like Freud's fetishist, disavows castration (her own rather than her mother's), takes on a fetishistic substitute for the phallus (another woman) 'and through this love-object is able to function as if she has . . . the phallus' (1995: 153). However, Grosz goes on to suggest that unlike the fetishist who, as Freud notes, is

183

the most contented of all perverts, the 'masculine' woman and/or lesbian 'remains the least contented' (Ibid.: 153) since she faces social ostracisation to a degree rarely experienced by Freud's fetishist. Her fetish, writes Grosz, 'is not the result of a fear of femininity but a love of it; it does not protect her from potential danger, for it introduces her to the effects of widespread social homophobia' (Ibid.: 153). So, given both the similarities and the differences between the 'masculine' lesbian and Freud's fetishist, is it possible or useful to conflate the two[12] in order to show that in fact female fetishism is not, despite claims to the contrary, a contradiction in terms? Grosz concludes her article by pondering what might be gained by describing (butch) lesbianism as fetishistic, and decides that in fact she, like Freud's fetishist, finds herself oscillating between believing (that (some) women can be fetishists), and not believing (that 'masculine' women can, or should, conceive of themselves in this way). She feels, on the one hand, that it is strategically necessary to stretch (perhaps to breaking-point) psychoanalytic paradigms, but on the other, is uncomfortable with the pathologising, and universalising tendencies inherent in psychoanalysis which, she acknowledges, seem impossible to destabilise without bringing down the whole theoretical edifice.

Whilst Grosz's strategic juxapositioning of the butch lesbian and the fetishist does undermine Freud's account of fetishism by bringing to light its internal contradictions, it could nevertheless be said to simultaneously reinforce the primacy of the phallus, the equation of lesbianism with 'masculinity', the invisibility of the femme, the image of the lesbian as a somewhat sad benighted creature, and a hierarchy of forms of female embodiment. Similar criticisms could be made of the project undertaken by Murray Healy in his book entitled *Gay Skins: Class, Masculinity, and Queer Appropriation* (1996). One of the things that intrigues Healy about the gay male skin is his love of clothes and symbols traditionally associated with a relatively narrow and rigid working-class image of masculinity, and worse still, with a hatred of difference, in particular, racism and homophobia. Why is it, Healy asks, that gay skins are attracted to the DM boots, the tight jeans with rolled-up legs, the cropped hair, the braces, and tattoos worn by other (gay) skins. In response to this question, Healy draws on Freud's account of fetishism in order to suggest that gay skins fetishise masculinity: that 'the fervent extremes of the masculine signifiers used may be seen as a symptom of traumatic amnesia: an attempt to forget that queers are not real men' (Ibid.: 107). Healy goes on to explain that having a penis does not guard against the castrating effects of a phallocentric system in which the gay man (as feminised invert) is constructed as both having and not having the signifier of masculinity. He says:

Where one is the same as one's sexual partner, the partner's [symbolic] castration would infer one's own, so the femininity of both must be denied through fetish . . . The [gay skins'] phallic fetishes guard against castration inherent in earlier homosexual identities, reinstating them as real men. (Ibid.: 107)

This, he goes on to claim, would explain why some gay skins prefer to keep their clothes on during sex, since without these phallic signifiers their 'masculinity' would once again be called into question.

Consequently, it may seem that rather than posing a challenge to Freud's heteronormative understanding of fetishism, Healy's account of the fetishisation of masculinity by gay skins functions to (re)inscribe gay male bodies and the relations between them as perverse, that it may, in effect, pathologise them. However, in a later chapter entitled 'The Queer Appropriators', Healy, drawing on the work of Judith Butler, suggests that the image cultivated by gay skins could be read as a 'queer tactic' (Ibid.: 185), as a performative (re)appropriation of (hyper)masculinity that functions to subvert phallic law through a process of denaturalisation. In doing so, Murray seems – at least implicitly – to share with Heather Findlay the belief that parody 'is a fundamentally fetishistic strategy' (Findlay 1996: 161) that may prove politically pertinent for lesbians and gays. In a sense, then, this second account of gay male clone styles as a fetishistic parody that at once appropriates and queers normative notions of masculinity, could be said to function as a (queer) critique of Healy's earlier explanation of gay skin style as the fetishistic disavowal of castration, rather than simply as an alternative to it.

Finally, we will consider the role that fetishism plays in the construction of racial difference, by briefly discussing two significantly different but connected analyses developed by Kobena Mercer in a paper entitled 'Reading Racial Fetishsism: The Photographs of Robert Mapplethorpe'. This paper consists of two essays, the first of which was originally published in 1986, and the second – which consists of a reevaluation of the position outlined in the first – in

185

1989. In the first essay Mercer argues that Robert Mapplethorpe's photographs of black male nudes[13] exemplify racial and sexual fantasies regarding black men's bodies, and thus illustrate the fetishistic structuring of the white colonialist gaze. Through his use of the generic codes and conventions associated with 'the nude', Mapplethorpe allegedly immobilises and silences the black man, reducing him to nothing more than a big black penis 'in the name of a transcendental aesthetic ideal' (Mercer 1993: 312). Drawing on Freud's account of fetishism, Laura Mulvey's notion of the gaze (see Chapter 11), and Homi Bhabha's[14] and Frantz Fanon's[15] analyses of racial stereotypes and colonialism, Mercer suggests that Mapplethorpe's colonialist gaze is (in)formed by an oscillation between the 'sexual idealization of the racialized other and anxiety in defense of the white male ego' (Ibid.: 312), by an 'ambiguous axis on which negrophilia and negrophobia intertwine' (Ibid.: 316). In short, then, Mapplethorpe inhabits the position of Freud's fetishist, but in this case the fantasy of mastery over difference is played out in relation to race, rather than gender. In order to overcome his fascination and fear, Mapplethorpe creates fetishistic images (such as *Man in a Polyester Suit*) that simultaneously affirm and deny the colonialist myth/fantasy/fear of the (omni)potent black penis, or as Mercer puts it, 'Mapplethorpe enacts a disavowal of this ideological "truth": *I know* (it's not true that all black men have huge penises) *but* (in my photo they do)' (Ibid.: 317).

In 'The Mirror Looks Back: Racial Fetishism Reconsidered', published three years later, Mercer acknowledges that 'ambivalence cuts both ways' (Ibid.: 318) and that consequently, what is needed is an account of ambivalence 'not as something that occurs "inside" the text, but as a "complex structure of feeling" experienced across the contingent relations among authors, texts, and readers, which are always historically specific to the context in which they arise' (Ibid.: 319). To cut a long story short, a number of cultural changes occurred after the publication of the first article, that caused Mercer to consider (rather than simply disavow) his own ambivalent position in relation to Mapplethorpe's images. For example, Mapplethorpe's death from AIDS-related illnesses led to a retrospective at the Whitney Museum which became the focus of a censorship initiative led by prominent members of the New Right, and also to more public and widespread discussions of his work as the documenting of a specific urban gay male community and lifestyle – of which Mapplethorpe was a well-known and trusted member rather than a voyeuristic outsider – that has changed irrevocably in the wake of HIV/AIDS. Consequently, Mercer recognises that Mapplethorpe's subject position is much more complex than he had previously imagined: he is at once a white man and a gay man, an *avant-garde* artist and a member of a marginalised subculture, whose work could be said to upset universalising (humanist) dichotomies such as subject/object, high culture/low culture, black/white, hetero/homo by evoking the interdependency of such terms. Mercer is thus led to rethink the theoretical dichotomous stereotypes (the white man, the black man) posited in his earlier article, and to acknowledge the complexities and ambiguities of his own subject position, particularly as it is constituted in relation to Mapplethorpe's images: that is, the fact that as a black man he identifies with the black men 'objectified' in the photographs, and as a gay man he identifies with the white subject of the (homo)sexual gaze (with Mapplethorpe).

One of the most interesting things about this shift is that it does not involve a withdrawal of the claim that Mapplethorpe's work is fetishistic. Rather, Mercer 'revises the assumption that fetishism is necessarily a bad thing' (Ibid.: 319), and suggests that it is possible to read the logic of fetishisation at work in Mapplethorpe's photographs as having a deconstructive or queer function. Mercer says:

the logic of fetishization as [Mapplethorpe] uses it actually *makes visible* the supplementary and interdependent relation between elite and everyday culture, between 'pure' and 'polluted' types, between official and vernacular tastes, at issue in the representability of black male subjectivity. (Ibid.: 323)

In other words, Mercer's revised reading of Mapplethorpe's work foregrounds undecidability ('I know, but . . . ') rather than attempting to bring about closure in and through the (re)production of binary logic and the disavowal of the 'messy, ambivalent, and incomplete character' (Ibid.: 324) of identity(s) and difference(s) as they are lived and experienced in historically and culturally specific ways. And insofar as the fetish is shown to be the site of undecidability, of radical difference, of interrelationality, what becomes poignantly clear is that 'the fetish itself embodies the failure of a single narrative of origins' (McClintock 1993a: 21). Consequently Mercer's rereading could be said to queer fetishism, opening it up to possibilities that exceed and disrupt 'the master narrative of the

Western family romance' (Ibid.: 21) that is central to psychoanalysis and to phallocentrism more generally. What we have then, is fetishisms, or, to paraphrase Irigaray, this fetishism which is not one.

NOTES

1. *Nkisi* is the singular of *minkisi*.
2. For a discussion of the latter, see Gamman and Makinen (1994) pp. 18–27.
3. See section 4 of *Capital*, Vol. I, entitled 'The Fetishism of Commodities and the Secret Thereof'.
4. *The Theory of the Leisure Class*, first published in 1899.
5. *History and Class Consciousness*, published in 1923.
6. First published in 1988 in Louise Rose's 'Freud and Fetishism: Previously Unpublished Minutes of the Vienna Psychoanalytic Society', *Psychoanalytic Quarterly*, 57.
7. Weegee – born Arthur Fellig – a New York-based photographer famous for his depictions of crime and brutality, also used this method of gaining access to crime and/or accident scenes before they had been cleared. In one sense, then, the figure of Vaughan could be interpreted as a commentary on the fetishising of death and disaster by photographer's such as Weegee, and increasingly so, by mainstream media.
8. For example, *The Parasite Murders*, also known as *Shivers*, and *They Came From Within* (1974), and *Dead Zone* (1983).
9. For a more wide-ranging and detailed account of why it is that female fetishism is a contradiction in terms, see Grosz (1995) pp. 149–54.
10. For a detailed critique of the phallocentric inability to imagine difference beyond the limits of what Irigaray refers to as and economy of the same, see de Lauretis (1988).
11. For a significantly different approach to the question of lesbian fetishism, see de Lauretis (1994).
12. In her foray into the dildo debates Heather Findlay raises some interesting and important questions concerning the dangers of conflating the lesbian and Freud's fetishist, particularly given that the latter is misogynistic in his belief in women's castration, his understanding of sexual difference in terms of women's deficiency, and his aversion to the female genitals. See Findlay (1996) pp. 157–9.
13. As found in Mapplethorpe (1982; 1986).
14. Bhabha (1996)
15. Fanon (1970)

11

Queering Popular Culture

IN THIS CHAPTER WE WILL examine the ways in which the relation between queer (and/or Queer Theory) and popular culture has been, or could be, configured. But, first, it is important to note that there is no single correct way to queer popular culture. Rather, the queering of popular culture has taken multifarious forms, has focused on different issues, and has drawn on a range of theoretical positions, often to contradictory or conflicting ends. In this chapter I will discuss some of the questions that are raised when we ponder what queer(y)ing popular culture might mean, how it might be practised, and what the implications of various practices might be.

I want to begin with a quote from Jean Genet in which he states that 'standing before the work of art requires you to act . . . The tension you bring to the work of art is an action' (cited in Doty 1993: 1). What this suggests is that one's relation to works of art, to texts, if you like – whether these are literary, televisual, filmic, photographic, or whatever – involves something other than passive reception. We are never simply consumers of popular cultural texts, but in and through our very 'reading' of them we actively (re)create them. So, drawing on the model of textuality developed by Roland Barthes[1] and others, we could say that the relation between reader and text is one which goes beyond the assumed dichotomies of passive/active, consumption/production, subject/ object, reading/writing, and so on. We are always, as Foucault would claim, implicated in the production of meaning and identity, and hence are both agents and effects of systems of power/knowledge. Given this, it seems valid to claim that the relationship between Queer Theory and popular culture is both political and cultural. Queering popular culture involves a range of reading/writing practices that are political insofar as they seek to expose and prob-lematise the means by which sexuality is textually constituted in relation to dominant notions of gender. And Queer Theory is cul-tural insofar as it concerns itself with the ways in which cultural texts – books, films, television programs, magazines, political manifestos, scientific theories, and so on – (in)form our under-standings and experiences of sexuality and subjectivity. Queering popular culture, then, involves critically engaging with cultural artefacts in order to explore the ways in which meaning and identity is (inter)textually (re)produced. But, whilst this notion of queering popular culture may sound pretty straightforward, the question of how we go about this is not quite as easily answered. The four main approaches that we are going to consider in this chapter are concerned with audience and reception theories, the-ories of 'the gaze', the notion and practice of 'camp', and what might be thought of as a sort of guerrilla tactics. In one sense, each of these approaches to queering popular culture could be said to shares resonances with the others, and in another, they are significantly different, and at times, seemingly incompatible. What I want to do now is briefly outline each approach.

Audience and reception theories are concerned with the ways in which audiences receive and respond to texts. Traditionally this has involved identifying audiences and categorising them as, for example, 'women' readers, 'lesbian' viewers, 'teenager' readers, and so on. So, for example, in some analyses of the reception of particular popular cultural texts an examination is undertaken of the differences between men's and women's responses to porno-graphic magazines. Others explore the differences between black women's and white women's responses to films, sitcoms, and so on, . in which black women are either non-existent, or play a peripheral role. Others examine the ways in which daytime soap-operas or Mills & Boon romances are engaged with by 'housewives', or women of a particular age and class. Whilst these studies are important, the main criticism aimed against them is that they tend to homogenize groups such as 'women', 'black women', 'middle-aged, working-class housewives', and so on.[2] Moreover, it has been claimed by theorists such as Alexander Doty that these kinds of analyses overlook the complex ways in which certain reception strategies are shared by otherwise disparate groups and individuals (1993: 2).

It is for this reason that Doty proposes 'queerness' as 'a mass culture reception practice that is shared by all sorts of people in varying degrees of consistency and intensity' (Ibid.: 2). What interests Doty is not so much how or why gays and/or lesbians read and respond to texts differently to so-called heterosexuals, but rather, the possibility that texts assumed to be heteronormative may contain queer elements, and/or that straight-identifying people can, and do, experience what he calls 'queer moments' when engaging with such texts. Whilst Doty is not explicit about exactly what might constitute these so-called 'queer moments' it seems feasible think of them as perhaps akin to the experience of what Freud refers to as 'the uncanny'. For Freud, the uncanny is tantamount to the return of the repressed, and thus, one might argue that the uncanny constitutes the recognition of the absurd but nevertheless life-producing effects of heteronormativity, founded as it is on dichotomous logic. In other words, the 'queer moments' that Doty refers to could be described as moments of narrative disruption which destabilise heteronormativity, and the meanings and identities it engenders, by bringing to light all that is disavowed by, and yet integral to, heteronormative logic.

Doty goes on to explain that 'queer readings and positions can [and do] become modified or change over time as people, cultures, and politics change' (Ibid.: 8), thereby suggesting that queerness does not reside in the text, but rather is produced in and through the ever-changing relations between texts, readers, and the world. Nevertheless, there is a sense in which Doty's methodology compels him to imply otherwise. For example, in his discussion of the musical number 'The Lady in the Tutti-Frutti Hat' in Busby Berkeley's *The Gang's All Here*, Doty describes the number as one in which 'Carmen Miranda triggers an all-woman group masturbation fantasia involving banana dildos and foot fetishism' (Ibid.: 13). Being a great fan of Busby Berkeley musicals, I was delighted to come across a piece of writing in which such films are treated as something other than ridiculous. However, I am not quite convinced that this so-called description of one of my favourite numbers is altogether apt. On the one hand it could explain why, without my knowing it, this particular number has always appealed to me so much, but on the other, I'm reluctant to concede that the colour, glamour, and exoticness – the aesthetic pleasure, if you like – of this scene is simply reducible to the covert presence of banana-dildos and foot fetishism. In short, what I want to suggest is that it is not so much the case that this scene is, in itself, queer, but rather, that for Doty, the viewing of it constitutes a queer moment. In other words, queer does not function here as a label that one can appropriately (or otherwise) apply to (the essence of) a particular text. Rather than functioning as a noun, queer can be used as a verb, that is, to describe a process, a movement between viewer, text, and world, that reinscribes (or queers) each and the relations between them.

Despite the misgivings outlined above, many viewers and critics believe it is theoretically and politically productive to attempt to locate the queer elements and undercurrents in specific texts. Such an approach to queer textuality is apparent in the 1995 film *The Celluloid Closet*, directed by Rob Epstein and and Jeffrey Friedman. The film is based on a book entitled *The Celluloid Closet: Homosexuality in the Movies* (1981) written by Vito Russo (a gay activist, and co-founder of ACT-UP) – a text which Andy Medhurst has described as 'an impressive act of gay archaeology' (cited in Drukman 1995: 86). Russo, to a much greater extent than Doty, could be said to practise a particular form of queering popular culture, which is perhaps best described as 'spot the queer' in which the primary aim is to dis-cover the (repressed) homosexual or homoerotic elements (the 'dirty secrets') contained in mainstream cinematic texts. What motivates Russo's attempts to 'out' such texts – or at least specific aspects of them – is apparent in the following quotation. Russo writes:

The big lie about lesbians and gay men is that we do not exist. The story of the ways in which gayness has been defined in American film is the story of the ways in which we have been defined in America. As expressed on screen, America was a dream which had no room for the existence of homosexuals, And when the fact of our existence became unavoidable, we were reflected on screen and off, as dirty secrets. We have cooperated for a very long time in the maintenance of our own invisibility. And now the party is over. (cited in GLAAD 1996: 1)[3]

Russo, who died in 1990 before the release of the film version of his book, wrote a number of articles on the relation of film to the construction of (homosexual) identity, which were published in *The Advocate*, *Rolling Stone*, and *The Village Voice*. In his book, Russo explores the way in which the 'invisibility' of gays and lesbians effects reading practices. He does this through elaborating the notion of a 'gay sensibility' or gay savvy as that which allows gays to 'detect "reality" about sexual pleasures even when [they are] obfuscated by a smoke-screen of "appearance"' (Drukman 1995: 87).

The film version of *The Celluloid Closet* repeats this 'archaeological' gesture, by attempting to unearth queer moments in Hollywood films, and thus to destabilise their heterocentric foundations. As a consequence most people who have seen *The Celluloid Closet* are unable to view *Ben Hur*,[4] *Calamity Jane*,[5] *The Maltese Falcon*,[6] *Red River*,[7] *Gentlemen Prefer Blondes*,[8] or *Rebecca*,[9] in quite the same way ever again. This is an important approach that has been significant in the development of gay and lesbian engagements with popular culture. It has, for example, allowed discussion of the different ways in which different people read certain scenes in relation to their own lives and their own perceived position in the world. Its limitation, however, is that it seems to imply, at least on one level, that cultural critics can, like good detectives, dis-cover the queer content – the 'reality' as Drukman puts it – which has supposedly been veiled over or obfuscated within mainstream cinematic narratives.

The notion of so-called 'gay sensibility' as a potentially transgressive response to marginalisation, and vilification, inevitably leads us to a consideration of what is often referred to as 'camp'. As Andy Medhurst notes:

[Camp] is a part of gay men's daily lives, one of the ways in which we (sic) have managed to make sense of a world which at best tolerates and at worst exterminates us, a method for negotiating our way through what Jonathan Dollimore has called 'the lived contradictions of subordination' . . . Camp is one of our most fearsome weapons . . . and one of our most enriching experiences. (1997: 275)

For Medhurst, camp is a practice, a 'relationship between queens and their circumstances' (Ibid.: 276) that is firmly rooted in gay male culture. It is a survival strategy that, as Medhurst's fondly recounted tales of the 'in your face' queer antics of Jane/Wayne County, and of himself and his close circle of queens and divas demonstrates, is at once political and pleasurable.

So, how does one recognise camp when one sees it? Camp is most often associated with parody, exaggeration, theatricality, humour, and insofar as it foregrounds the performative character of gender, sexuality, race, class, and so on, it functions – at least potentially – to denaturalise, or queer, heteronormative notions of identity, as Esther Newton noted in her landmark study of female impersonators.[10] It was perhaps Susan Sontag's analysis of camp as 'a sensibility that, among other things, converts the serious into the frivolous' (1966: 276) that jettisoned the term into the realm of popular culture and away from its roots in gay male subcultures. Sontag's now somewhat notorious essay 'Notes on Camp'[11] (re)presented the concept as a playful, ironic, aesthetic strategy that anyone could deploy in order to upset conservative beliefs, practices, and forms of representation. Consequently, camp, Medhurst claims, 'is now absolutely everywhere' (1997: 289). It has become, as Jon Savage notes, 'an all-pervasive ingredient in a pop culture [that] has become reified, ironicised, once-removed from the impulses that called it into being' (cited in Drukman 1995: 88). The fear, then, is that in and through its commercialisation, camp may have lost its subversive edge, or at least its ties to a specifically gay, lesbian, or queer politics. Whether or not this is the case is debatable, nevertheless, critics continue to use this tem in order to explore the ways in which particular texts, or elements thereof, queer – in the broadest sense of the term – heteronormative values, beliefs, and institutions.

In an article entitled 'Holy Homosexuality Batman!: Camp and Corporate Capitalism in *Batman Forever*', Freya Johnson examines the ways in which *Batman Forever* functions in and through camp techniques of mirroring and exaggeration which simultaneously 'trouble' or denaturalise heteronormative institutions and enable their survival as artificial. Johnson begins her article with a quote from a psychiatrist Fredric Wertham, who, in 1953 in a text entitled *Seduction of the Innocent*, warned parents and lawmakers of 'the "factually proven" method by which comic books turned innocent children into homosexually and pederastically inclined deviants and perverts' (cited in Johnson 1995: 1). Wertham, disturbed by what he saw as 'a subtle atmosphere of homoeroticism which pervades the adventure of the mature "Batman", and his young friend "Robin"', makes a list of the signifiers that seem to imply that this relationship may not be a healthy one. These include the fact that Bruce Wayne, an unmarried 'socialite' and 'Dick' Grayson, his much younger ward, 'live in sumptuous quarters, with beautiful flowers in large vases, and have a butler, Alfred' (Ibid.: 1). In effect what Wertham does, is to search for what we, following Doty, might think of as queer moments or queer signifiers, and as much as Werther's politics is opposed to Johnson's, her task could be described similarly.

As I said, Johnson's focus is *Batman Forever* which, she claims, is saturated with campness, and/or with queer signification. Whilst, as Johnson sees it, camp homoerotic encounters between the

Caped Crusaders abound and are juxtaposed to the sterile hetero-sexual 'love-scenes' with Nicole Kidman in which Val Kilmer (Batman) remains fully clothed, the villain of the piece – Jim Carrey's Riddler, who prances around in a sparkly tiara and bright green lyotard screaming 'Spank Me!' – is 'much much camper' (Ibid.: 2).The Riddler's overtly queer behaviour draws the audi-ence's 'attention away from the homoerotic electricity between the heroes and invites the misreading that "if the bad guy's gay, the good guys must be straight"' (Ibid.: 2). Further, argues Johnson, the film aligns 'Bad Capitalism' with 'Bad Sexuality' embodied in the figure of the Riddler and opposes this to 'Good/Democratic Corporate Capitalism' which is aligned with the rejection of bad sex (and of the Riddler's/Nygma's advances) and embodied in the figure of Bruce Wayne. In short, Johnson suggests that in this text 'Bat-Camp' as she calls it, functions to eclipse the anti-normative potential of the more radical elements of camp that are nevertheless at work here. 'Bat-Camp', she says, converts what 'Sontag once termed a "secret sensibility" into a mass market symbolic currency' (1995: 5) by drawing attention to its own artificiality, its own status as a vehicle for mass marketing, and thereby flattering the media-savvy postmodern audience. In effect, then, it seems that camp may have not only lost its subversive edge – as many gay theorists post-Sontag feared it would – but worse still, has ironically become a successful strategy with which to market heteronormative values and lifestyles.

But, despite Johnson's reading of camp as it functions in *Batman Forever*, there are those who claim that this particular sensibility, or set of textual strategies, continues to have queer currency even in so-called mainstream (con)texts. One such example is Judith Halberstam's reading of what she refers to as 'English abject mas-culinity films' of the 1990s, in a paper entitled 'Oh Behave! Austin Powers and the Drag Kings' (2001). But before we look at Halberstam's thesis in more detail, I want to locate it within the debate about whether there has been, or could be, something called 'lesbian camp'. To cut a very long story short, there are, on the one hand, those who claim that lesbian camp does exist and that butch/femme role playing and female-to-male transvestism are evidence of this. On the other, there are those who argue that given that gay men and lesbians have, historically speaking, been positioned significantly differently in relation to dominant dis-courses and social institutions, the use of an umbrella term that conflates the practices and positions of the two groups and over-looks the differences between them, is highly problematic.[12]

In her analysis of what she refers to as 'kinging', Halberstam carefully avoids the pro/anti logic of the polarised positions out-lined above, arguing instead, that:

While camp may have originated in and may be peculiar to drag-queen cultures, it also travels as a cultural style and allows for a gay counter-public site to influence and ironize the depiction of femininity in mainstream venues . . . [C]amp shows up in many sites that are not gay, as an aesthetic mode detached from one type of identity. (2001: 427)

In similar ways, Halberstam claims, kinging – the hyperbolic and yet heterogeneous performance of masculinities – could be said to 'exceed the boundaries of lesbian and transgender subcultures and to circulate independently of the drag-king act itself'(Ibid.: 427). Hence the existence of, for example, the figure of Austin Powers, 'international man of mystery', who Halberstam suggests 'represents a variation of drag-king masculinity', and 'is marked irredeemably as queer' (Ibid.: 245). In other words, *Austin Powers, International Man of Mystery* – as an exemplar of what Halberstam refers to as the 'new king comedies' – not only poignantly illustrates Judith Butler's claim that gender is the product of repeated, culturally specific, gestures or performances, but also shows that masculinity (like femininity) is an idea(l) that can never be achieved, but which men must nevertheless anxiously attempt to (re)produce if the 'heterosexual matrix'[13] is to remain intact. And insofar as *Austin Powers, International Man of Mystery*, draws on, and further parodies, the *Carry On* image of two interdependent aspects of masculinity embodied in the figures of Sid James (homophobic) and Kenneth Williams (homoerotic), Mike Myers, Halberstam claims, 'exposes English masculinity as a peculiar combination of camp and com-pulsory heterosexuality' (Ibid.: 442). Or, to put it more simply, the effect of camp, or kinging – at least in Halberstam's reading of this particular text – is to denaturalise, and/or queer masculinity, and the heteronormative institutions that are informed by, and inform, gender and sexuality.

According to Steven Drukman, camp could be thought of as 'a "means" or a "method" for the gay gaze' (1995: 88). As the title of his (1995) article 'The Gay Gaze, or Why I Want My MTV' sug-gests, Drukman's aim is to elaborate a notion of the 'gay gaze' which would queer heterocentric accounts of the relationship

between viewing practices and modes of desire. In order to understand Drukman's project, we must first turn to Laura Mulvey's
(1975) landmark essay 'Visual Pleasure and Narrative Cinema',[14]
which, many would claim, began the still on-going debates on the
gaze.

As those familiar with film theory will know, the gaze is a theoretical concept which has been used in a range of many and varied
attempts to think through the relation between ways of seeing and
ways of being. Theories of the gaze raise the question of how we
look, and what the relation is between ways of looking and the
(re)production of gender identity. In her account of the gaze
Mulvey drew on the psychoanalytic notions of scopophilia, ego-
identification, and fetishism in order to analyse the relation
between sexual difference and the production and consumption of
Hollywood films. In short, Mulvey argued that classic Hollywood
cinema was primarily (in)formed by an attempt to satisfy the
unconscious desires of male viewers.

In the article Mulvey identifies three types of looking. The first
of these is the look of the camera as it records the filmic events.
Mulvey argues that this is inherently voyeuristic and male. The
second is the look of the characters in the film at each other.
Mulvey suggests that most films tend to be edited in such a way
that the male characters do most of the looking, and the female
characters are, more often than not, looked at. Men, then, are the
active subjects of most films whereas women are the passive
objects. The third is the look of the spectator, and this, claims
Mulvey, is directed or shaped by the first two looks. Since the
spectator can only see what the camera shows, then the spectator
is forced to identify with what Mulvey calls 'the male gaze'. She
says:

In a world ordered by sexual imbalance, pleasure in looking has been
split between active/male and passive/female. The determining male
gaze projects its fantasy onto the female figure which is styled accordingly. In their traditional exhibitionist role women are simultaneously
looked at and displayed, with their appearance coded for strong visual
and erotic impact so they can be said to connote *to-be-looked-at-ness*.
(1989a: 19)

Mulvey supports these claims by drawing on various psychoanalytic
concepts to argue that woman (as she is represented in Hollywood
films) connotes something that the male gaze continually circles

around but disavows, that is, her castration or lack. Thus she suggests that the glamour of women in film is linked to castration anxiety and provides the male viewer with a fetishistic object in and through which he can both acknowledge and disavow or displace such anxieties. The gaze then, as a fetishistic form of scopophilic pleasure, belongs, Mulvey, following Freud, concludes, to the male alone.[15] In 1981, in response to calls for an explanation of female viewing pleasure – a phenomenon whose very existence was negated in Mulvey's original conception of the gaze – Mulvey published another paper entitled 'Afterthoughts on "Visual Pleasure and Narrative Cinema"'. Here she argues that whilst the female spectator may (cross-) identify with the (male) subject of the film, this is achieved with some level of difficulty through what she calls 'visual transvestism', that is, the female spectator's temporary 'masculinisation' in memory of her so-called active phase.[16] Consequently, Mulvey's model of the gaze has been accused of remaining caught up in, and reproducing, phallocentric, heterocentric, and/or eurocentric logic. Moreover, if, as was suggested in the previous chapter, women also fetishise, then the foundation of Mulvey's account of the gaze becomes untenable.

There have since been many attempts to rework Mulvey's theory of the gaze and to address its shortcomings. Mary Anne Doane, for example, has argued that female viewing positions may well be multiple and much more fluid than Mulvey recognises.[17] As we saw in the previous chapter, Kobena Mercer demonstrates that race and ethnicity impact significantly on viewing practices. As Z. Isiling Nataf notes, insofar as the black lesbian spectator 'has a schizophrenic relationship' (1995: 61) with mainstream cinema she can, and often does, radically misread and thus subvert dominant meanings and the institutions they support. In this sense, claims Nataf, such spectators queer mainstream texts by elaborating camp subtexts which work against the grain. Theorists such as Richard Dyer,[18] Andy Medhurst,[19] and Yvonne Tasker[20] have all convincingly argued that male bodies are also objectified in cinema, and that this is increasingly the case. And, Dyer,[21] Jackie Stacey,[22] and, as I said, Drukman, have explore the feasibility of a theory of gay and/or lesbian spectatorship.

For Drukman, who openly acknowledges that subject positions are ultimately undecidable, the elaboration of a taxonomy of gay male spectatorship is nevertheless politically necessary despite the obvious pitfalls – that is, the tendency to homogenise and universalise gayness, and to therefore overlook the complex ways in which certain reception strategies are shared, as Doty has noted, by otherwise disparate groups and individuals (1993: 2). Drukman, who, unlike many other contemporary theorists, believes that psychoanalytic theory can be appropriated as a political weapon, draws on Mulvey's work, but raises the question of where/how the gay male spectator is, or can be, situated in the scenario that Mulvey envisages: as he puts it: 'if one is not a male heterosexual spectator, why pay the price for the ticket?' (1995: 84). It is Drukman's contention that 'for the gay male spectator, the object of scopophilic pleasure is the man [whilst in Mulvey's schema it is the woman] and the subject of ego-identification is . . . in constant flux between the woman and the man' (Ibid.: 84–5). What enables Drukman to make this claim – rather then, as we might suppose, the claim that the male who is subjected to the gaze of the gay male viewer becomes objectified, and thus feminised – is the notion of transitivism outlined in Mulvey's (1981) article. For Drukman, the 'gaze-shifting' character of transitivism shares resonances with the notion of a gay sensibility that 'enables the twist of traditional Oedipal narrative', and it is this possibility, says Drukman 'that makes the gay male want to gaze at all' (1995: 87). For Drukman, then, the gay gaze is less an empirical phenomenon that can be pinned down and explained, than a sort of shifting process that (at least potentially) engenders the multiplication of meanings and identities, and thus undermines the logic of Sameness that is central to heteronormative accounts of sexual (in)difference. But if, as Diana Fuss claims, 'because subject-positions are multiple, shifting and changeable, readers can occupy several "I-slots" *at the same time*' (1989: 35), it seems unnecessary, perhaps even misguided, to refer to the phenomenon Drukman discusses as the 'gay gaze' – a term that implies the existence of a unified, singular and identifiable ontological category (gayness).

For many theorists, particularly those more influenced by the work of Foucault than by psychoanalysis, any attempt to identify a specific form of the gaze – particularly the queer gaze – is decidedly unqueer in as much as such a task necessarily presumes the viability of identity categories. Consequently, Caroline Evans and Lorraine Gamman suggest that cultural critics and queer theorists focus not on identities, but on identifications, which, they claim, 'are multiple, contradictory, shifting, oscillating, inconsistent, and fluid' (1995: 45), rather than fixed and singular, as Mulvey's thesis implies. Whilst they acknowledge that texts do position viewers/readers, or at least could be said to a construct 'preferred readings', in and through the use of a range of textual mechanisms, Evans and Gamman are nevertheless of the opinion that all texts, even those that have 'overt heterosexual narratives', 'can be viewed queerly' (Ibid.: 46). This claim is supported, it seems to me, in the queer re-readings of Barbie that now abound and that have been discussed in much detail by Erica Rand, and Lucinda Ebersole and Richard Peabody.

The task that Rand sets herself in *Barbie's Queer Accessories* is 'to determine how and why such products transmit value [and meaning] in order to design effective strategies of cultural activism' (1995: 8). For Rand, Mattel (the company that has produced Barbie for the past thirty odd years) is an exemplar of successful hegemonic heteronormative discourse. Mattel, she argues, promotes compulsory heterosexuality by representing it as natural, as a *fait accompli*, promotes capitalism by glamourising a character with a necessarily outrageous amount of apparently unearned disposable income, and promotes ageism and racism by suggesting that the epitome of feminine beauty and desirability is white, thin, and young (Ibid.: 8–9). Given this, Rand is compelled to explore the queer potential of the seemingly conservative figure of Barbie.

The title of Rand's book – *Barbie's Queer Accessories* – refers to all those who have, at some time in their lives, engaged with Barbie and thus invested this figure with a range of meanings, identities, desires, and fears. Of interest to us, however, is those who Rand claims 'act as accessories to the crime of helping Barbie escape from the straight world into which Mattel has tried to enclose her' (Ibid.: 11), who 'queer Barbie's intended meanings by giving her queer artifactual and narrative accessories' (Ibid.: 12). One of the most interesting examples that Rand discusses is the Barbie Liberation Organization (BLO),[23] who, in 1993, procured a number of 'Teen Talk Barbies' and 'Talking Duke GI Joe' dolls and switched their voice-boxes. The group then returned the dolls to the shelves of a local department store and included in the boxes the phone numbers of local television stations so that horrified shoppers would make public their outrage at purchasing an effeminate GI Joe or a butch Barbie. The campaign was successful and the BLO did indeed get national media coverage. One article in *The New York Times* described the dolls as 'A mutant colony of Barbies-on-steroids who roar things like "Attack!", "Vengeance is mine!", and "Eat lead, Cobra!". The emasculated GI Joes meanwhile, twitter "Will we ever have enough clothes?", and "Let's plan our dream wedding!"' (cited in Ibid.: 159).

The BLO's queering of popular culture – what I am going to refer to as a form of guerrilla tactics – achieves a number of things. First, the voice-box switch reveals, through a denaturalisation of the relation between woman and 'femininity' (connoted by an interest in fashion, and marriage) and man and 'masculinity' (connoted by a warrior-like attitude), the artificiality or social-constructedness of gender. Second, it simultaneously draws our attention to the extent to which these idea(l)s about gender become consolidated, and thus rendered invisible, in and through the everyday practices in which we are all implicated. In other words, the guerrilla tactics employed by the BLO seem to nicely illustrate Cherry Smith's claim that queer 'defines a strategy, an attitude . . . a radical questioning of social and cultural norms, notions of gender, reproductive sexuality, and the family' (1996: 280). But, if we cast our minds back to Chapter 3 we may remember Lisa Duggan's description of queer as a radical potentiality that is sometimes realised and sometimes not. Rand also addresses this issue, raising the question of if, and how, it might be possible to ensure the subversiveness of particular queer strategies or guerrilla tactics. In response to this question we would do well to keep in mind the distinction between performance and performativity discussed in Chapter 5.

For Butler, the term performativity refers to a precondition of subjectivity, it is that which constitutes subjectivity in and through relations with others and with a world. Performance, on the other hand, is most often used to refer to a set of actions which a presumably always already constituted subject intentionally and knowingly choreographs, in some cases for subversive means. But, if we follow Butler's logic insofar as any performance presupposes performativity, intentional forms of subversion will always be open to multiple meanings, to being (re)read/(re)written. Rand gives an example of this when she cites the case of the Barbie slasher who, as we saw in Chapter 5, somewhat ambiguously mutilated two dozen Barbies by slashing their breasts and crotches and leaving them in public places. So if, as Halperin suggests, queer practice constitutes 'a horizon of possibility whose precise extent and heterogeneous scope cannot in principle be delimited in advance' (1995: 62), how do we interpret and evaluate the kinds of guerilla tactics undertaken by, in this case, the BLO? In the final chapter of *Barbie's Queer Accessories*, Rand writes:

If we measure cultural interventions and strategies of resistance by whether they catalyze big social changes by themselves and fast, Barbie subversions, like most, will not pass the test: you can't shoot down an antigay referendum by wheatpasting Subversive Barbie all over the state of Oregon ... But, if we measure resistance and [queer] transformation in smaller increments, Barbie's subversivability and visible cracks matter a lot. It matters that lots of people recognize and think about Mattel's silences, camouflages, and dubious claims, and come prepared to a Barbie subversion that uses Mattel's line to expose social injustice by drawing connections that they might not have considered before. (1995: 161)

For Rand, then, queer activism necessarily involves engaging with the discourses, the institutions and idea(ls), the products and practices, that one identifies as inextricably bound up with heteronormativity. It involves 'remain[ing] within [heteronormative] consciousness and ... proceed[ing] to dismantle it, to weaken it, to break it down on the spot, as we would do with a lump of sugar by steeping it in water' (Barthes 1977: 63). In other words, rather than presuming that it is possible to entirely destroy heteronormativity, or to exist somehow outside of it, Rand proffers, what we might think of as a deconstructive account of the queering of popular culture in which any strategy will necessarily produce heterogeneous and unpredictable effects.

Given the claim made by various theorists throughout this chapter that all texts are open to interpretation and thus all are potentially queer, I want to turn now to a somewhat notorious counter-cultural comic strip – that could be said to constitute an example of guerrilla tactics – created by Diane DiMassa and entitled *Hothead Paisan Homicidal Lesbian Terrorist*. Hothead, the Italian-American homicidal homegirl heroine of the piece, who is most often to be found toting guns, machetes and other such implements in her assault on hetero-patriarchy, is described by Lia Kiessling in the following way: 'She's Pippi Longstocking with more firepower than Rambo ever dreamed of. She's got a bigger mouth than Howard Stern could ever hope for. She's shed more blood than Freddy Krueger and Jason combined. And she has absolutely no balls.'[24] Consequently, for some, Hothead Paisan may seem to represent nothing more than a graphic and offensive reaffirmation of all that is most horrific about hetero-patriarchal power and violence. Indeed, it is this sort of interpretation that led Canada Customs to confiscate shipments of the zine and to ban its sale in Canada on the grounds that it constitutes hate literature. Others have argued, however, that rather than literally promoting violence Hothead 'delegitimises the symbolic power of the "straight white male"' (Dean 1997: 200) as a paradigm for hetero-patriarchy, through graphic castration – and, in fact, this could well be the threat that institutions such as Canada Customs cannot tolerate.

In all of the strips Hothead finds herself in a hostile heteronor-mative world in which she is not only marginalised, but constantly assaulted by doctors, newsreaders, advertisers, Neo-Nazis, misogy-nists, 'femme-bots', homophobes, educators, and so on, all of whom she responds to with murderous rage. The question, to recast a concern of Audrey Lourde's, is whether or not its possible to use the (symbolic) father's tools to dismantle the father's house. Can Hothead's violence undermine dominant systems of power/ knowledge, or, does her behaviour undermine the gains made by feminist and gay and lesbian movements? Should we read Hothead as a queer political satire, a revenge fantasy that is deadly only at a metaphorical level, but deadly nevertheless, or, should we read the text as a reactive attempt to reverse dominant hierarchies that ulti-mately fails to challenge the logic against which it is apparently opposed, and in fact perpetuates it?

Kathleen Martindale proposes that the theoretical underpinnings of DiMassa's text are not, as some may presume, 'the post-identitar-ian queer theory of Judith Butler or the anti-essentialism of Diana Fuss – but the "lesbian chauvinism" of Mary Daly and Valerie Solanis,[25] particularly [the latter's] 1967 SCUM (Society For Cutting Up Men) Manifesto'[26] (1997: 70). The thrust of Solanis' Manifesto, which, as Martindale notes, Hothead is shown reading in one particular strip, is that women should destroy the male sex, since, because of his innate deviance and vagina/womb envy, he, is responsible for – amongst other things – war, money, marriage and prostitution, mental illness, prejudice, hate and violence, con-formity, censorship, and, in short, making 'the world a shitpile'. Whilst it may be valid to claim that Hothead seems to be driven by an equally excessive rage, it could also be said that Hothead's rancour, unlike Solanis', is vented not so much at men, but at what we might think of as the Law of the Phallus.

In a psychoanalytic reading of *Hothead Paisan* Gabrielle Dean argues that just as feminist psychoanalytic theorists have attempted to explode Lacan's claim that the Phallus and the penis are not indexically related, so too does Hothead. In issue 12, for example, a series of stereotypical males, all making various complaints about their treatment in an earlier issue, are lined up beside a phallic pillar. The pillar which bears the inscription 'For God, For Country, for Penis' then proceeds to be blown-up by a couple of dykes with a classic cartoon box of TNT whose laughter overtakes the entire frames (Dean 1997: 200). This is just one of many examples, claims Dean, of Hothead's attempt to reinscribe sexual difference in and through a kind of guerrilla practice that 'visibly dislocate[s] the phallus, and thus the chain of meaning emanating from its fixed position' (Ibid.: 201). She goes on to explain that the text 'articulates a countersubjectivity, a relation to the symbolic order that is, at times, successfully oppositional' but, she stresses, does not 'function by outright negation of the existing symbolic order' (Ibid.: 201). In Dean's opinion, Hothead inhabits and thus infiltrates the symbolic order in much the same way as water infuses a lump of sugar that has been immersed in it, breaking it down, changing its structure, and simultaneously being changed by it.

More particularly, Dean claims that because lesbian desire cannot be represented in psychoanalytic terms except as a form of disavowal that leads to a masculinity complex (that is, as a stereotype of the phallic woman), then the only option for the (always already) 'phallicised dyke' is to take up this fetishised position – which is itself the result of disavowal on the part of the phallocentric imaginary – and simultaneously accept and repudiate it. The task, she says, is to 'occupy the stereotype, in the sense of a military occupation, a guerrilla colonization; to fetishize this fetish . . . in order to both identify with it and reject it' (Ibid.: 207). And this, she argues, is exactly what Hothead does. Thus Dean reads Hothead's rage not as constituted by a desire for the phallus, but by a desire to *resignify* or to queer the phallus; Hothead wants control over signification (Ibid.: 209–10), and more particularly, over the ways in which subjectivity, sexuality, and social relations, are constituted in through the relation to this so-called Transcendental Signified (the Phallus) which Lacan claims defines each subject's access to the Symbolic Order.

Whilst this particular approach to queering popular culture, unlike the strategies discussed earlier, involves the explicit production of alternative images, each of the approaches in different

ways, and to varying degrees, read/(re)write 'mainstream' culture
for resistory purposes. Whether or not, the various engagements
do queer popular culture and the discourses that inform it, is, of
course, open to debate. But then how could it be otherwise?

NOTES

1. See Barthes (1990; 1994; 1995).
2. For a more detailed discussion of the positive and negative aspects
    of this sort of approach see O'Sullivan *et al.* (1983).
3. See www.glaad.org/glaad/news/9603/vito-russo.html Vito Russo
    was one of the founders of GLAAD (the Gay Lesbian alliance
    Against Defamation), and the associated Center for the Study of
    Media and Society.
4. 1959, directed by William Wyler.
5. 1953, directed by David Butler.
6. 1931, directed by Roy del Ruth and based on a novel by Dashiell
    Hammet.
7. 1948, directed by Howard Hawks.
8. 1953, directed by Howard Hawks and based on a novel by Anita
    Loos.
9. 1940, directed by Alfred Hitchcock, and based on a novel by Daphne
    du Maurier.
10. See Newton (1972).
11. The following writers have all commented on Sontag's use of the
    term camp: Dollimore (1983); Dyer (1992a); Medhurst (1997); Meyer
    (1994); Miller (1993).
12. See, for example, Davy (1994); Graham (1995); Medhurst (1997);
    and Robertson (1996).
13. See Chapter 5 for an explanation of this term coined by Butler.
14. It is important to note that Mulvey's essay was published at a time
    when feminists were extremely concerned with what they saw as the
    objectification of women in all forms of media. The issue of repre-
    sentation, and its relation to gender has, since the popularisation of
    postmodernism, taken quite a different turn.
15. Linda Williams (1999) argues against Mulvey's claim that the work of
    fetishisation is always the same, and claims that Freud's scenario of
    the little boy's encounter with the his mother's genitals is signifi-
    cantly different from the experience of classic Hollywood narrative.
16. That is, in the Freudian schema, the phase prior to the girl's relin-
    quishing of her mother as her primary love object, and the replace-
    ment of the ('active') clitoris as the primary erotogenic zone with the
    ('passive') vagina. For an account of the Oedipal development of
    females, see Freud (1931).

17. See Doane (1982); (1988/9).
18. Dyer (1992b)
19. Medhurst (1985)
20. Tasker (1993)
21. Dyer (1987)
22. Stacey (1988)
23. For more information on the Barbie Liberation Organisation, see www.rtmark.com/blo.html
24. www.charlatan.carleton.ca/jan23_97/arts/
25. For a cinematic account of Valerie Solanis' infamous attack on Andy Warhol, see *I Shot Andy Warhol*, written and directed by Mary Harron.
26. The SCUM Manifesto is available at: www.envirolink.org/orgs/coe/e-sermons/scum.html and also at www.bcn.net/~jpiazzo/scum.htm

Bibliography

Abott, Sidney and Love, Barbara (1972), *Sappho Was a Right on Woman*, New York: Stein and Day.

Adam, Barry D. (1995), *The Rise of a Gay and Lesbian Movement* (revised edition), New York: Twayne Publishers.

Albury, Kath (2002), *Yes Means Yes: Getting Explicit about Heterosex*, Sydney: Allen & Unwin.

Alcoff, Linda Martín (2001), 'Toward a phenomenology of racial embodiment', in Bernasconi (ed.) *Race*, Oxford: Blackwell Publishers, pp. 267–83.

Alexander, Brian Keith (2000), 'Reflections, riffs and remembrances: the Black queer studies in the millennium conference (2000)', *Callaloo*, 23: 4, 1285–305.

Allison, Dorothy (1993), *Bastard Out of Carolina*, New York: Plume Books.

Allison, Dorothy (1995), *Skin: Talking about Sex, Class and Literature*, London: Pandora.

Althusser, Louis (1971), 'Ideology and ideological state apparatuses', in Brewster (trans.), *Lenin and Philosophy*, London: New Left Books, pp. 121–73.

Altman, Dennis (1972), *Homosexual Oppression and Liberation*, Sydney: Angus and Robertson.

Antoniou, Laura (1995), *Some Women*, New York: Masquerade Books Inc.

Anzaldúa, Gloria (1987), *Borderlands/La Frontera: The New Mestiza*, San Francisco: Aunt Lute.

Anzaldúa, Gloria (1991), 'To(o) queer the writer: loca, escrita y chicana', in Warland (ed.), *InVersions: Writing by Dykes, Queers and Lesbians*, Vancouver: Press Gang, pp. 249–63.

Appleby, Yvon (1993), 'Disability and "compulsory heterosexuality"', in Kitzinger and Wilkinson (eds), *Heterosexuality: A Feminism and Psychology Reader*, London: Sage Publications, pp. 266–9.

Apter, Emily and Pietz, William (eds) (1993), *Fetishism as Cultural Discourse*, Ithaca, NY: Cornell University Press.

Austin, J. L. (1962), *How to Do Things with Words*, Oxford: Oxford University Press.

Balibar, Etienne (1994), *Masses, Classes, Ideas*, New York: Routledge.

207

Bibliography

Barnard, Ian (1999), 'Queer race', *Social Semiotics*, 9: 2, 199–212.

Bar-On, Bat Ami (1982), 'Feminism and sadomasochism, self-critical notes', in Linden *et al.* (eds), *Against Sadomasochism: A Radical Feminist Analysis*, San Francisco: Frog In The Well.

Barthes, Roland (1977), *Roland Barthes by Roland Barthes*, Howard (trans.), London: Macmillan Press.

Barthes, Roland (1990), 'The death of the author', in Rice and Waugh (eds), *Modern Literary Theory*, London: Edward Arnold, pp. 114–18.

Barthes, Roland (1994), *The Pleasure of the Text*, Miller (trans.), New York: Hill and Wang.

Barthes, Roland (1995), *S/Z*, Miller (trans.), New York: Hill and Wang.

Bauman, Zygmunt (2000), *Community: Seeking Safety in an Insecure World*, Oxford: Polity Press.

Baumeister, Roy. F (1988), 'Masochism as escape from self', *Journal of Sex Research*, 25: 1, 478–99.

Bell, David, Binnie, Jon, Cream, Julia and Valentine, Gill (1994), 'All hyped up and no place to go', *Gender, Place, and Culture: A Journal of Feminist Geography*, 1: 1, 31–47.

Benjamin, Harry (1966), *The Transsexual Phenomenon*, New York: The Julian Press.

Berlant, Lauren and Freeman, Elizabeth (1996), 'Queer nationality', in Morton (ed.), *The Material Queer: A LesBiGay Cultural Studies Reader*, Boulder, CO: Westview Press, pp. 305–9.

Berlant, Lauren and Warner, Michael (1998), 'Sex in public', *Critical Inquiry*, 24: 2, 547–66.

Bernasconi, Robert (1993), 'On deconstructing nostalgia for community within the west: the debate between Nancy and Blanchot', *Research in Phenomenology*, 23, 3–21.

Berry, Chris (1997), 'History, herstory, queerstory? *Stonewall* – the movie', *Critical InQueeries*, 1: 3, 133–43.

Berry, Chris and Jagose, Annamarie (1996), 'Australia queer', *Meanjin*, 551, 5–15.

Bersani, Leo (1987), 'Is the rectum the grave?', October, 43, 197–222.

Bersani, Leo (1995), 'Foucault, Freud, fantasy and power', *GLQ: A Journal of Lesbian and Gay Studies*, 2: 1–2, 11–33.

Bhabha, Homi (1996), 'The other question', in Mongia (ed.), *Contemporary Postcolonial Theory: A Reader*, London and New York: Arnold, pp. 37–54.

Birke, Lynda I. A. (1982), 'From sin to sickness: hormonal theories of lesbianism', in Hubbard, Henifin and Fried (eds), *Biological Woman: The Convenient Myth*, Cambridge, MA: Schenkman Publishing Company, pp. 71–90.

Bland, Lucy and Doan, Laura (eds) (1998), *Sexology Uncensored: The Documents of Sexual Science*, Cambridge: Polity Press.

Bollen, Jonathan (1996), 'The parties are for us', *Crosstext*, 1, 48–53.

Bordo, Susan (1993), *Unbearable Weight: Feminism, Western Culture, and the Body*, Los Angeles: University of California Press.

Bornstein, Kate (1994), *Gender Outlaw: On Men, Women, and the Rest of Us*, New York: Routledge.

Boyarin, Daniel (1995), 'Freud's bay, Fliess's maybe: homophobia, anti-Semitism, and the invention of Oedipus', *GLQ: A Journal of Lesbian and Gay Studies*, 2: 1–2, 115–47.

Brush, Pippa (1998), 'Metaphors of inscription: discipline, plasticity, and the rhetoric of choice', *Feminist Review*, 58, 22–43.

Burstin, Hinde Ena (1999), 'Looking out, looking in: anti-Semitism and racism in lesbian communities', in Jackson and Sullivan (eds), *Multicultural Queer: Australian Narratives*, New York: Harrington Park Press, pp. 143–58.

Butler, Judy (1982), 'Lesbian S&M: the politics of dis-illusion', in Linden *et al.* (eds), *Against Sadomasochism: A Radical Feminist Analysis*, San Francisco: Frog in the Well, pp. 168–75.

Butler, Judith (1990), *Gender Trouble: Feminism and the Subversion of Identity*, New York: Routledge.

Butler, Judith (1991), 'Imitation and gender insubordination', in Fuss (ed.), *Inside/Out: Lesbian Theories/Gay Theories*, London: Routledge, pp. 13–31.

Butler, Judith (1993a), *Bodies That Matter: On The Discursive Limits of 'Sex'*, New York: Routledge.

Butler, Judith (1993b), 'Critically queer', *GLQ: A Journal of Lesbian and Gay Studies*, 1: 1, 17–32.

Califia, Pat (1983a), 'A secret side of lesbian sexuality', in Weinberg and Kamel (eds), *S and M: Studies in Sadomasochism*, Buffalo, NY: Prometheus, pp. 129–36.

Califia, Pat (1983b), 'Gay men, lesbians, and sex: doing it together', *The Advocate*, 7 July, pp. 46–52.

Califia, Pat (1996), 'Feminism and sadomasochism', in Jackson and Scott (eds), *Feminism and Sexuality: A Reader*, New York: Columbia University Press, pp. 230–7.

Califia, Pat (1997), *Sex Changes: The Politics of Transgenderism*, San Francisco: Cleis Press.

Caprio, Frank S. (1954), *Female Homosexuality: A Psychodynamic Study of Lesbianism*, New York: The Citadel Press.

Caputo, John D. (1997), *Deconstruction in a nutshell: A Conversation with Jacques Derrida*, New York: Fordham University Press.

Carlston, Erin G. (1997), '"A finer differentiation": female homosexuality and the American medical community, 1926–1940', in Rosario (ed.), *Science and Homosexualities*, New York: Routledge, pp. 177–96.

Case, Sue-Ellen (1991), 'Tracking the vampire', *Differences: A Journal of Feminist Cultural Studies* 3: 2, 1–200.

Cauldwell, David O. (2001), 'Psychopathia transsexualis', *The International Journal of Transgenderism*, 5: 2, 1–6.

Champagne, John (1995), '"I just wanna be a rich somebody": experience, common sense, and *Paris Is Burning*', in *The Ethics of Marginality: A New Approach to Gay Studies*, Minneapolis: University of Minnesota Press, pp. 88–128.

Chang Hall, Lisa Kahaleole (1993), 'Bitches in solitude: identity politics and lesbian community', in Stein (ed.), *Sisters, Sexperts, Queers: Beyond the Lesbian Nation*, New York: Penguin Books, pp. 218–29.

Chetcuti, Joseph (1994), 'Continuing legal discrimination in Australia against homosexual men', in Aldrich (ed.), *Gay Perspectives II: More Essays in Australian Gay Culture*, Sydney: The Australian Centre for Gay and Lesbian Research, pp. 316–51.

Clarke, Cheryl (1983), 'The failure to transform: homophobia in the black community', in Smith (ed.), *Home Girls: A Black Feminist Anthology*, New York: Kitchen Table/Women of Color, pp. 197–208.

Cohen, Cathy J. (1997), 'Punks, bulldaggers, and welfare queens', *GLQ: A Journal of Lesbian and Gay Studies*, 3, 437–65.

Combahee River Collective (1983), 'The Combahee River Collective statement', in Smith (ed.), *Home Girls: A Black Feminist Anthology*, New York: Kitchen Table/Women of Color, pp. 272–82.

Cooper, Dennis (1996), 'Queercore', in Morton (ed.), *The Material Queer: A LesBiGay Cultural Studies Reader*, Boulder, CO: Westview Press, pp. 292–6.

Cornell, Drucilla (1991), *Beyond Accommodation: Ethical Feminism, Deconstruction, and the Law*, New York: Routledge.

Cornell, Drucilla (1992), 'The postmodern challenge to the ideal of community', *The Philosophy of the Limit*, New York: Routledge, pp. 39–61.

Costera Meijer, Irene and Prins, Baukje (1998), 'How bodies come to matter: an interview with Judith Butler', *Signs* 23: 2, 275–86.

Creet, Julia (1991), 'Daughters of the movement: the psychodynamics of lesbian S/M fantasy', *Differences: A Journal of Feminist Cultural Studies*, 3: 2, 135–59.

Creet, Julia (1995), 'Anxieties of identity: coming out and coming undone', in Dorenkamp and Henke (eds), *Negotiating Lesbian and Gay Subjects*, London: Routledge, pp. 179–99.

Crenshaw, Kimberlé (1991), 'Mapping the margins: intersectionality, identity politics, and violence against women of color', *Stanford Law Review*, 43, 1241–99.

Crenshaw, Kimberlé (2000), 'Demarginalizing the intersection of race and sex: a black feminist critique of antidiscrimination doctrine, feminist theory, and antiracist politics', in James and Sharpley-Whiting (eds), *The Black Feminist Reader*, Oxford: Blackwell Publishers, pp. 208–38.

Cromwell, Jason (1998), 'Fearful others: medico-psychological constructions of female-to-male transgenderism', in Denny (ed.), *Current Concepts in Transgender Identity*, New York: Garland Publishing, pp. 117–61.

Cromwell, Jason (1999), 'Passing women and female-bodied men: (re)claiming FTM history', in More and Whittle (eds), *Reclaiming Genders: Transsexual Grammars at the Fin de Siècle*, London: Cassell, pp. 34–61.

Cummings, Katherine (1993), *Katherine's Diary: The Story of a Transsexual*, Melbourne: Mandarin.

Davis, Kathy (1999), '"My body is my art": cosmetic surgery as feminist utopia?', in Price and Schildrick (eds), *Feminist Theory and the Body: A Reader*, Edinburgh: Edinburgh University Press, pp. 454–65.

Davis, Whitney (1992), 'Homovision: a reading of Freud's "fetishism"', *Genders*, 15.

Davy, Kate (1994), 'Fe/Male impersonation: the discourse of camp', in Meyer (ed.), *The Politics and Poetics of Camp*, London: Routledge, pp. 130–48.

Dean, Gabrielle (1997), 'The "phallacies" of dyke comic strips', in Foster, Seigel and Berry (eds), *The Gay 90's: Disciplinary and Interdisciplinary Formations in Queer Studies*, New York: New York University Press, pp. 199–223.

de Beauvoir, Simone (1973), *The Second Sex*, Parshley (trans.), New York: Vintage.

de Lauretis, Teresa (1988), 'Sexual indifference and lesbian representation', *Theatre Journal*, 40: 2, 155–77.

de Lauretis, Teresa (1994), *The Practice of Love: Lesbian Sexuality and Perverse Desire*, Bloomington, IN: Indiana University Press.

de Lauretis, Teresa (1999), 'Popular culture, public and private fantasies: femininity and fetishism in David Cronenberg's *M. Butterfly*', *Signs: Journal of Women in Culture and Society*, 24: 2, 303–33.

Deleuze, Gilles and Guattari, Felix (1983), *On the Line*, Johnston (trans.), New York: Semiotext(e) Inc.

D'Emilio, John (1983), *Sexual Politics, Sexual Communities: The Making of a Homosexual Minority in the United States 1940–1970*, Chicago: University of Chicago Press.

Denny, Dallas (1995), 'How we use the surgeon's lancet to define and divide ourselves', *TransSisters: The Journal of Transsexual Feminism*, 10, 52–3.

Derrida, Jacques (1978), *Writing and Difference*, Bass (trans.), London: Routledge.

Derrida, Jacques (1991), 'Signature, event, context', in Kamuf (ed.), *Between the Blinds: A Derrida Reader*, Hemel Hempstead: Harvester Wheatsheaf, pp. 82–111.

Derrida, Jacques and Deutscher, Penelope (2001), 'Hospitality, perfectability, responsibility', in Patton and Smith (eds), *Jacques Derrida: Deconstruction Engaged, The Sydney Seminars*, Sydney: Power Publications, pp. 93–104.

DiMassa, Dianne (1994), *Hothead Paisan, Homicidal Lesbian Terrorist*, San Francisco: Cleis Press.

Diprose, Rosalyn (1994), *The Bodies of Women: Ethics, Embodiment and Sexual Difference*, London: Routledge.

Diprose, Rosalyn (1995), 'Performing body identity', *Writings on Dance*, 11/12, 7–15.

Doane, Mary Anne (1982), 'Film and the masquerade: theorising the female spectator', *Screen*, 23: 3–4, 74–87.

Doane, Mary Anne (1988/89), 'Masquerade reconsidered: further thoughts on the female spectator', *Discourse*, 11, 42–54.

Dollimore, Jonathan (1983), 'The challenge of sexuality', in Sinfield (ed.), *Society and Literature 1945–1970*, London: Methuen, pp. 51–86.

Donoghue, Emma (1993), *Passions between Women: British Lesbian Culture 1668–1801*, London: Scarlet Press.

Doty, Alexander (1993), *Making Things Perfectly Queer: Interpreting Mass*

Culture, Minneapolis: University of Minnesota Press.

Doyle, Gerry (1996), 'No man's land: lesbian separatism revisited', in Godwin, Hollows and Nye (eds), *Assaults on Convention: Essays on Lesbian Transgressors*, London: Cassell, pp. 178–97.

Drukman, Steven (1995), 'The gay gaze, or why I want my MTV', in Burston and Richardson (eds), *A Queer Romance: Lesbians, Gay Men, and Popular Culture*, London: Routledge, pp. 81–95.

Duggan, Lisa (1992), 'Making it perfectly queer', *Socialist Review* 22: 1, 11–31.

Duggan, Lisa and Hunter, Nan D. (1996), *Sex Wars: Sexual Dissent and Political Culture*, New York: Routledge.

Dworkin, Andrea (1987), *Intercourse*, London: Secker & Warburg.

Dyer, Richard (1987), *Heavenly Bodies*, New York: St Martin's Press.

Dyer, Richard (1992a), 'It's being so camp as keeps us going', *Only Entertainment*, London: Routledge, pp. 135–48.

Dyer, Richard (1992b), 'Don't look now: the male pin-up', in Screen Editorial Collective (eds), *The Sexual Subject: A Screen Reader in Sexuality*, London: Routledge, pp. 265–76.

Dyer, Richard (1997), *White*, London: Routledge.

Ebershoff, David (1999), *The Danish Girl*, Sydney: Allen & Unwin.

Ebersole, Lucinda and Peabody, Richard (eds) (1993), *Mondo Barbie*, New York: St Martin's Press.

Edgar, Andrew and Sedgwick, Peter (eds) (1999), *Key Concepts in Cultural Theory*, London: Routledge.

Ellis, Havelock (1908), *Studies in the Psychology of Sex*, Philadelphia: F. A. Davis Company.

Eng, David L. (1997), 'Out here and over there: queerness and diaspora in Asian American studies', *Social Text*, 52/53, 15: 3–4, Fall/Winter, 31–51.

Epstein, Julia (1990), 'Either/or-neither/both: sexual ambiguity and the ideology of gender', *Genders*, 7, 99–142.

Eugenides, Jeffrey (2002), *Middlesex*, London: Bloomsbury.

Evans, Caroline and Gamma, Lorraine (1995), 'The gaze revisited, or reviewing queer viewing', in Burston and Richardson (eds), *A Queer Romance: Lesbians, Gay Men, and Popular Culture*, London: Routledge, pp. 13–56.

Faderman, Lillian (1991), *Odd Girls and Twilight Lovers: A History of Lesbian Life in Twentieth-Century America*, New York: Columbia University Press.

Fanon, Frantz (1970), *Black Skin, White Masks*, London: Paladin.

Farr, Susan (1982), 'The art of discipline: creating erotic dramas of play and power', in Samois (ed.), *Coming to Power*, Boston: Alyson, pp. 183–91.

Feinberg, Leslie (1993), *Stone Butch Blues: A Novel*, New York: Firebrand.

Fenster, Mark (1993), 'Queer punk fanzines: identity, community, and the articulation of homosexuality and hardcore', *Journal of Communication Inquiry* 17: 1, 73–94.

Ferguson, Ann, Zita, Jacquelyn and Addleson, Kathryn (1981), 'On "com-

pulsory heterosexuality and lesbian existence": defining the issues',
Signs, 7: 1, 158–99.

Findlay, Heather (1996), 'Freud's "fetishism" and the lesbian dildo debates',
in Vicinus (ed.), *Lesbian Subjects: A Feminist Studies Reader*, Bloomington, IN: Indiana University Press, pp. 151–66.

Foertsch, Jacqueline (2000), 'In theory if not in practice: straight femi-
nism's lesbian experience', in Thomas (ed.), *Straight with a twist: Queer
Theory and the Subject of Heterosexuality*, Chicago: University of Illinois
Press, pp. 45–59.

Foucault, Michel (1979), *Discipline and Punish: The Birth of the Prison*,
Sheridan (trans.), New York: Vintage Books.

Foucault, Michel (1980), *The History of Sexuality* Volume I: *An Introduction*,
Hurley (trans.), New York: Vintage.

Foucault, Michel (1987), *The Use of Pleasure: The History of Sexuality*
Volume II, Hurley (trans.), Harmondsworth: Penguin.

Foucault, Michel (1991), 'On the genealogy of ethics: an overview of a
work in progress', in Rabinow (ed.), *The Foucault Reader*, Harmondsworth: Penguin, pp. 340–72.

Foucault, Michel (1997), 'Sex, power, and the politics of identity', in
Rabinow (ed.), *Michel Foucault: Ethics, Subjectivity, and Truth*, New York:
The New Press, pp. 163–73.

Fraser, Mariam (1999), 'Classing queer: politics in competition', *Theory,
Culture and Society*, 16: 2, 107–32.

Freud, Sigmund (1925), 'Some psychical consequences of the anatomical
distinction between the sexes', *The Standard Edition of the Complete
Psychological Works of Sigmund Freud*, Vol. 19, Oxford: The Hogarth Press.

Freud, Sigmund (1931), 'Female sexuality', *The Standard Edition of the
Complete Psychological Works of Sigmund Freud*, Vol. 21, London: The
Hogarth Press.

Freud, Sigmund (1977a), 'Fetishism', in Strachey (ed.), *On Sexuality*,
Pelican Freud Library, Vol. 7, Harmondsworth: Penguin Books, [1927],
pp. 345–58.

Freud, Sigmund (1977b), 'Three Essays on Sexuality', in Strachey (ed.),
On Sexuality, Pelican Freud Library, Vol. 7, Harmondsworth: Penguin
Books, [1905], pp. 33–170.

Freud, Sigmund (1996), 'The Sexual Aberrations', in Morton (ed.), *The
Material Queer: A LesBiGay Cultural Studies Reader*, Boulder, CO:
Westview Press, pp. 77–94.

Friedan, Betty (1963), *The Feminine Mystique*, Harmondsworth: Penguin.

Frye, Marilyn (1983), 'Lesbian feminism and the gay rights movement:
another view of male supremacy, another separatism', in *The Politics of
Reality: Essays in Feminist Theory*, New York: The Crossing Press,
pp. 128–51.

Fuss, Diana (1989), *Essentially Speaking: Feminism, Nature, and Difference*,
New York: Routledge.

Fuss, Diana (1991), 'Inside/Out', in *Inside/Out: Lesbian Theories, Gay
Theories*, New York: Routledge, pp. 1–10.

Gabb, Jacqui (1998), 'Marginal differences? An analysis of the imag(in)ed bodies of Del LaGrace', *Journal of Gender Studies*, 7: 3, 297–305.

Gamman, Lorraine and Makinen, Merja (1994), *Female Fetishism*, London: Lawrence & Wishart.

Garber, Linda (2001), *Identity Poetics: Race, Class, and the Lesbian-Feminist Roots of Queer Theory*, New York: Columbia University Press.

Gatens, Moira (1988), 'Towards a feminist philosophy of the body', in Caine, Grosz and de Lepervanche (eds), *Crossing Boundaries: Feminism and the Critique of Knowledges*, Sydney: Allen & Unwin, pp. 59–70.

Gatens, Moira (1991), *Feminism and Philosophy: Perspectives on Difference and Equality*, Cambridge: Polity Press.

Gatens, Moira (1996), *Imaginary Bodies: Ethics, Power, and Corporeality*, London: Routledge.

Gates, Henry Louis Jr. (1993), 'The black man's burden', in Warner (ed.), *Fear of a Queer Planet*, Minneapolis: University of Minnesota Press, pp. 230–8.

Gibson, Margaret (1998), 'The masculine degenerate: American doctors' portrayal of the lesbian intellect, 1880–1949', *Journal of Women's History*, 9: 4, 78–103.

Goldflam, Annie (1999), 'Queerer than queer: reflections of a kike dyke', in Jackson and Sullivan (eds), *Multicultural Queer: Australian Narratives*, New York: Harrington Park Press, pp. 135–42.

Goldman, Ruth (1996), '*Who is that queer queer?* Exploring norms around sexuality, race, and class in queer theory', in Beemyn and Eliason (eds), *Queer Studies: A Lesbian, Gay, Bisexual and Transgender Anthology*, New York: New York University Press, pp. 169–82.

Gopinath, Gayatri (1997), 'Nostalgia, desire, diaspora: South Asian sexualities in motion', *Positions: East Asia Cultures Critique*, 5: 2, 467–89.

Goto, Hiromi (1994), *A Chorus of Mushrooms*, Edmonton: NeWest Press.

Graham, Paula (1995), 'Girl's camp? The politics of parody', in Wilton (ed.), *Immortal, Invisible: Lesbians and the Moving Image*, London: Routledge, pp. 163–81.

Griffin, Christine (1993), 'Fear of a black (and working-class) planet: young women and the racialization of reproductive politics', in Kitzinger and Wilkinson (eds), *Heterosexuality: A Feminism and Psychology Reader*, London: Sage Publications, pp. 239–42.

Grosz, Elizabeth (1990), 'Inscriptions and body maps: representation and the corporeal', in Threadgold and Cranny-Francis (eds), *Feminine/ Masculine and Representation*, Sydney: Allen & Unwin, pp. 62–74.

Grosz, Elizabeth (1994a), *Volatile Bodies: Toward a Corporeal Feminism*, Sydney: Allen & Unwin.

Grosz, Elizabeth (1994b), 'Experimental desire: rethinking queer subjectivity', in Copjec (ed.), *Supposing the Subject*, New York: Verso, pp. 133–58.

Grosz, Elizabeth (1995), 'Lesbian fetishism?', in *Space, Time and Perversion: The Politics of Bodies*, Sydney: Allen & Unwin.

Halberstam, Judith (1994), 'F2M: the making of female masculinity', in

214

Doan (ed.), *The Lesbian Postmodern*, New York: Columbia University Press, pp. 210–28.

Halberstam, Judith (1997), 'Mackdaddy, superfly, rapper: gender, race, and masculinity in the drag king scene', *Social Text* 52/53, 15: 3–4, Fall/Winter, 104–31.

Halberstam, Judith (1998), *Female Masculinity*, Durham, NC: Duke University Press.

Halberstam, Judith (2001), 'Oh behave!: Austin Powers and the drag kings', *GLQ: A Journal of Gay and Lesbian Studies*, 7: 3, 425–52.

Hale, C. Jacob (1998a), 'Consuming the living, dis(re)membering the dead in the butch/FTM borderlands', *GLQ: A Journal of Lesbian and Gay Studies*, 4: 2, 311–48.

Hale, C. Jacob (1998b), 'Tracing a ghostly memory in my throat: reflections on FTM feminist voice and agency', in Digby (ed.), *Men Doing Feminism*, New York: Routledge.

Halperin, David (1995), *Saint Foucault: Towards A Gay Hagiography*, Oxford: Oxford University Press.

Halperin, David (1996), 'The queer politics of Michel Foucault', in Morton (ed.), *The Material Queer: A Lesbigay Cultural Studies Reader*, Boulder, CO: Westview Press, pp. 317–23.

Hankin, Kelly (2000), '"Wish we didn't have to meet secretly?": negotiating contemporary space in the lesbian bar documentary', *Camera Obscura*, 15: 3, 34–69.

Harper, Phillip Brian (1999), '"The subversive edge": *Paris Is Burning*, social critique, and the limits of subjective agency', in *Private Affairs: Critical Ventures in the Culture of Social Relations*, New York: New York University Press, pp. 33–59.

Harris, Daniel (1997), *The Rise and Fall of Gay Culture*, New York: Hyperion.

Hart, Lynda (1998), *Between the Body and the Flesh: Performing Sadomasochism*, New York: Columbia University Press.

Hart, Lynda and Dale, Joshua (1997), 'Sadomasochism', in Medhurst and Munt (eds), *Lesbian and Gay Studies: A Critical Introduction*, London: Cassell, pp. 341–55.

Healey, Emma (1996), *Lesbian Sex Wars*, London: Virago.

Healy, Murray (1996), 'Fetishizing masculinity', in *Gay Skins: Class, Masculinity, and Queer Appropriation*, London: Cassell, pp. 102–21.

Hegel, G. W. F. (1977), *Phenomenology of Spirit*, Miller (trans.), Oxford: Oxford University Press.

Hein, Hilde (1982), 'Sadomasochism and the liberal tradition', in Linden *et al.* (eds), *Against Sadomasochism: A Radical Feminist Analysis*, San Francisco: Frog in the Pond, pp. 83–9.

Henderson, Lisa (1999), 'Simple pleasures: lesbian community and *Go Fish*', *Signs: Journal of Women in Culture and Society*, 25: 1, 37–64.

Hennessey, Rosemary (1995), 'Queer visibility in commodity culture', in Nicholson and Seidman (eds), *Social Postmodernism: Beyond Identity Politics*, Cambridge: Cambridge University Press, pp. 142–86.

215

Hill, Mike (ed.) (1997), *Whiteness: A Critical Reader*, New York: New York University Press.

Hoagland, Sarah Lucia (1982), 'Sadism, masochism, and lesbian-feminism', in Linden *et al.* (eds), *Against Sadomasochism: A Radical Feminist Analysis*, San Francisco: Frog in the Well, pp. 153–63.

Hobbes, Thomas (1997), *Leviathan*, Cambridge: Cambridge University Press.

hooks, bell (1992a), 'Is Paris burning?', in *Black Looks: Race and Represen-tation*, Boston: South End Press, pp. 145–56.

hooks, bell (1992b), 'Eating the other: desire and resistance', in *Black Looks: Race and Representation*, Boston: South End Press, pp. 21–39.

Hopcke, Robert H. (1991), 'S/M and the psychology of male initiation: an archetypal perspective', in Thompson (ed.), *Leatherfolk: Radical Sex, People, Politics, and Practice*, Boston: Alyson, pp. 65–76.

Hopkins, Patrick D. (1994) 'Rethinking sadomasochism: feminism, inter-pretation, and simulation', *Hypatia*, 9: 1, 116–39.

Hoyers, Niels (ed.) (1933), *Man Into Woman: An Authentic Record of a Change of Sex. The Story of the Miraculous Transformation of the Danish Painter Einar Wegener*, Stenning (trans.), New York: E. P. Dutton.

Ion, Judith (1997), 'Degrees of separation: lesbian separatist communities in Northern New South Wales, 1974–95', in Matthews (ed.), *Sex in Public: Australian Sexual Cultures*, Sydney: Allen & Unwin, pp. 97–113.

Irigaray, Luce (1985a), *Speculum of the Other Woman*, Gill (trans.), Ithaca, NY: Cornell University Press.

Irigaray, Luce (1985b), *This Sex which is Not One*, Porter (trans.), Ithaca, NY: Cornell University Press.

Irigaray, Luce (1992), *Elemental Passions*, in Collie and Still (trans.), New York: Routledge.

Jackson, Peter and Sullivan, Gerard (eds) (1999), *Multicultural Queer: Australian Narratives*, New York: Harrington Park Press.

Jagose, Annamarie (1996), *Queer Theory*, Melbourne: Melbourne University Press.

Jakobsen, Janet R. (1998), 'Queer is? Queer does?: Normativity and the problem of resistance', *GLQ: A Journal of Gay and Lesbian Studies*, 4: 4, 511–36.

Jeffreys, Sheila (1986), 'Sado-masochism: the erotic cult of fascism', *Lesbian Ethics*, 2: 1, 65–82.

Jeffreys, Sheila (1990), *Anticlimax: A Feminist Perspective on the Sexual Revolution*, London: The Women's Press.

Jeffreys, Sheila (1993), *The Lesbian Heresy: A Feminist Perspective on the Lesbian Sexual Revolution*, Melbourne: Spinifex Press.

Jeffreys, Sheila (1994), 'Sadomasochism, art and the lesbian sexual revo-lution', *Artlink*, 14: 1, 19–21.

Jeffreys, Sheila (1998), 'Heterosexuality and the desire for gender', in Richardson (ed.), *Theorising Heterosexuality: Telling it Straight*, Buckingham: Open University Press, pp. 75–90.

Johnson, Freya (1995), 'Holy homosexuality Batman!: Camp and corporate capitalism in *Batman Forever*', *Bad Subjects: Political Education for Everyday Life*, 23, December, http://eserver.org/bs/23/johnson.html

Johnston, Craig (1999), *A Sydney Gaze: The Making of Gay Liberation*, Sydney: Schiltron Press.

Jordan, Lloyd (1990), 'Black gay v gay black', *BLK*, 6, 25–30.

Kando, Thomas (1973), *Sex Change: The Achievement of Gender Identity among Feminized Transsexuals*, Illinois: Charles C. Thomas Publishers.

Kanneh, Kadiatu (1993), 'Sisters under the skin: a politics of heterosexuality', in Kitzinger and Wilkinson (eds), *Heterosexuality: A Feminism and Psychology Reader*, London: Sage, pp. 46–7.

Katz, Jonathan Ned (1996), *The Invention of Heterosexuality*, New York: Plume.

Kelly, Sharon (1996), 'Queer heterosexuality', *body politic*, http://www.bodypolitic.co.uk/body4/queer.html

Kennedy, Elizabeth Lapovsky and Davis, Madeline (1992), '"They was no one to mess with": the construction of the butch role in the lesbian community of the 1940s and 1950s', in Nestle (ed.), *The Persistent Desire: A Femme-Butch Reader*, Boston: Alyson Books, pp. 62–80.

Kennedy, Elizabeth Lapovsky and Davis, Madeline (1993), *Boots of Leather, Slippers of Gold: The History of a Lesbian Community*, New York: Routledge.

Kennedy, Hubert (1997), 'Karl Heinrich Ulrichs: first theorist of homosexuality', in Rosario (ed.), *Science and Homosexualities*, New York: Routledge, pp. 26–45.

Kirby, Vicki (1991), '*Corpus delicti*: the body at the scene of writing', in Diprose and Ferrell (eds), *Cartographies: Poststructuralism and the Mapping of Bodies and Spaces*, Sydney: Allen & Unwin, pp. 88–100.

Kitzinger, Celia and Wilkinson, Sue (1993), *Heterosexuality: A Feminism and Psychology Reader*, London: Sage Publications.

Krafft-Ebing, Richard von (1965), *Psychopathia Sexualis*, Klaf (trans.), London: Staples Press.

Kristeva, Julia (1982), *Powers of Horror: An Essay on Abjection*, Roudiez (trans.), New York: Columbia University Press.

Lacan, Jacques (1953), 'Some reflections on the ego', *International Journal of Psychoanalysis*, 34, 11–17.

Lacan, Jacques (1977), 'The mirror stage as formative function of the I', *Ecrits*, London: Tavistock.

Leslie, Robert (1966), *Casebook: Homophile*, New York: Dalhousie Press Inc.

Lloyd, Moya (1999), 'Performativity, parody, politics', *Theory, Culture and Society*, 16: 2.

Lucas, Ian (1998), *Outrage!: An Oral History*, London: Cassell.

Lyotard, Jean-François (1984), *The Postmodern Condition: A Report on Knowledge*, Bennington and Massumi (trans.), Manchester: Manchester University Press.

McCaskell, Tim (1994), 'A history of race/ism', Toronto Board of Education, http://www3.sympatico.ca/twshreve/Inclusive/HistoryRacism.htm

McClintock, Anne (1993a), 'The return of female fetishism and the fiction of the phallus', *New Formations*, 19, Spring, 1–21.

217

McClintock, Anne (1993b), *Imperial Leather: Race, Gender, and Sexuality in the Colonial Contest*, New York: Routledge.

Macey, David (1993), *The Lives of Michel Foucault*, New York: Pantheon Books.

McIntosh, Mary (1993), 'Queer theory and the war of the sexes', in Bristow and Wilson (eds), *Activating Theory: Lesbian, Gay, Bisexual Politics*, London: Lawrence & Wishart, pp. 33–52.

McKee, Alan (1999), '"Resistance is hopeless": assimilating queer theory', *Social Semiotics*, 9: 2, August, 235–50.

MacKinnon, Catherine (1987), *Feminism Unmodified: Discourses on Life and Law*, Cambridge, MA.: Harvard University Press.

Mansfield, Nick (2000), *Subjectivity: Theories of the Self from Freud to Haraway*, Sydney: Allen & Unwin.

Mapplethorpe, Robert (1982), *Black Males*, Amsterdam: Gallerie Jurka.

Mapplethorpe, Robert (1986), *The Black Book*, Munich: Schirmer/Mosel.

Marlowe, Kenneth (1965), *The Male Homosexual*, Los Angeles: Sherbourne Press.

Marshall, John (1981), 'Pansies, perverts, and macho men: changing conceptions of male homosexuality', in Plummer (ed.), *The Making of the Modern Homosexual*, London: Hutchinson, pp. 133–54.

Martindale, Kathleen (1997), *Un/Popular Culture: Lesbian Writing after the Sex Wars*, Albany, NY: State University of New York Press.

Martino, Mario (1977), *Emergence: A Transsexual Autobiography*, New York: Crown Publishers.

Medhurst, Andy (1985), 'Can chaps be pin-ups?', *Ten 8*, 8: 17.

Medhurst, Andy (1997), 'Camp', in Medhurst and Munt (eds), *Lesbian and Gay Studies: A Critical Introduction*, London: Cassell, pp. 274–93.

Meeker, Martin (2001), 'Behind the mask of respectability: reconsidering the Mattachine Society and male homophile practice, 1950s and 1960s', *Journal of the History of Sexuality*, 10: 1, 78–116.

Mercer, Kobena (1993), 'Reading racial fetishism: the photographs of Robert Mapplethorpe', in Apter and Pietz (eds), *Fetishism as Cultural Discourse*, Ithaca, NY: Cornell University Press, pp. 307–29.

Mercer, Kobena (1994), *Welcome to the Jungle: New Positions in Black Cultural Studies*, New York: Routledge.

Merleau-Ponty, Maurice (1962), *The Phenomenology of Perception*, Smith (trans.), London: Routledge & Kegan Paul.

Merleau-Ponty, Maurice (1964), 'The child's relations with others', in *The Primacy of Perception and Other Essays*, Evanston, IL: Northwestern University Press.

Meyer, Moe (ed.) (1994), *The Politics and Poetics of Camp*, London: Routledge.

Meyerowitz, Joanne (2001), 'Sex research at the borders of gender: transvestites, transsexuals and Alfred C. Kinsey', *Bulletin of the History of Medicine*, 75: 1, 72–90.

Miles, Kevin Thomas (1997), 'Body badges: race and sex', in Zack (ed.), *Race/Sex*, New York: Routledge, pp. 133–43.

Miller, D. A. (1993), 'Sontag's urbanity', in Abelove *et al.* (eds), *The Lesbian and Gay Studies Reader*, London: Routledge, pp. 212–20.

Millett, Kate (1977), *Sexual Politics*, London: Virago.

Mirzoeff, Nicholas (1999), *An Introduction to Visual Culture*, London: Routledge.

Montag, Warren (1997), 'The universalization of whiteness: racism and enlightenment', in Hill (ed.), *Whiteness: A Critical Reader*, New York: New York University Press, pp. 281–93.

Moore, Clive (2001), *Sunshine and Rainbows: The Development of Gay and Lesbian Culture in Queensland*, St Lucia, Qld: University of Queensland Press.

Mootoo, Shani (1999), *Cereus Blooms at Night*, Austin, TX: Bard Books.

Moraga, Cherríe (1983), *Loving in the War Years*, Boston: South End Press.

Moraga, Cherríe (1996), 'Queer Aztlán: the re-formation of Chicano tribe', in Morton (ed.), *The Material Queer: A LesBiGay Cultural Studies Reader*, Boulder, CO: Westview Press, pp. 297–304.

Moraga, Cherríe and Anzaldúa, Gloria (eds) (1981), *This Bridge Called My Back: Writings by Radical Women of Color*, New York: Kitchen Table/Women of Color.

Morkham, Bronwyn (1995), 'From parody to politics: bodily inscriptions and performative subversions in *The Crying Game*', *Critical In Queeries*, 1: 1, 47–68.

Morris, Jan (1974), *Conundrum*, New York: Harcourt, Brace, Jovanovich.

Mulvey, Laura (1989a), 'Visual pleasure and narrative cinema', in *Visual and Other Pleasures*, Basingstoke: Macmillan, pp. 14–26.

Mulvey, Laura (1989b), 'Afterthoughts on "Visual pleasure and narrative cinema"', in *Visual and Other Pleasures*, Basingstoke: Macmillan, pp. 29–38.

Namaste, Ki (1996), 'Tragic misreadings: queer theory's erasure of transgender subjectivity', in Beemyn and Eliason (eds), *Queer Studies: A Lesbian, Gay, Bisexual, and Transgender Anthology*, New York: New York University Press, pp. 183–203.

Nancy, Jean-Luc (1991), *The Inoperative Community*, Connor and Garbus (trans.), Minneapolis: University of Minnesota Press.

Nancy, Jean-Luc (2000), *Being Singular Plural*, Richardson and O'Byrne (trans.), Stanford, CA: Stanford University Press.

Nataf, Zachary I. (1995), 'Black lesbian spectatorship and pleasure in popular cinema', in Burston and Richardson (eds), *A Queer Romance: Lesbians, Gay Men and Popular Culture*, London: Routledge, pp. 57–80.

Nataf, Zachary I. (1996), *Lesbians Talk Transgender*, London: Scarlett Press.

Neath, Jeanne F. (1987), 'Let's discuss dyke S/M and quit the name calling: a response to Sheila Jeffreys', *Lesbian Ethics*, 2: 3, 95–9.

Nietzsche, Friedrich (1974), *The Gay Science*, Kaufmann (trans.), New York: Vintage Books.

Nietzsche, Friedrich (1989), *On the Genealogy of Morals and Ecce Homo*, Kaufmann (trans.), New York: Vintage Books.

Nestle, Joan (1992), *A Persistent Desire: The Femme-Butch Reader*, Boston: Alyson Publications.

Newton, Esther (1972), *Mother Camp: Female Impersonators in America*, Chicago: Chicago University Press.

Ng, Vivien (1997), 'Race matters', in Medhurst and Munt (eds), *Lesbian and Gay Studies: A Critical Introduction*, London: Cassell, pp. 215–31.

Nye, Robert (1993), 'The medical origins of sexual fetishism', in Apter and Pietz (eds), *Fetishism as Cultural Discourse*, Ithaca, NY, and London: Cornell University Press, pp. 13–30.

OnlyWomen Collective (eds) (1984), *Love Your Enemy? The Debate Between Heterosexual Feminism and Political Lesbianism*, London: OnlyWomen Press.

Oosterhuis, Harry (1997), 'Richard von Krafft-Ebing's "step-children of nature": psychiatry and the making of homosexual identity', in Rosario (ed.), *Science and Homosexualities*, New York: Routledge, pp. 67–88.

O'Sullivan, Kimberley (1997), 'Dangerous desire: lesbianism as sex or politics', in Matthews (ed.), *Sex in Public: Australian Sexual Cultures*, Sydney: Allen & Unwin, pp. 114–26.

O'Sullivan, Tim *et al.* (eds) (1983), *Key Concepts in Communication*, London: Methuen.

Overall, Christine (1999), 'Heterosexuality and feminist theory', in Lebacqz and Sinacore-Guinn (eds), *Sexuality: A Reader*, Ohio: The Pilgrim Library of Ethics, pp. 295–309.

Parnaby, Julia (1996), 'Queer straits', in Harne and Miller (eds), *All the Rage: Reasserting Radical Lesbian Feminism*, London: The Women's Press, pp. 3–10.

Phelan, Shane (1993), '(Be)Coming out: lesbian identity and politics', *Signs: A Journal of Women in Culture and Society*, 18: 4, 765–90.

Phelan, Shane (1994), 'Getting specific about community', in *Getting Specific: Postmodern Lesbian Politics*, Minneapolis: University of Minnesota Press, pp. 76–97.

Pietz, William (1985), 'The problem of the fetish, I', *Res*, 9, 5–17.

Pietz, William (1987), 'The problem of the fetish, II, the origins of the fetish', *Res*, 13, 23–45.

Polhemus, Ted and Randall, Housk (1994), *Rituals of Love: Sexual Experiments, Erotic Possibilities*, London: Picador.

Prosser, Jay (1997), 'Transgender', in Medhurst and Munt (eds), *Lesbian and Gay Studies: A Critical Introduction*, London: Cassell, pp. 309–26.

Prosser, Jay (1998a), *Second Skins: The Body Narratives of Transsexuality*, New York: Columbia University Press.

Prosser, Jay (1998b), 'Transsexuals and the transsexologists: inversion and the emergence of transsexual subjectivity', in Bland and Doan (eds), *Sexology in Culture: Labelling Bodies and Desires*, Cambridge: Polity Press, pp. 116–31.

Prosser, Jay and Storr, Merl (1998), 'Introduction to Part III: transsexuality and bisexuality', in Bland and Doan (eds), *Sexology Uncensored: The Documents of Sexual Science*, Cambridge: Polity Press, pp. 75–7.

Rand, Erica (1995), *Barbie's Queer Accessories*, Durham, NC: Duke University Press.

Rasmussen, Brigid Brander, Nexica, Irene J., Klinenberg, Eric and Wray,

Matt (eds) (2001), *The Making and Unmaking of Whiteness*, Durham, NC: Duke University Press.

Raymond, Janice (1998), 'Sappho by surgery: the transsexually constructed lesbian-feminist', in Hopkins (ed.), *Sex/Machine: Readings in Culture and Technology*, Bloomington, IN: Indiana University Press, pp. 306–21.

Rechy, John (1979), *The Sexual Outlaw*, London: Futura.

Reynolds, Robert (1994), 'Postmodernism and gay/queer identities', in Aldrich (ed.), *Gay Perspectives II: More Essays in Australian Gay Culture*, Sydney: The Australian Center for Gay and Lesbian Research, pp. 245–74.

Reynolds, Robert (2002), *From Camp to Queer: Remaking the Australian Homosexual*, Melbourne: Melbourne University Press.

Rich, Adrienne (1986), *Blood, Bread and Poetry: Selected Prose 1979–1985*, London: Virago.

Rivière, Joan (1986), 'Womanliness as a masquerade', in Burgin, Donald and Kaplan (eds), *Formations of Fantasy*, London: Methuen, pp. 35–44.

Robertson, Pamela (1996), *Guilty Pleasures: Feminist Camp from Mae West to Madonna*, Durham: Duke University Press.

Roen, Katrina (2001), 'Transgender theory and embodiment: the risk of racial marginalisation', *Journal of Gender Studies*, 10: 3, 253–63.

Rorty, Richard (1989), *Contingency, Irony, and Solidarity*, Cambridge: Cambridge University Press.

Rosario, Vernon A. (ed.) (1997), *Science and Homosexualities*, New York: Routledge.

Rose, Kieran (1994), *Diverse Communities: The Evolution of Lesbian and Gay Politics in Ireland*, Cork: Cork University Press.

Rousseau, Jean-Jacques (1968), *The Social Contract*, Harmondsworth: Penguin.

Rubin, Gayle (1981), 'The leather menace', in Samois (ed.), *Coming to Power: Writings and Graphics on Lesbian S/M*, Berkeley, CA: Samois, pp. 194–229.

Rushton, Philippe (2000), *Race, Evolution, and Behavior: A Life History Perspective* (3rd edition), Port Huron, MI: Charles Darwin Research Institute.

Russell, Diana (1982), 'Sadomasochism: a contra-feminist activity', in Linden *et al.* (eds), *Against Sadomasochism: A Radical Feminist Analysis*, San Francisco: Frog in the Well.

Russo, Vito (1981), *The Celluloid Closet: Homosexuality in the Movies*, New York: Harper & Rowe.

Said, Edward (1996), 'Orientalism', in Mongia (ed.), *Contemporary Postcolonial Theory: A Reader*, London & New York: Arnold, pp. 20–36.

Sandell, Jillian (1994), 'Shopping for a change: *The House of Mirth* and *Paris Is Burning*', *Bad Subjects: Political Education for Everyday Life*, issue #11, http://eserver.org/bs/11/Sandell.html

Sandell, Jillian (1997), 'Telling stories of "queer white trash"', in Wray and Newitz (eds), *White Trash: Race and Class in America*, New York: Routledge, pp. 211–30.

Sandoval, Chela (1991), 'U.S. Third World feminism: the theory and method of oppositional consciousness in the postmodern world', *Genders*, 10, 1–24.

Sartelle, Joe (1992), 'As if we were a community', *Bad Subjects: Political Education for Everyday Life*, Issue #1, http://eserver.org/bs/01/sartelle.html

Sartelle, Joe (1994), 'Rejecting the gay brain (and choosing homosexuality)', *Bad Subjects: Political Education for Everyday Life*, Issue #14, May, http://eserver.org/bs/14/sartelle.html

Scheman, Naomi (1997), 'Queering the center by centering the queer: reflections on transsexuals and secular Jews', in Tiejens Meyers (ed.), *Feminists Rethink the Self*, Oxford: Westview Press, pp. 124–62.

Schor, Naomi (1986), 'Female fetishism: the case of Georges Sand', in Suleiman (ed.), *The Female Body in Western Culture*, Boston: Harvard University Press, pp. 363–72.

Schrift, Alan (1995), 'Reconfiguring the subject as a process of self: following Foucault's Nietzschean trajectory to Butler, Laclau/Mouffe, and Beyond', *New Formations*, 25.

Schultz, Gretchen (2001), 'Daughters of Bilitis: literary genealogy and lesbian authenticity', *GLQ: A Journal of Lesbian and Gay Studies*, 7: 3, 377–89.

Schwarz, Judith (1979), 'Questionnaire on issues in lesbian history', *Frontiers* 4: 3.

Scott, Darieck (1994), 'Jungle fever?: Black gay identity politics, white dick, and the utopian bedroom', *GLQ: A Journal of Lesbian and Gay Studies*, 1, 299–321.

Secomb, Linnell (1997), 'Queering community', *Queerzone*, Nepean: University of Western Sydney Women's Research Centre, pp. 9–16.

Secomb, Linnell (2000), 'Fractured community', *Hypatia*, 15: 2, 133–50.

Sedgwick, Eve Kosofsky (1990), *The Epistemology of the Closet*, Berkeley, CA: University of California Press.

Sedgwick, Eve Kosofsky (1993), *Tendencies*, Durham, NC: Duke University Press.

Segal, Lynne (1994), *Straight Sex: Rethinking the Politics of Pleasure*, Berkeley, CA: University of California Press.

Segal, Lynne (1997), 'Feminist sexual politics and the heterosexual predicament', in Segal (ed.), *New Sexual Agendas*, New York: New York University Press, pp. 77–89.

Seidman, Steven (1993), 'Identity and politics in a "postmodern" gay culture', in Warner (ed.), *Fear of a Queer Planet: Queer Politics and Social Theory*, Minneapolis: University of Minnesota Press, pp. 105–42.

Seidman, Steven (1995), 'Deconstructing queer theory or the under-theorization of the social and the ethical', in Nicholson and Sediman (eds), *Social Postmodernism: Beyond Identity Politics*, Cambridge: Cambridge University Press, pp. 116–41.

SGLMG (1995), *Defining Membership: A Discussion Paper*, Sydney: Sydney Gay & Lesbian Mardi Gras.

SGLMG Committee (1998), *Twenty Years of Revolution*, Sydney: Sydney Gay and Lesbian Mardi Gras Festival Guide.

Shapiro, Judith (1991), 'Transsexualism: reflections on the persistence of gender and the mutability of sex, in Epstein and Straub (eds), *Body Guards: The Cultural Politics of Gender Ambiguity*, New York: Routledge, pp. 248–79.

Shrage, Laurie (1997), 'Passing beyond the other race or sex', in Zack (ed.), *Race/Sex*, New York: Routledge, pp. 183–90.

Smith, Barbara (1993), 'Queer politics: where's the revolution?', *The Nation*, 257: 1, 5 July.

Smith, Cherry (1996), 'What is this thing called queer?', in Morton (ed.), *The Material Queer: A LesBiGay Cultural Studies Reader*, Boulder, CO: Westview Press, pp. 277–85.

Smyth, Cherry (1992), *Lesbians Talk Queer Notions*, London: Scarlet Press.

Somerville, Siobhan (2000), *Queering the Color Line: Race and the Invention of Homosexuality in American Culture*, Durham, NC: Duke University Press.

Sontag, Susan (1966), 'Notes on Camp', in *Against Interpretation*, New York: Delta.

Spelman, Elizabeth (1988), *Inessential Woman: Problems of Exclusion in Feminist Thought*, Boston: Beacon.

Stacey, Jackie (1988), 'Desperately seeking difference', in Gamman and Marshment (eds), *The Female Gaze: Women as Viewers of Popular Culture*, London: The Women's Press.

Steakley, James (1997), '*Per scientiam ad justitiam*: Magnus Hirschfeld and the sexual politics of innate homosexuality', in Rosario (ed.), *Science and Homosexualities*, New York: Routledge, pp. 133–54.

Stone, Sandy (1991), 'The empire strikes back: a posttranssexual manifesto', in Epstein and Straub (eds), *Body Guards: The Cultural Politics of Gender Ambiguity*, New York: Routledge, pp. 280–304.

Stryker, Susan (1994), 'My words to Victor Frankenstein above the village of Chamounix', *GLQ: A Journal of Gay and Lesbian Studies*, 1, 237–54.

Stryker, Susan (2001), *Queer Pulp*, San Francisco: Chronicle Books.

Sullivan, Nikki (1997), 'Fleshing out pleasure: canonisation or crucifixion?', *Australian Feminist Studies*, 12: 26, 283–92.

Sullivan, Nikki (1999), 'Queer pleasure(s): some thoughts', *Social Semiotics*, 9: 2, 251–5.

Tasker, Yvonne (1993), *Spectacular Bodies: Gender, Genre, and the Action Cinema*, London: Routledge.

Taylor, Robert (1996), 'Black on Black and White', *Body Politic*, http://www.bodypolitic.co.uk/body2/BonBW.html

Terry, Jennifer (1995), 'Anxious slippages between "us" and "them": a brief history of the scientific search for homosexual bodies', in Terry and Urla (eds), *Deviant Bodies: Critical Perspectives on Difference in Science and Popular Culture*, Indianapolis: Indiana University Press, pp. 129–69.

Thomas, Calvin (2000), *Straight with a Twist: Queer Theory and the Subject of Heterosexuality*, Chicago: University of Illinois Press.

Thompson, Denise (1985), *Flaws in the Social Fabric: Homosexuals and Society in Sydney*, Sydney: Allen & Unwin.

Thompson, Denise (1991), *Reading between the Lines: A Lesbian Feminist*

Bibliography

Critique of Feminist Accounts of Sexuality, Lesbian Studies and Research Group, Sydney: Gorgon's Head Press.

Tucker, Robert C. (ed.) (1978), *The Marx-Engels Reader*, New York and London: W. W. Norton and Company.

Ulrichs, Karl Heinrich (1994), *The Riddle of 'Man-Manly' Love*, Lombardi-Nash (trans.) New York: Prometheus Books.

Vicinus, Martha (1996), '"They wonder to which sex I belong": the historical roots of modern lesbian identity', in Vicinus (ed.), *Lesbian Subjects: A Feminist Studies Reader*, Bloomington and Indianapolis: Indiana University Press, pp. 233–60.

Waldby, Catherine (1995), 'Destruction: boundary erotics and refigurations of the heterosexual male body', in Grosz and Probyn (eds), *Sexy Bodies: The Strange Carnalities of Feminism*, New York: Routledge, pp. 266–77.

Walker, Lisa (1995), 'More than just skin-deep: fem(me)ininity and the subversion of identity', *Gender, Place and Culture: A Journal of Feminist Geography*, 2: 1.

Ware, Vron and Back, Les (2001), *Out of Whiteness: Color, Politics, and Culture*, Chicago: Chicago University Press.

Warner, Michael (ed.) (1993), *Fear of a Queer Planet: Queer Politics and Social Theory*, Minneapolis: University of Minnesota Press.

Waters, Chris (1998), 'Havelock Ellis, Sigmund Freud and the state: discourses of homosexual identity in interwar Britain', Bland and Doan (eds), *Sexology in Culture: Labeling Bodies and Desires*, Cambridge: Polity Press, pp. 165–79.

Weeks, Jeffrey (1977), *Coming Out: Homosexual Politics in Britain from the Nineteenth Century to the Present*, London: Quartet Books.

Weeks, Jeffrey (1981), *Sex, Politics, and Society: The Regulation of Sexuality Since 1800*, London and New York: Longman.

Weinber, Thomas and Levi Kamel, G. W. (eds) (1983), *S and M: Studies in Sadomasochism*, Buffalo, NY: Prometheus.

Werhane, Patricia (1996), 'Community and individuality', *New Literary History*, 27: 1.

Wheelwright, Julie (1990), *Amazons and Military Maids*, London: Pandora.

Wilchins, Riki Anne (1997), *Read My Lips: Sexual Subversion and the End of Gender*, New York: Firebrand Books.

Willett, Graham (2000), *Living Out Loud: A History of Gay and Lesbian Activism in Australia*, Sydney: Allen & Unwin.

Williams, Linda (1999), *Hard Core: Power, Pleasure, and the 'Frenzy of the Visible'*, (2nd edition), Berkeley, CA: University of California Press.

Wotherspoon, Garry (1991), *'City of the Plain': History of a Gay Sub-Culture*, Sydney: Hale & Monger.

Young, Iris Marion (1986), 'The ideal of community and the politics of difference', *Social Theory and Practice*, 12: 1, 1–26.

Yue, Audrey (2000), 'New Asian queer funk: sticky rice and chinky chicks', *Photofile*, 61, 243–6.

Index

Index

equality
    difference(s) and, 124
    sadomasochism and, 159–61
essentialism, 81, 110, 111, 123
    strategic, 146
ethics, 47, 49–50
eugenics, 17, 58
Eugenides, Jeffrey, 80n
eunuchs, 110
Evans, Caroline, 199–200
Evans, Rodney, 80n
evolutionary theory, 58
exclusivity, 32, 47, 48, 68, 140–2

family, 67, 134
    community and, 138
    fetishism and, 188
Fanon, Frantz, 186
fantasy, and construction/psychic reality,
    60–2, 64, 78
fascism, 12, 164
fatalism, 92
Fellig, Arthur (Weegee), 188n
Felski, Rita, 116
feminism and feminist groups, 29, 32–5, 43,
    48, 68
    and community, 137, 138
    and essentialism, 110
    and heterosexuality, 124–8
    'policing' by, 34
    and private/public spheres, 24
    and sadomasochism, 158, 159, 164–6
femme/butch relations and culture, 27–9
Fernie, Lynne, 36n
fetishism, 168, 171–88, 191
    anthropological, 169–70
    commodity, 170–1
    as continuum, 171–2
    and 'normality', 174
    and race, 185–6
    and theory of the gaze, 197, 198
    women and, 175, 180, 183–4, 198
film, 61, 193; see also individual films
Finch, Nigel, 25; see also Stonewall
Findlay, Heather, 185, 188n
Fire, 74
Fireworks, 19
Fiveash, Tina, 133–4
Foertsch, Jacqueline, 135n
Forbidden Love: The Unashamed Stories of
    Lesbian Lives, 36n
forgetting, 106
Foucault, Michel, 39, 40, 47, 50, 119, 189
    de Beauvoir and, 81
    on fetishism, 172–3
    Freud and, 15
    on history, 1–2
    The History of Sexuality, 3, 4, 40, 53–4,
      155
    on power/knowledge, 42, 93, 123, 189
    on racism, 58
    on resistance, 42
    on sadomasochism, 153–4, 155–6, 158,
      159, 160
    Segal and, 128, 129
    on self-knowledge, 53–4
    and theory of the gaze, 199

freedom, security and, 144, 145
Freud, Sigmund, 14–15, 174–8, 188n, 205nn
    on fetishism, 171–3, 174–8, 180, 181–4,
      185, 186, 188n
    on lesbianism, 180
    Mulvey and, 198
    on sadomasochism, 151, 152, 153
    on self and group, 144
    and Ulrichs, 7
    on the uncanny, 191
    see also psychoanalytic theory
Friedan, Betty, 32
Friedman, Jeffrey, 192
From Wimps to Warriors, 167n
fundamentalism, 11, 20n
Fuss, Diana, 51, 199, 203

Gamman, Lorraine, 169, 170, 171, 172, 175,
    176, 183, 199–200
Gang's All Here, The, 191–2
Gatens, Moira, 129
Gates, Henry Louis, Jr., 59, 68
Gay (and Lesbian) Liberation Movement, 26,
    29–32
    heterogeneity, 36n
    Mattachine Society and, 35–6n
    and race issues, 67
    women and, 32, 34–5
Gay Black Group, 67
gay men
    and femininity, 162
    and sadomasochism, 161, 162
    as spectators, 198–9
    see also homosexuality
Gay Pride, 29–31, 67
gaze, the, 186, 190, 196–200
Gebhard, Paul, 171–2
gender, 81, 83–6, 128–30
    abstractions of, 100
    community and, 138
    as constructed, 84, 85–6, 123, 201
    as fiction, 115
    and the gaze, 197–8
    ideals, 107, 196
    as learned, 54
    ontologies of, 83, 84
    performativity, 82, 86–93, 106–7, 196
    project of abolition of, 124
    and representation, 197, 205n
    views of, and laws, 3–4
    see also masculinity, men and women
gender ambiguity, 99–102, 112, 113–17
    'rectifying', 107
    see also transsexualism/transgenderism
gender identity clinics, 102
gender norms, transsexualism and, 105
gender pronouns, 110, 113–15
Genet, Jean, 189
genres, mixing, transsexualism and, 106
Gentlemen Prefer Blondes, 193
Germany, 7, 12
Glover, Edmund, 16
Go Fish, 141–2, 144, 146–7, 149
Goldman, Ruth, 66
Gopinath, Gayatri, 74–5
Goto, Hiromi, 62–3
Greeks, ancient, 2, 15, 155–6

227

Index

Grosz, Elizabeth, 49–50, 128, 176, 177, 183–4
guerrilla tactics, 92–3, 133–4, 190, 200–2
Gutheil, Emil, 18

Haeckel, Ernst Heinrich, 58
Halberstam, Judith, 115, 116–17, 195–6
Hale, C. Jacob, 113–14, 115–16
Hall, Radclyffe, 18–19
Halperin, David, 2, 43–4, 45–6, 49, 201
Hammet, Dashiell, 205n
harassment, 27–8
Harlem Renaissance, 79n
Harper, Phillip Brian, 78, 89
Harris, Daniel, 23, 24, 25, 30–1
Harry Benjamin International Gender
    Dysphoria Association Incorporated, 104
Hart, Lynda, 159–60, 165–7
Hawks, Howard, 205nn
Healy, Murray, 184–5
Hedwig, Sophie, 103
Hegel, G. W. F., 145
Hein, Hilde, 164
hermaphroditism, theory of original, 7–8
heterocentricity, 120
heterogeneity see variability
heteronormativity, 59, 91, 107, 132–3, 200
    camp and, 193
    fetishism and, 185
    Queer Theory and, 81
    remaining within to deconstruct, 202
    sadomasochism and, 161
    see also heterosexual matrix
heterosexual desire, 124, 142, 159
heterosexuality, 39, 119–28
    butch/femme roles and, 28
    compulsory, 200
    as constructed, 120, 126–7
    feminism and, 124–8
    and homosexuality, 17–18, 40, 51
    whether an institution, 121
    and life/death, 52
    whether natural, 14, 15, 119–20
    whether oppressive to women, 120, 122–7
    and privilege, 133–4
    queering, 121, 127–8, 129, 130–4
    see also heteronormativity
heterosexual matrix, 86, 196
'Hey, Hetero!', 133–4
Hirschfeld, Magnus, 7, 11–12, 14, 99, 100–2,
    107
history, 1–2, 39–40
Hitchcock, Alfred, 205n
HIV/AIDS, 186, 187
Hobbes, Thomas, 145
homophile groups/movement, 22–5, 26, 29,
    48
homophobia
    racism and, 58–9, 66–75
    sadomasochism and, 158
'homosexual advance defence', 130
homosexual desire, 124
homosexuality
    and heterosexuality, 17–18, 40, 51
    history of views of, 2–19, 30, 99–100, 101
    and life/death, 52
    and transsexualism/transgenderism, 10,
    108

views of causes of, 4–12
see also gay men and lesbians/lesbianism
hooks, bell, 79n, 96–7
Hopcke, Robert, 161, 162
Hopkins, Patrick, 160
hospitality, 149
Hoyers, Niels, 103
Hum Aapke Hain Koun, 74
human being and human doing, 50
humanist ontology, 50
human rights, basis of claiming, 23
Huston, Angelica, 80n
Hwang, David, 61
hybridity, 73, 74

'I Am What I Am', 29–30
identity, 83–4
    and activism, 135n
    ambiguity, 93
    Cartesian dualism and, 41–2
    categorisation of, 15, 38, 199–200
    community and, 137–50
    competing aspects of, 32–5, 37–8, 66–72,
    139
    and the gaze, 199
    growth in belief in, 3, 4
    and heterosexual matrix, 86
    intersectional, 49, 72
    opposition and, 41–50
    other and, 93–4
    parody and, 90
    perception and, 93–4
    and performance, 87–93, 96–7
    policing of, 34, 84, 97
    race and, 37–8, 66–72, 139
    sadomasochism and, 154, 158–67
    sex and, 133
    sexuality and, 85
    transgender and, 112
    Ulrichs' views on, 4–7
identity politics, 66–78, 81–2
    Queer Theory and, 66–8, 79n
ideology, 42
If These Walls Could Talk 2, 32, 33
inclusivity, 44–5, 47, 116, 139, 142–3
individualism, community and, 136–7
individuality/individualisation, 54, 81; see also
    identity and variability
individuals, institutions and, 126
Institute for Scientific Treatment of
    Delinquency, 16
Institute for Sexology, 12
intelligibility, 115
intercourse, 123, 130; see also heterosexuality
intersectionality, 49, 72
'inversion', 8–11, 14, 41, 99–100, 103, 108,
    173; see also homosexuality and
    transsexualism/transgenderism
Irigaray, Luce, 40, 130, 165, 176, 183

Jagose, Annamarie, 39, 43–4, 46
Jakobsen, Janet, 50
Jeffreys, Sheila, 122, 133, 160
    on butch/femme relationships, 28, 142
    on homosexual/heterosexual desire, 124,
    142, 160
    on sadomasochism, 158–9, 164

Index

PUSSY (Perverts Undermining State
    Scrutiny), 37

QUASH (Queers United Against Straight
    Acting Homosexuals), 46
queer
    as male, 48
    and race, 48
    as radical potentiality, 43–4, 201
    treated as opposed to lesbian and gay,
        45–6
    as umbrella, 44–5
    uses of word, vii, 43–50, 52, 192, 201
    see also queering and Queer
        Theory/Theories
queer community, 148
Queercore, 45
queering, 50, 52, 192
    of culture, 189–205
    of heterosexuality, 121, 127–8, 129, 130–4
'queer moments', 191, 192, 194
Queer Nation, 37
queer practice, 78
queer tactics, 185
Queer Theory/Theories, vii–viii, 43–50
    canon of, 66
    and community, 143–4
    and culture, 189–90
    as deconstructive, 50–2, 81
    and identity politics, 66–8, 79n
    as monstrous, 52, 73
    and race issues, 48, 72–4, 78

race
    community and, 138
    fetishism and, 185–6
    identity and, 37–8, 66–72, 139
    mixed, 73, 80n
    origins and use of term/concept, 57–60,
        65–6, 75–8
    perception and, 83, 88, 186, 198
    purity/impurity, 72–3
    Queer Theory and, 48, 72–4, 78
    as sexualised, 72
    transsexualism and, 116, 117n
    see also Orientalism
racism, 58, 75–8, 200
    and homophobia, 58–9, 66–75
    and sexism, 58–9, 66–75
Radicalesbians, 33
radical groups, 29
Rand, Erica, 82–3, 200–1, 202
rape, 129–30
    sadomasochism and, 160, 163
    transsexualism and, 109, 115
Raymond, Janice, 33–4, 108–12
reacting, to popular culture/art, 189–205; see
    also resistance
reality, fantasy and, 64
Rebecca, 193
reception theories see audience and reception
    theories
Rechy, John, 158
Red River, 193
reification, 171; see also fetishism
relationships, and fetishism, 173
religion, 11, 20n, 168, 169–70

repression, 40
resistance
    and power, 42, 91
    Queer Theory and, 47–9
    whether a requirement, 106
Rich, Adrienne, 120–1, 122, 124, 127, 133
Riggs, Marlon, 70, 74
Rituals of Love see Polhemus, Ted
Rivière, Joan, 81
Roen, Katrina, 116
roles, 27–9; see also gender and
    sadomasochism
Rorty, Richard, 145
Rosanoff, Aaron, 17
Ross, Thomas, 15–16
Rotello, Gabriel, 44, 45
Rousseau, Jean-Jacques, 145
Rushton, Philippe, 59–60
Russell, Diana, 158, 159, 160, 163–4
Russo, Vito, 192

S/M see sadomasochism
Sacher-Masoch, Leopold von, 151, 152
Sade, Marquis de, 151, 152
sadism, 151–2; see also sadomasochism
sadomasochism, 38, 151–67
Sagan, Leontine, 21n
Said, Edward, 60
Sartelle, Joe, 30, 31
Sartre, Jean-Paul, 131
Savage, Jon, 194
Schaw, Janet, 75–7
schools, 9, 10, 40
Schor, Naomi, 176
Scientific-Humanitarian Committee, 12
scopophilia, 197, 198; see also gaze
Scott, Darieck, 68, 69–70, 72
SCUM (Society for Cutting Up Men), 203
Secomb, Linnell, 145–8
security, freedom and, 144, 145
Sedgwick, Eve Kosofsky, 38, 66
seduction, 9–10
    whether possible, 20n
Segal, Lynne, 126, 127–9, 130–1, 133
segregation, 9, 10
Seidman, Stephen, 47, 51–2
self-examination and self-knowledge, 53–4
self-help, 30
Selvadurai, Shyam, 74
separatism, 36n
sex, 17, 133
    heteropatriarchy and, 164
    identity and, 133
    as intersubjective, 130–1
    lesbians and, 165–6
    masculinity and, 131
    patriarchy and, 160
    'rough', 164
    see also pleasure
sexism, racism and, 58–9, 66–75
'sex radicalism', 38
sex reassignment, 102–5, 107
sexuality
    categorisations of, 2–17, 38–9
    whether a choice, 30–1, 125–7
    community and, 138
    as constructed, 1, 2, 40

231

232